SECRET BELIEVERS

Also by Brother Andrew

With John and Elizabeth Sherill
God's Smuggler
With Al Janssen
Light Force

SECRET BELIEVERS

What Happens when Muslims Turn to Christ?

Brother Andrew
and Al Janssen

HODDER

Unless indicated otherwise, Scripture quotations are taken from the
HOLY BIBLE, NEW INTERNATIONAL VERSION.
Used by Permission. All rights reserved.

Scripture marked NLT is taken from the *Holy Bible, New Living
Translation*. Copyright © 1996. Used by permission of Tyndale House
Publishers, Inc., Wheaton, Illinois 60189. All rights reserved.

Scripture marked NKJV is taken from the *New King James Version*.
Copyright © 1982 by Thomas Nelson, Inc. Used by permission.
All rights reserved.

The right of Brother Andrew and Al Janssen to be identified as the
Authors of the Work has been asserted by them in accordance with the
Copyright, Designs and Patents Act 1988.

1

British Library Cataloguing in Publication Data
A record for this book is available from the British Library

ISBN 978 0340 954843

Typeset in Century by Avon DataSet Ltd,
Bidford on Avon, Warwickshire

Printed in the UK by CPI Bookmarque, Croydon, CR0 4TD

The paper and board used in this paperback are natural recyclable
products made from wood grown in sustainable forests.
The manufacturing processes conform to the environmental
regulations of the country of origin.

Hodder & Stoughton
A Division of Hodder Headline Ltd
338 Euston Road
London NW1 3BH
www.madaboutbooks.com

Contents

Prologue: The Good Jihad   vii

Part 1 Secret Believers   1

Part 2 How Shall We Respond?   223

Epilogue   264

Appendix: A Letter from the Afghan
    Persecuted Church in Christ   265

Notes   269

Selected Bibliography   271

Prologue
The Good Jihad

The good jihad. It sounds like an oxymoron, until you look in your Bible at 2 Timothy 4:7. Paul says, 'I have fought the good fight'. In the Arabic translation those last three words are rendered 'the good jihad'.

We are engaged in a fight. Actually a war. It involves the challenge of Islam. Millions of Muslims have settled in Europe and North America, and we must acknowledge that at least some of them hate the West. We've seen the evidence: 9/11, the nightclub attack in Bali, the Madrid train bombings, the London Underground attacks, Iran, Iraq. Thousands of people have died, and extremist groups like Al-Qaeda promise that more attacks are on the way.

But this isn't the war it appears to be. It isn't the war Paul the apostle talked about with Timothy. Rather, these events are a reflection of a spiritual war, an unseen conflict. How are we Christians going to respond? With guns and bombs? Is that really our only option? We can assure you this approach won't win a spiritual war. For one thing, it's a purely defensive, reactionary approach. It's time for Christians to go on the offensive.

So just how do we fight a good spiritual jihad? To answer this question, let's look at a group of Christians who live under Islam. Yes, there is a church in the Islamic world, in countries like Iran, Iraq, Indonesia, Pakistan, Egypt and the countries of the Middle East and Central Asia. In some cases, the church is hidden and barely surviving. In other countries there has been a church since the time of Pentecost. These churches have seen the rise and advance of Islam. Often they have suffered terribly. If we want to know what might be coming to Europe and North America, we should study these churches. We can learn from their successes and failures.

But how do we tell this story? We want you to meet these amazing people, but if we tell you their names and where they live, we will endanger their lives and their churches. They have told us, however, that they *want* their stories told. So the method we have chosen is rather unusual. Part 1 of *Secret Believers*, about 85 per cent of the book, is a narrative. Everything you read here is true; we haven't made up any of this, though in some situations we have filled in gaps based on input from friends who live and minister in the Islamic world.

You will notice that the story takes place in an unnamed Middle Eastern country. The names of the characters, except for Brother Andrew's, are generic, and in many cases characters are composites of more than one individual. In this way we hope to protect our friends and still allow you to enter into the real world in which these brothers and sisters of ours live. And while I (Brother Andrew) am a participant in this story, mine is not a major role. My responsibility is to encourage and help the church in this Muslim country in any way that I can. But this is not my story, which is why I'll step into the background and refer to myself in the third person as I let my friends take centre stage.

At the end of this book, we will present some thoughts on how to respond to this story. We in the West have a crucial part to play in the good fight, and we plan to present for your consideration a strategy for responding to the challenge of Islam.

But first, we want to introduce some amazing people. Join us as we travel to a typical Arab town, Suq al Khamis. There you will meet Ahmed, a Muslim who's facing a major life-changing decision, and Abuna Alexander, the local priest of St Mark's Church, who is trying to nurture his congregation in the midst of a hostile Muslim society. Next, you will meet Butros, who is finishing his education in England and must decide whether to stay in England or return home. Later, you will meet Nadira, Butros's wife; Mustafa, who plays an important role in the local chapter of the fundamentalist group

Muslim Brotherhood; Hassan, one of Ahmed's closest friends; Salima, a teenage girl who discovers something amazing on satellite television; Kareem, a senior government official; and Layla, a Christian girl whose uncle has converted to Islam.

Now settle in and enter their story. We'll be back after you've finished reading it to talk about where we go from here.

Part 1

SECRET BELIEVERS

1

A Middle Eastern country

It was Sunday morning in the town of Suq al Khamis, and Ahmed was considering the unthinkable. The lanky teenage boy paced around his room, trying to decide whether to take the risk. He looked up at the poster over his bed, even though he had the words memorised:

> Allah is our objective.
> The messenger is our leader.
> The Quran is our law.
> Jihad is our way.
> Dying in the way of Allah is our highest hope.

It was that last statement that made Ahmed shudder. Just last night he'd suffered another nightmare. He was in a pit filled with all kinds of snakes. They were coiled around him, striking at him with their terrifying fangs. He'd awoken in a sweat, recognising again the threat of eternal punishment that Allah promised to all who did not faithfully follow the pillars of Islam. The dreams varied – sometimes he could feel flames scorching his flesh; other times he was hung by his hair as the skin was scraped off his body. This was the terrifying message of Islam as taught by the faction of Muslim Brotherhood that often met in his home. Yes, Allah was merciful; but he was also a god of horror and fear who took pleasure in torturing infidels. And according to the teaching, every Christian was *kafir*, an infidel. His only hope for escaping the horrors of hell was to live an exemplary life of Islam. Or to die in jihad.

Then Zaki went to university and soon wrote back to Ahmed with his outrageous questions that challenged the core of their religion. Zaki was Ahmed's lifelong friend. Together the two boys had attended the mosque and listened to the fiery sermons of their imam every Friday. Together they had also attended the local Christian school – their fathers had agreed that it provided the best education for their sons. Religion had been an important part of their education. Every day students spent time studying their faith – Christians in one room led by Abuna Alexander, a local priest; Muslims in another room, taught by a recent graduate of the major Islamic university in the capital city. Ahmed had to admit that even though he'd attended a school run by Christians, he really had never talked with them about their beliefs, except in a mocking way when he and Zaki and their mutual friend Hassan tried to convert the Christian students to Islam.

Now his best friend was proposing the unthinkable: maybe there was something to Christianity. Zaki had got hold of an *Injil*, the Christian gospel, and was secretly reading about *Isa* (Jesus). It wasn't that Jesus was unknown to them – there were many references to him in the Quran – but the Christian Scriptures presented a very different portrait of this prophet.

Ahmed pulled the rumpled letter out of his pocket and reread Zaki's shocking words: 'Isa is the most amazing man who ever lived. I can't help but compare Him to our Prophet, peace be upon him. I won't say anything more. Get a copy of the Injil and read it for yourself. We'll talk when I'm home for the holiday.'

Ahmed stuffed the letter back in his pocket and thought again about his options. The dreams were getting worse. If there was any chance that he could find answers at the church, it was worth the risk. But he had to be careful. No one in his family could know. He hurried through the living room and out the door to his motor scooter, parked by the front door. He kickstarted the bike and blew up a cloud of dust as he tore down the dirt street to the main paved road through town. He weaved his way through the morning traffic, passing donkey carts, lorries driving through town to the capital city, and overstuffed vans that served as local mass transportation.

Along the way he passed rows of shops, several mosques, and a bustling farmers' market – the *suq* for which the town was named – until he reached the edge of town where a mud-brick church named after St Mark stood. Ahmed could see several people heading to the door where Abuna Alexander, dressed in a black cassock and wearing a simple wooden cross, stood to greet the worshippers.

Ahmed parked his bike by the school fence across the street from the church. Uncertainty welled up inside him. What if someone recognised him? How would he explain this behaviour to his father? He looked around him but didn't recognise anyone. He walked down the street, crossed over, and headed back toward the church. He would quickly dash up the steps and sit in the very back.

But the priest saw him coming and a look of concern came over his face. 'I know you,' Father Alexander said, cutting off the boy's approach to the church. 'From the school, right?'

Ahmed nodded.

'What a surprise to see you! What brings you to St Mark's Church?'

'I just want to visit. I promise I'll be no problem.'

Father Alexander gave a nervous laugh and said, 'No, that's not a good idea. You just turn around and go back home. This place is for Christians. If you want to worship God, go to the mosque.'

The words stunned the boy. It hadn't occurred to him that the church wouldn't welcome him. Haltingly he tried to explain: 'I just want to find out what you believe.'

'I'm sorry. This is not the time or place.' The priest's voice became severe. Clearly he would not let Ahmed into the building.

'Then can I at least borrow the Injil?'

'Why do you want the Injil? You have your Quran. Now go. The service is about to start, and you should not be seen here.'

Ahmed started to protest, then noticed that several of the parishioners had stopped to stare at the strange scene. He'd lost any chance to slip quietly into the church. If he lingered any longer, someone might report this to his father. He turned and quickly dashed across the street to his bike.

—☙—

Why would this Muslim boy want to come to church? Abuna Alexander stroked his beard, perplexed as he watched the teenager jump on his motorbike and take off. The priest squinted in the bright sunlight that reflected off the sandy road. A lazy donkey pulled a farmer on a cart by the church and out into the fields that stretched beyond Suq al Khamis towards a village two miles away. Inside the church, about fifty faithful worshippers waited for Father Alexander to begin the liturgy.

It wasn't that the priest didn't like Muslims. He'd worked hard to be a good neighbour, even after a new mosque had been built next door to St Mark's Church. Sometimes its loudspeakers were cranked up, trying to drown out his services. He maintained cordial relationships with several imams. Each year he wished them a happy Eid al-Fitr, the feast that celebrated the end of Ramadan, and some of them wished him a happy Christmas. During the Easter season, though, the imams reminded him that Muslims don't believe that Jesus died on the cross but was simply taken away by God. He felt helpless in trying to defend Christianity against such attacks.

Theirs was an uneasy coexistence. Less than 10 per cent of the town's 75,000 people identified themselves as Christian, and that was higher than in most communities. Officially, in this country everyone had the right to choose his or her religion, but in reality that meant that everyone had the right to choose Islam. The Quran said anyone who left Islam was an infidel and infidels must be killed. Besides, Sharia law, being actively promoted by the local group of Muslim Brotherhood, trumped any other legal system in the eyes of dedicated Muslims. In fact, these fundamentalists were starting to cause problems for some in his congregation. One of his members, a gold dealer and the major contributor to the church treasury, had his shop robbed by some of these young men. The local police had done nothing about it. In smaller communities the pressure was even worse. The extremists had burned down a church in one nearby village.

So what was the point of allowing a Muslim to visit his church? It would destroy the stability of his little flock. As a priest he was responsible for the people in his congregation. He had to protect them from the wolves, and make no mistake, some of the Muslims in his neighbourhood were wolves. Though an uneasy truce prevailed in the community, there had been times in the past when Muslims had tried to deceive and devour the faithful. Even now inducements were sometimes offered to members of his flock to convert to Islam.

At one point, centuries ago, the church had been strong. Arabs were among those who heard Peter preach at Pentecost, and it was soon after this that the church was established in the Arab world. Christianity had spread and dominated the area until Islam arose in the seventh century. The armies of Islam soon overran the area and forced Christian communities to convert. For 1400 years those who didn't convert to Islam suffered from its rules. Under the philosophy of *dhimmitude*, Christians were permitted to exist, but they were penalised by extra taxes and second-class status.

'We must be careful and remember that in the past some Muslims have fooled us,' Abuna Alexander had reminded the parish leadership. 'They've pretended to convert, only to seduce our daughters, marry them, and then return to Islam.' Young Muslim men had pretended to be seekers but in reality they came to see girls with bare legs and without head scarves. No, he could not invite the persecutors into his church so they could leer at the women.

While he told himself that he had to protect his flock, a pang of guilt stabbed the priest. He knew that God had invited *all* to come and be saved. But really, how could Muslims be saved? Why would any Christian want them to be saved? Didn't they deserve God's judgement? If he had let this young man come in, the entire church would have been put in danger. The secret police would come and question him. They could even order the church to be closed permanently. He couldn't take that risk. Surely the boy knew that. He shouldn't have put the priest in such a precarious situation.

The chimes rang inside the sanctuary, calling Abuna Alexander. He went in to begin the service.

2

England, two years later

The train to London rocked as it sped through the countryside. Normally, if he wasn't catching up on much-needed sleep, Butros enjoyed gazing out the window at the lush green landscape, hoping to catch sight of an old farmhouse with a thatched roof. Distinctive hedgerows divided farms and the rolling fields, populated by sheep and cows and occasionally a flock of Shetland ponies. The scene was such a stark contrast to the dry, rugged desert of his home in the Middle East. Soon he would complete his post-graduate studies and a major decision loomed over him. Should he stay in England, where there were several mission agencies that could utilise his talents? Or should he return to his home country, where the church was withering under the oppressive power of a culture dominated by Islam?

The internal struggle had intensified as he neared graduation, complicated by a young woman, Nadira. They were studying at neighbouring universities and had met at a gathering for Christian students. Like Butros, Nadira was from a Middle Eastern country. They enjoyed meeting in a coffee shop to talk in Arabic about their Christian faith. They had not officially 'dated', but he knew that soon he would talk with her father and request her hand in marriage. Since they were from different countries, it would be simpler if they settled in neutral England, and the opportunities here provided him many more options for supporting a family.

But he sensed God had a different plan and he was praying for some clear indication of what that might be. As the train crept into Victoria Station, passengers rose to collect their belongings. Still deep in thought, Butros waited. Only after everyone had departed his coach, did he slowly rise and step on to the platform. Carrying a shoulder bag, he made his way through the terminal and down to the London Underground where he would catch a tube to his flat.

Suddenly a voice called out to him in his native Arabic: 'My dear Muslim brother, don't forget to come to the mosque for Friday prayers. Don't let the ways of the West ensnare you. If we follow the way of Allah, we will one day win England for Islam.'

Butros stopped and stared at the bold missionary, then gently answered, 'You are mistaken. I am not a Muslim brother. I am a follower of the Lord Jesus Christ.'

A look of disgust came over the missionary and he turned on his heel and walked to the other end of the platform. Butros boarded the tube, and as the doors closed and the train began to move, he saw the missionary speaking passionately to another unsuspecting foreigner.

And then, in his mind, Butros heard: *This Muslim missionary is determined to change a western country for Islam. What about the Great Commission that I have given you?* Butros recognised that this was not his own thought but the gentle nudging of the Holy Spirit. And his heart answered, *That is for the whole world, Lord. Surely I can stay here in England and do my part to help fulfil the Great Commission.*

Then he remembered the words of Jesus in Acts 1:8: 'You will be my witnesses in Jerusalem, and in all Judea and Samaria, and to the ends of the earth.' The evangelistic thrust of the disciples started at their home and then moved outwards. In the same way, Butros sensed that he was being compelled to return to his home country. Butros shuddered as he considered the implications, remembering from his Greek classes that the word *witnesses* is the same word as *martyrs*. Did that mean that he might have to pay the ultimate price to be a witness back home?

While the train jostled him gently as it roared through the tunnel, Butros wrestled with God. Hadn't missionaries served for many years in his country? And while missionary activity was no longer permitted, there were foreign Christians working in various secular occupations, providing a witness by their lives. Besides, if he returned home, how would he support a family? He could pastor a church, but church salaries were paltry. If he attempted any type of expanded work, he'd need help, and how would he find co-workers in a nation where 95 per cent of the population was Muslim? What did God have to say about that? All he heard in reply was the rumble of the train.

Butros had almost missed his stop. It was raining now as he climbed the stairs to street level and hurried the short distance to his flat. He pushed open his door and picked up the stack of mail that had accumulated in the few days he'd been away. Quickly, he sorted through the bills and advertisements. One envelope caught his attention. It was from the Netherlands. He slit the envelope and pulled out a letter from Brother Andrew.

A year earlier Butros had met Brother Andrew during a summer mission project on the island of Cyprus. The veteran missionary had delivered several talks to the mission team. After the publication of his book *God's Smuggler*, which told about delivering desperately-needed Bibles to churches in Eastern Europe and the Soviet Union, Andrew was prevented from personally going back to the Communist countries. So he had given more attention to the Islamic world, and his messages focused on the challenges that Islam presented to Christian mission agencies. Between meetings, Andrew had listened to Butros tell about the trials facing the church in his Middle Eastern country and had suggested that God might have a special job for him to do in that field.

Eagerly Butros read the words from his mentor: 'I want to encourage you to return home after graduation.' Butros's eyes filled with tears as he read the sentences that gently reminded him that he was needed in his country to do the work he knew God had just called him to do. If any doubt remained about his responsibility, it was erased as he read the final lines of the letter: 'I know you feel it must be an impossible assignment. However, remember, one man with God is a majority.'

―◦◦◦―

A few weeks later Butros made the short flight from London to Amsterdam and spent a day with Brother Andrew talking about the possibilities for ministry in his home country. Andrew's office felt like a refuge from a noisy and harsh world. There was a quiet hum of the heater running near the ceiling above Andrew's desk. Through one door was another workroom that looked out on a lush garden where Andrew spent much of his time when it wasn't raining. The moisture from the morning's showers added a luminous sheen to the rich green of trees, bushes and a tall hedge that separated Andrew's property from that of his neighbours. Brother Andrew seated himself in a rocking chair while Butros sat back in a well-worn, imitation leather sofa.

Butros looked around the room, enjoying the library feel with floor-to-ceiling bookshelves lining two walls, and another wall filled with mementoes of Andrew's years of travel. In the centre of the room was a set of large, old bellows that served as a coffee table. Andrew explained that it was from a smithy. 'It reminds me that I was once a blacksmith and my father was a blacksmith. In a book my father is called "The Rembrandt of blacksmiths". He tried desperately to teach me the trade, but he failed utterly.' Andrew pulled out a small stuffed dog that plugged the end of the bellows. 'Now don't be naughty and start pumping or I'll have soot all over the carpet.'

Butros laughed. 'Thank you for taking the time to meet with me,' he said.

Andrew raised his hand. 'No, the honour is mine. I am here to serve you in any way that I can.'

'Well, first let me say that I have decided to return to my country. I believe God has called me to work there, but I don't know where to begin.'

'At the *beginning*!' Andrew said with a laugh. 'The first step is to *go*. When I found that brochure for the Communist youth congress in Poland, all I did was grab my passport and buy a ticket and go. Once I was there, then I looked for my brothers. Once I found the churches, the rest followed naturally.'

'I've heard you say that before: "I seek the brethren." But what then?'

'You *listen*.' Andrew grabbed one of the many Bibles that filled several shelves of his office and opened it. 'The book of Revelation, chapters 2 and 3.'

'The letters to the seven churches,' Butros said.

'That's correct. It was the words written to the church in Sardis, Revelation 3:2, that became my life call. "Wake up! Strengthen what remains and is about to die." But I want you to notice two things about these seven letters. First, each one ends with the same phrase: "Hear what the Spirit says to the churches." That means God is going to say something that is not in the Bible. That means the Spirit has something to say in every time, in every generation, in every situation. I spoke on this at a pastors' conference on the Mount of Olives many years ago. One pastor got up and said, "Andrew, tell us, what *is* the Spirit saying to the churches?" That is exactly what I cannot tell you. You must listen. What is the Spirit saying to the church in *your* country?'

Butros closed his eyes for a moment to reflect on these words. They seemed so natural to Andrew, as though this was a message he'd preached hundreds of times – and not just preached but lived. 'So should I talk to the denominational leaders? The bishops?'

'You should let the leaders know what you are doing. But go to the towns and villages. Sit with the pastors and listen to them. Ask them to tell you their hopes and fears. Learn about the spiritual health of their congregations. Are the people weak or strong spiritually?'

'I don't think we're very strong,' Butros lamented.

'Find out why. For example, the Scriptures say that every person in the world has a right to hear the gospel. How is the church doing in that regard? Are they reaching out? Are they having an impact in their communities? Are they seeing people come to faith in Jesus Christ?'

'But we live in a Muslim society. We're maybe 5 per cent of the population.'

'Does God want Muslims to hear the gospel?'

'Yes, I know He does. That is my heart's desire, but most Christians are afraid to witness for Jesus.'

'So what is the Spirit saying to *your* situation? Does He want you to help strengthen the churches so that they will be an effective witness to Muslims? I know this makes you vulnerable. Consider that God was vulnerable. He saved others. He could not save Himself. We have to manoeuvre ourselves into a position where we are vulnerable, but for one purpose: to save others. I don't know what that means. Maybe Christians give their property to serve Muslims in their community. Maybe they take a risk and go and speak to terrorist leaders. Remember that we are here to save others.'

Butros let out a big sigh, clearly troubled by the implications of what he heard. In his country people were rarely so direct in their conversations. But Andrew had quickly forced him to confront the core issues he would need to face when he returned home. 'You said there were two things in all seven letters.'

'The second thing is that in each letter Jesus speaks about the one "who overcomes". That tells me that the church should attack. It should reach out. Not just survive but go on the offensive. And when it does, we are promised that the gates of hell will not prevail against the attack of the church. But when Jesus says "He that overcomes", He also implies that we may *not* overcome. That's where my call came, in Revelation 3:2: "Strengthen what remains and is about to die".'

'I think the church is just trying to survive in my country.'

'Then strengthen her. God has an important job for her to do. The work of the church is not survival. She exists to fulfil the Great Commission. Her work is making disciples of all nations. You know that Islam is an aggressive evangelistic religion. Much of the church isn't meeting that challenge. We are not doing what God told us to do. Our aim is that the world will be full of the knowledge of the Lord.'

'Do you have any programmes I could use that have worked in other countries?'

Andrew shook his head. 'We've never gone to any country and prescribed the medicine for the sick or suffering church. We've always gone and asked, "What can we do for you?" Because the Spirit has to speak to them. We go and strengthen the church, so it can function in their situation, living under any regime, whether political or religious, that hinders or weakens their ability to fulfil the Great Commission. In Eastern Europe the desperate need was for Bibles. But in other places there are no seminaries and the pastors need training. In many Muslim countries most of the Christians can't read, so to help strengthen the church, we provide literacy training. In other countries the Christians are at the bottom of the economic ladder; we help them start small businesses so that they become self-sufficient and have greater witness in the community.'

'I can already hear the protests. The Muslims will not allow us to evangelise. Islamic culture oppresses Christians. Pastors will say it's dangerous for the church to reach out to Muslims.'

'Of course it's dangerous, but it's a lot more dangerous for all of us if we don't do it. Even in a conquering army there are casualties. Safety is not the issue when we look at the Great Commission. The purpose of the church cannot be to survive, or even to thrive, but to serve. How do you serve?'

Andrew paused before he said, 'Sometimes servants die in the serving.'

There was silence for a few moments. The heater had cut off and the only sound was of a gentle rain tapping on the skylight overhead.

Then Butros said, 'I have to be honest. I don't know if I can do this.'

Andrew gazed intently at his friend. 'I know,' he said, his voice gentle. 'You feel inadequate. That's exactly how I felt when I launched out behind the Iron Curtain. However, in time, others joined me. Remember, you aren't doing this alone. The Holy Spirit is with you. He will guide you. He will raise up others in the country to work with you. And in time you will meet others like you who are serving the persecuted church in Muslim countries and Communist countries and Hindu countries. The church in the West is helping. When people hear what God is doing through you, they will want to pray and give of their resources. If you obey God, He will provide all that you need to do His work. I want you to know that I will pray for you every day. And if there is *anything* I can do to help, I will do it.'

3

A Middle Eastern country, one year later

Ahmed could feel the depression tugging at his mind, ready to suck him down again into a pit of despair. The nightmares would surely return tonight if he didn't conquer his thoughts. He grabbed his notebook and pen. *The rational person who raises questions, doubts, and believes is a hundred times greater than a god who carries a censor's scissors and a police informant's eye to spy and pilfer.* He felt the anger pour through his pen. Arabic was the perfect language to express such emotions, and the tradition of Arabic poetry was honoured in his family. These were dangerous thoughts, but the twenty-year-old university student knew of no other way to process the war in his mind. *A man who can disagree and yet remain gracious with you is a hundred times greater than a god who cannot bear divergence of opinion or criticism – the dictator's fragile throne.*

Poetry filled the void when Zaki was away. Zaki, the one friend who knew about Ahmed's spiritual journey – who, in fact, had encouraged him to ask the forbidden questions about Islam and had brought him a Bible – was overseas, starting postgraduate studies to become a doctor. Zaki was the only one who knew about his fear of death. At night when he couldn't sleep, Ahmed visualised the tortures that would be inflicted on all who did not measure up to Allah's standards.

Ahmed knew he was playing with fire and in his nightmares he was always burned. Yet he couldn't escape from the pages of the Bible. They

provided stark contrast to all other literature. He had read several poets of
his culture, and the subtle message that he noticed was of the god of Islam
who treated people as slaves. He had read the works of Jean-Paul Sartre and
Karl Marx and considered for a time the utopian vision of Communism.
Those dreams had shattered when he learned about the brutal regimes of
Stalin and Mao in his university studies. Then Zaki had introduced him to a
Sufi poet who wrote about the *Mahdi*, the coming messiah of Islam. 'When
God wanted to see His face, He sent Jesus to the world,' he'd read. What a
strange idea! Through this poet he heard for the first time about the cross
and the crucifixion.

The call of the *adhan* from the neighbourhood mosque interrupted his
concentration. Today's midafternoon prayer was to be followed by the
weekly discussion of the Quran for local university students. Ahmed had
skipped several sessions, and a couple of friends had enquired about his
absence. So he grabbed his prayer rug and Quran from the top shelf and
walked quickly down the street to the local mosque, a small, simple building
with wood floors and a single minaret. He removed his sandals, washed his
face, hands, and feet at one of the taps used for ablutions, and hurried inside.
It was a small gathering – most of the regulars performed their prayers at
their place of business.

The hall was spacious but devoid of ornamentation except for the
mihrab, a niche in the front wall indicating the direction of Mecca. On the
frame of the *mihrab* were painted verses of the Quran in beautiful
calligraphy. Ahmed placed his prayer rug down facing the *mihrab* just as the
imam began recitation of the opening verses of the Quran: 'Praise be to God,
the Lord of the Universe, the Compassionate, the Merciful, Sovereign of the
Day of Judgement. You alone we worship, and to You alone we turn for help.
Guide us to the straight path, the path of those whom You have favoured . . .'

How many times had he recited those words? Thousands. Did he believe
them? Of course. And yet he was changing. Whom did God favour? Over the
past year he had read and reread the Injil, and the teachings of Jesus, the
Prophet called Isa in the Quran, still astonished him. He memorised several
of the Prophet's statements from the Injil: 'If someone strikes you on one
cheek, turn to him the other also.' The Quran by contrast commanded him to
fight and kill. 'I tell you that anyone who looks at a woman lustfully has

already committed adultery with her in his heart.' The Quran permitted him to marry up to four women, and to keep all women captured in any invaded country. He knew the arguments against the Bible – that it was distorted and required the corrective of the Quran. But the man Jesus, He attracted Ahmed like a butterfly drawn to a colourful flower.

Ahmed bowed, hands on knees, his back straight, as the imam recited a short *sura*, a chapter of the Quran. With the assembly he raised his head and responded, 'God hears those who praise Him.' Then all went to their knees and bowed so that forehead and nose touched the floor. 'God is most great!' recited the imam.

How great was the prophet Jesus, Ahmed thought.

You were rich in being . . . poor in things.

How could You give when You had not even a place to lay Your head? You gave us Your heart – that vast expanse that still encompasses us, weary and heavy laden.

Many have wealth – salt water that will not quench their thirst. You can see them in their towers, hungry. There they are in their air-conditioned castles, famished. The metal cash boxes don't satisfy. They only rust.

Standing again, as the prayers continued, Ahmed thought about his meditations on Jesus. Something had happened to him. When had the change occurred? Perhaps he would never discern the exact moment, but he knew now that he was convinced. It was impossible to live without Jesus Christ, because only Jesus gave real meaning to life. Because Jesus Christ was, in fact, divine!

What was a Muslim to do with such a conclusion? To see God in any human being was *shirk*, the worst sin in Islam. *Shirk* meant to ascribe divinity or divine attributes to someone other than Allah. Muhammad, not Jesus, was the seal of all prophets. Allah didn't have a son; he only had messengers. So this was nonsense. Yet Ahmed couldn't deny what he'd learned, and such passionate conviction couldn't be kept forever in check. He had to speak the truth. But where? How?

As the prayers ended, Ahmed turned to his neighbour and said, 'Peace be upon you', and noticed that the young man was already developing a dark spot in the centre of his forehead, caused by repeatedly bowing and forcefully touching his head to the floor. This was a mark of pride for a devout Muslim, demonstrating for all to see that he faithfully prayed five times a day.

They sat down on the floor as the imam placed the Quran on a *rehal*, an ornate wooden stand. In his youthful exuberance, in his thirst for truth, Ahmed felt compelled to speak. Maybe others in the room had similar thoughts but only lacked the boldness to voice their doubts. He would raise the right question, the honest question. Politely addressing the imam, he asked: 'Why do we, the religion that honours the prophets, ignore the greatest Prophet of all?' The imam looked at him, stunned that anyone would speak before he had started his lesson. Ahmed couldn't stop now: 'Is there anyone greater than the Prophet Isa? I look at Him and see perfection. I look at Him and see God.'

That's when all hell was unleashed on Ahmed.

—◦◦◦—

Abuna Alexander met Butros at the entrance to St Mark's Church and led him down the right side of the sanctuary, past the altar, and through a door that put them in the vestry or dressing room where the priest's vestments were hanging. In one corner was a wooden desk, opposite it a sink and a tiny, cracked linoleum counter where an electronic kettle and a few glasses sat.

'I apologise – this is my office,' the priest said, offering a folding chair to his guest. 'It isn't much, but it's quiet, and I can think and study and pray here.'

'I am grateful that you would see me,' Butros replied.

'Actually, I'm very curious about what you are doing. Oh, I should plug in the kettle. Would you have some tea or coffee?'

'I would love some tea.'

The priest filled the pot with water and prepared two small glasses, placing loose tea leaves and a generous spoonful of sugar in each as he waited for the water to boil. 'How long have you been back home?' Father Alexander asked.

'Six months. When I finished my doctoral dissertation in England, I felt God calling me back to this country.'

The priest looked at him quizzically. 'But you are not a shepherd?'

'Well, I could be. I've filled in several pulpits to give Protestant pastors a break. But I think I'm called to minister to other pastors.'

'Are you married?' Alexander asked as he poured the hot water into the two glasses and stirred the mixture.

'Yes. My wedding was three months ago.'

'Congratulations! May you be blessed with many sons.' Gripping the rim with his fingers, the priest handed a glass of hot tea to Butros, then took the other, set it on his desk, and sat down on his creaky office chair. 'You seek to help pastors? My bishop is my pastor.'

Butros understood the hierarchy in liturgical denominations and said immediately, 'I will not undermine the authority of your bishop. I've already met with him to tell him what I am doing and will report back to him after I've finished my survey.'

'You are trying to meet all the priests and ministers in the country?'

'If possible, yes. There aren't that many.'

'May I ask why?'

'I'm trying to learn the health of the church.'

'We're surviving,' Alexander said with a weary laugh.

'Yes, but I wonder, perhaps God wants more than survival.' Butros took a deep breath and launched into a statement he'd repeated in every pastoral study he'd visited. 'Our Lord said we are to be salt and light. Are the churches in this country, here in Suq al Khamis, being salt and light?'

'We're not doing badly for a church that's been here for nearly two thousand years.'

Butros recognised that the priest was testing him. Butros was a Protestant, and his denomination was started by a British mission agency about one hundred years ago. There was a chronic tension between Protestants and the historical liturgical denominations. As a result there had been little co-operation between them. But Butros felt that God had called him to strengthen *every* church that would allow him to help.

'Abuna Alexander, I thank God that you and your fellow priests and bishops preserved the faith for centuries. You remained faithful when Islam invaded, and you persevered under terrible persecution. Today, as you know, we Christians are probably no more than 5 per cent of the population. Those who have the means leave and move to the West . . .'

'I've lost two families this year,' Alexander interrupted. 'They have relatives in Europe.'

'So we struggle against severe odds. However, I believe God wants a strong church here. I believe it's necessary. I came home to serve the church – not Protestant or Catholic or Orthodox or any specific denomination but the body of Jesus Christ. I want to see her be a vibrant witness. I want to see her fulfil her God-given mission.'

He stopped and waited. The priest had finished his tea and set the glass on his desk. He played with his long, grey beard as he studied Butros, who shifted uncomfortably on the rickety folding chair. Finally, Father Alexander asked, 'Do you know what my biggest problem is?'

'Please, tell me.'

'Protestants. They can't make any converts among the Muslims, so they proselytise my people. There are several families who have left St Mark's and started attending the Pentecostal church across town.'

The accusation hung in the room. Butros had heard this before. But he'd also heard from some of the 'converts' that they wanted more Bible teaching and that they found more life in Protestant services. He had seen vibrant Orthodox and Catholic congregations – in some places the clergy had responded to the challenge with Bible classes and programmes for the youth. Still, Butros was uncomfortable with the situation.

'I understand your frustration. We shouldn't be competing for church members. We are such a minority that our only hope is to work together. My desire is to help unify us rather than divide us further.'

As his hand played absentmindedly with the wooden cross that hung around his neck, the priest asked, 'How do you intend to serve the church?'

'That's what I am trying to discover. I want to listen and learn. And then with your bishop and other denominational leaders, I hope to develop a plan.'

'Who is funding you?'

This was a sensitive subject, but there was no sense hiding the truth. Clearly there was little in the way of resources in the country to support what Butros was doing. He thought of Brother Andrew and breathed a prayer of thanksgiving that his ministry along with others had provided seed money to start this work. 'There is an organisation in the Netherlands that provides some money. Once I have a plan, they may give more, and I will also contact other agencies.'

The priest nodded. He had served the church in Suq al Khamis for many years and no one, except his bishop, had enquired about his work and sought to help. He wanted, yes needed, to talk.

'May I show you the church?' Alexander rose and led Butros out of the vestry to a small closet and unlocked it. Inside was a toilet and washbasin.

'The toilet broke years ago. If any of my parishioners want to go to the bathroom, they must use my flat down the street. Or they must wait until they return home.'

He locked the door and led Butros into the sanctuary. 'Now, look up at the ceiling.'

Butros tilted his head back and noticed several holes.

'When it rains, we put bowls and basins on the pews and floor. Now, look at the walls.' They walked over to the nearest wall and Butros observed the cracks and peeling paint. 'You see, yes?'

Butros nodded. He understood the problem. Any church that wanted to make repairs needed to get permission from government authorities. And permission was almost never granted.

'Do you know how many years we've tried to fix the roof or the bathroom? I can't remember the first time we filed for a permit. And yet look outside.' The priest grabbed Butros by the arm and led him out the door of the sanctuary and pointed to the building abutting the church. 'Anyone can get permission to build a mosque. They built that four years ago, even though there is another mosque two blocks away. Look at those loudspeakers pointed right at us. Sometimes during our services, they turn on the speakers and try to drown us out with their noise.'

Butros sighed. He'd heard similar complaints throughout the country. The condition of church buildings was deplorable. But there was a greater burden that kept him awake at night. 'Please, allow me to ask one more, very important question. Could you tell me, what is the spiritual health of your congregation?'

Father Alexander stood mute for a moment. Butros thought he detected a deep sadness in the man's eyes. He studied the priest's face and saw in the wrinkles and spots a man who loved God and had laboured hard for years.

Finally, Alexander spoke: 'Yes, that is a good question. I have some very committed people in my church. There are about seventy-five families in my congregation. But not all of them attend. On a good Sunday, we might have forty or fifty people. For others, Christianity is simply what distinguishes them from their Muslim neighbours. Their families have been Christians for generations, centuries. So naturally they are Christian. But they don't come to church except for Christmas and Easter and to get married and to have their babies baptised.'

The young man felt compassion well up for the faithful old priest. At that moment Butros was willing to do whatever he could to encourage and help. 'Father, I'm afraid I can't repair your church building,' he said quietly, 'but maybe together we can find a way to repair hearts in your congregation.'

—◦◦◦—

One month later

Ahmed groaned from the pain of his bruises. Several times in the last few weeks, his father had severely beaten him with a bamboo stick. His siblings had kicked him, shouting, 'You infidel, come back to Islam', as he writhed on the ground. Somehow he had crawled back to his room and climbed on to his bed.

The local imam, on hearing Ahmed's revolutionary statement, had shouted in anger. The students had grabbed Ahmed, dragged him out of the mosque, and roughed him up as they returned him to his home. The imam urged the family to beat sense into the young man. 'Beat him until he recites the *shahadah*.' Ahmed needed only to hold a Quran and recite the words, 'I testify that there is no God but God and Muhammad is his messenger', and the punishment would cease. The honour of his family would be restored. His younger sister, Farah, had even whispered to him, 'Just say the words. You don't have to believe them.'

But Ahmed couldn't deny what he had learned about Jesus. He was so radically different from Muhammad. The Prophet was honoured for his military successes, while Jesus never led an army and was known for His message of love. There was no record of Muhammad performing a miracle, while dozens of Jesus's miracles were recorded in the Injil. Why would he want to return to the Prophet, who was so human, when Jesus clearly was divine? That seemed to be the choice. Still, how long could he endure the unrelenting pressure? Already members of his extended family had discussed killing him. Several of them had screamed, 'You have brought shame on us. You deserve to die.' One of his cousins even grinned when he said, 'God will be pleased when I kill you.'

He thought about death and how for so long it had terrified him. Yet now, death didn't seem so frightening. He was surprised by this, and as he tried to find a comfortable position on his bed, he forced his mind to comprehend the change. In Islam there was only one way a Muslim could know he was headed for paradise – to die in jihad. The glories of martyrdom were frequently preached in the mosque and taught in classes on the Quran. For those who died in the struggle for Islam, there was the promise of many virgins and unending pleasure. Some also believed that a martyr could bring members of his family with him to paradise. It was all so glorious, and Ahmed didn't believe a word of it.

What did he believe? The words he'd read in the Gospel, when Jesus raised Lazarus to life, flooded into his mind: 'I am the resurrection and the life. He who believes in me will live, even though he dies; and whoever lives and believes in me will never die.' Ahmed believed this, and he wasn't afraid to die for the truth he had discovered. Yet he sensed that if he was to die for loving Jesus, now wasn't the time.

The next day he managed to muster the strength to slip out of the house, climb on to his motorbike, and ride to the edge of town. He parked the bike in an alley two blocks from St Mark's Church and walked gingerly on a roundabout route until he arrived at the priest's residence on a side road half a block from the front of the church. Ahmed knocked gently. When there was no answer, he knocked harder. The door opened slightly and a woman, the priest's wife, took a look at him, registered an expression of shock, and shut the door. Ahmed glanced at his reflection in a window, saw his bruised and cut face, and guessed his appearance had frightened the woman. Before he could move away, the door opened again. Father Alexander glanced quickly both ways up and down his street, then opened the door wider, and said, 'Quick, come in before someone sees you.'

Inside the door the priest studied Ahmed's face. 'We've met, but I can't recall where,' he said.

Ahmed nodded. 'I tried to visit your church.'

Father Alexander told Ahmed to sit at the dining table and for the next few minutes he ministered to the cuts and bruises on Ahmed's face and upper body. When he had finished, the priest sat down across from him. At first, he said nothing. In the silence, Ahmed bowed his head, unable to look the priest in the eyes, afraid of rejection.

Finally, the older man said, 'It's all right. You are safe here, at least for the moment. Please, tell me what happened.'

After Ahmed had finished his story, there was another long silence. Finally, the priest rose and went to the kitchen. A few minutes later he returned, followed shortly by his wife who placed in front of Ahmed a plate of fried eggs, pitta bread, and cheese. The priest sat down to think while Ahmed ate eagerly for the first time in several days.

After he'd satisfied his hunger, Ahmed looked up at the priest.

Father Alexander looked stern as he said, 'You cannot stay here. Soon your family will be looking for you, and you're safer if you can get out of town. Do you have any money?'

Ahmed shook his head. 'No, I escaped at the first opportunity. They took everything away except the clothes I'm wearing. And my motorbike – it was still parked outside my home.'

'Do you have a job?'

'No, I've been attending the local college. Of course now I can't go back. I don't know what to do.'

'Okay, I know someone who I think may be able to help. Are you strong enough to ride your bike for an hour?' Ahmed nodded. 'Then I will make a phone call and if he says it is okay, I will give you some money for gas and food. After that . . . we will see what God wills.'

4

Three months later

A Bible and a Quran lay open on the desk. A man in his thirties stroked his black beard as he stared at the texts. 'This is incredible,' he muttered to himself.

The window was open and noise of traffic drifted into Mustafa's flat. He seemed unusually alert to sounds that normally provided a subconscious background noise. Cars and buses and lorries had distinctive horn tones and their constant beeps and blares performed a kind of symphony. He could almost tell each driver's mood – everything from the friendly little taps to long angry blasts, none of which seemed to change the constant snarl of traffic that tried to manoeuvre through the narrow old streets of the city. Sometimes it seemed as though every vehicle were honking its displeasure at having to wait another thirty seconds before moving forward a few metres.

The oppressive heat of summer had not yet descended on the desert nation and Mustafa's ceiling fan turned slowly on its lowest setting. The muezzin's call to prayer sounded from the university mosque just two streets away. Often he attended afternoon prayers there, followed by meetings with his Muslim Brotherhood disciples. Usually they remained in the mosque, sitting in a circle on the floor and studying the Quran. But today he couldn't make himself go and pray. He, who had insisted there was never an excuse for a Muslim to miss prayers – even when he was sick, he could pray with his eyes, opening and closing them to indicate kneeling and bowing toward Mecca – couldn't break away from his study today.

Mustafa leaned back in his chair and thought for a moment about his youth growing up in a village near Suq al Khamis. What would his father think of him now? He had three brothers and four sisters, but his father had always expected the most from him. Mustafa had attended the Islamic school in the village, and his father had pushed him to memorise large portions of the Quran to earn the monetary prizes offered each time a student successfully recited three *suras*.

A cousin had recruited him for the Muslim Brotherhood, which had started in upper Egypt in the 1920s and spread to other countries throughout the Middle East. The cousin had fed his thirst for knowledge by giving him books by Hassan al-Banna, founder of the Muslim Brotherhood, and other fundamentalist thinkers such as Sayyid Qutb, whose book *Milestones*, written while he was in prison, had inspired thousands of jihadists throughout the Muslim world.

Over time Mustafa had become too radical even for his father. The son had accused his parents of being unbelievers. When his father protested: 'I pray and fast and do everything required by the Prophet, peace be upon him', Mustafa had countered, 'It is not enough. You have to confess that the society in which we live is infidel and that everyone who doesn't pray is an atheist.' Then he'd told his father, 'My mother is an unbeliever because she doesn't pray, so if you are a real Muslim, you have to divorce her because Islam forbids being married to an unbelieving woman.' His father had struck him and banished him from the house, so he'd slept at the home of a fellow Muslim Brotherhood member.

As part of their total abandonment to radical Islam, Mustafa and his friends had terrorised the small Christian community, stealing from Christian businesses in Suq al Khamis and surrounding villages. He hadn't considered it stealing; it was jihad. The Islamic texts taught that Christians should either pay the *jizya*, a special tax levied on Jews and Christians, or embrace Islam. Or they should be killed. The fact that his country was more tolerant of the *dhimmi* made him angry. That was the problem – no Muslim country was really fully committed to Islam and Sharia law. The Brotherhood was determined to correct that.

Mustafa had carried this message to surrounding nations in the Middle East. He was passionate in declaring that kings and emirs and high government officials must rule by Islam alone and reject any semblance of western legal systems. His outspokenness had landed him in prison, after which he was deported back to his home country. Since then he'd concentrated his efforts on the university campus in the capital city, recruiting for the Brotherhood. The sheikh who led the local cell group liked Mustafa's commitment and harnessed his articulate intellect by having him write several small tracts.

It was one of these assignments that led to his crisis. He'd heard about some Christian missionaries who were arrested for trying to convert Muslims to Christianity. This had made Mustafa so angry that the sheikh had suggested he write a book revealing the distortions of the Christian faith. To do that, Mustafa had to read the Bible. He'd set out to prove the Bible had been altered or even corrupted, as many Islamic scholars taught. But how could he prove the book was false if he couldn't compare it with the original? He had drawn from critiques of the Holy Book by several writers, but when he looked up the verses the authors referenced in their arguments, they were different or, in some cases, didn't even exist. Then the sheikh had pointed him to the work of Izhar al-Haqq whose arguments seemed more rational, but his book had the same mistakes as those of the other scholars.

For the last several days Mustafa had decided to concentrate on the prophecies in the Torah (the first five books of the Bible) and the Injil that referenced the Prophet Muhammad. Though he couldn't find the name Muhammad in the Holy Book, there were twenty-six texts that supposedly pointed to him. Eagerly he had read the first one, Genesis 49:10: 'The sceptre will not depart from Judah, nor the ruler's staff from between his feet, until he comes to Shiloh.' Al-Haqq had said that 'Shiloh' was Muhammad, but when Mustafa had investigated to prove this linguistically and rhetorically and legally, he'd concluded that Isa the Christ clearly fulfilled the prophecy much more than Muhammad did.

He had turned to Deuteronomy 18:15: 'The Lord your God will raise up for you a prophet like me from among your own brothers. You must listen to him.' Al-Haqq had explained that Isaac's sons and Ishmael's sons were brothers, and thus Muhammad was a brother of Isaac's sons. But when he'd referenced the Quran, it said that the prophet would be from the Arab people and speak Arabic. The Torah text spoke of a prophet from the Hebrews who spoke Hebrew. *If this prophet was Muhammad, then I would distrust the Quran.* That was a dangerous thought.

Mustafa had exhausted himself with study and concluded that *none* of the twenty-six texts spoke of Muhammad. And now he stared at this verse from *sura* 'The Table' of the Quran: 'People of the Book, you will attain nothing until you observe the Torah and the Gospel and that which is revealed to you from your Lord.' The Quran affirmed the authority of the Jewish and Christian Scriptures. He turned to *sura* 3:84 and read: 'Say: "We believe in God and what is revealed to us; in that which was revealed to Abraham and Ishmael, to Isaac and Jacob and the tribes; and in that which their Lord gave Moses and Jesus and the prophets. We discriminate against none of them. To Him we have surrendered ourselves."' But how could the Christian God be the same as Allah? He'd read in the Gospels: 'Love your enemies and pray for those who persecute you, that you may be sons of your Father in heaven.' Allah commanded exactly the opposite in the Quran. In the *sura* 'Repentance', God commanded: 'Slay the idolaters wherever you find them. Arrest them, besiege them, and lie in ambush everywhere for them.' It was impossible that the two Gods were one and the same. It was impossible that the two books, the Holy Bible and Quran, were both right. While the two books agreed on some things, the differences were startling. *One of them had to be wrong.*

The prayer time was over and the flow of activity on the street was back to normal. But now Mustafa knew what he had to do – pray. *Allah, God, which is the real book? Show me which book is right.*

A peace washed over him, and Mustafa felt confident that God would reveal the truth.

———⟐∾⟐———

Butros enjoyed the quiet of his study when he rose early on most mornings. The flat where he and his wife, Nadira, lived was small but comfortable. One of the two tiny bedrooms served as his study, with bookshelves, a small desk, and a love seat that also converted into a bed for occasional guests. It was comforting to be surrounded by all the commentaries and theological books he had collected during his years of study in England. The authors were his friends and mentors who provided direction in this lonely work. Eventually he would have to pack most of these books and find a new office. He and Nadira had been married for six months, and two months ago his wife had given him the wonderful news that she was pregnant. Before long this room would become a nursery.

Soon after their wedding, Nadira had secured a job near their home as an elementary school teacher. That job, along with a small stipend from an organisation in Holland and occasional gifts from a few friends in England, provided their modest income. Also Butros had received a small inheritance when his father died, including a piece of land that was rented to farmers near Suq al Khamis.

It bothered Butros that he couldn't provide more for Nadira. She had grown up in a relatively wealthy family and several times her father had offered him a job in the family business. Now their lives were about to change significantly. In this country, once the first child was born, women rarely returned to work. But when Butros had wondered aloud if he should accept his father-in-law's offer, Nadira wouldn't hear of it. 'God has called you here,' she assured him, 'and I will help you. We are in this together. We must trust God that He will provide for all of our needs.'

There was so much to think about. Butros had visited almost every church in the country. He'd sipped innumerable cups of tea and coffee and listened to pastors and priests and lay leaders who were eager to pour out their hearts to a sympathetic peer. As a result, he'd learned a lot. Many of the pastors, especially those from more rural areas, had a very limited theological education. Most had never attended seminary or Bible school. Sometimes they earned their position because they were the only literate person in the congregation. There was also a lack of pastoral resources – commentaries and other tools that pastors in the West took for granted. Working through the Bible Forum in a neighbouring Arab country, Butros had obtained several valuable resources and distributed them to pastors for their personal libraries. He had also secured copies of *God's Smuggler* in Arabic, with the somewhat macho title translated: 'In Spite of the Impossible'. That, Butros felt, described his situation. He made sure that the literate young people in his church in the capital city and around the country had a chance to be inspired by Brother Andrew's story of faith.

Besides considering the needs of his family, Butros worried also about the resources he would need to expand the work. There were no extra funds to start any large programmes, especially after the arrival of Ahmed, sent to him by the priest in Suq al Khamis. Through a landlord at his church, he had found a tiny flat for the young convert. Ahmed had searched for work but had found only odd jobs. He looked to Butros for spiritual guidance and once or twice a week a meal. Somehow God had provided all that was needed for his family, for the literature, for his travels around the country, for Ahmed and others who came looking for help, but if Butros was going to implement his vision, he would need a lot more resources.

Nadira slipped into the room. 'You are up earlier than usual,' she said. She sat down next to Butros and laid her head on his shoulder.

'I'm sorry I woke you. I have a lot to think and pray about. How are you feeling this morning?'

'A little better. It's been nearly three months, so maybe the morning sickness will begin to let up.'

'Would you like some tea?'

Nadira smiled her assent, and Butros padded to the tiny kitchen to prepare a pot of tea that he hoped would calm his wife's queasy stomach. He knew that many men in his culture never spent time in the kitchen. Butros and Nadira had talked a great deal about how their marriage needed to reflect their Christian faith. Butros didn't accept the popular perspective in which men viewed their wives as property. In his country few women worked in businesses or shops. They were supposed to stay at home, have babies, raise children, and have their heads covered whenever they left home. It's not that family was any less important to them as Christians. On the contrary, Nadira was much more to Butros than a bearer of his children. She was a friend and confidante, and she was able to minister to women. They were partners in this work, and Butros often sought his wife's counsel.

Butros returned to the study with a tray containing a pot of steeping tea, two cups, milk and sugar. While she waited, Nadira had dozed on the love seat. Now as her husband set the tray on his desk, she stretched and sat up.

After she had been served and had taken a couple of sips of tea, Nadira asked, 'So why is my husband getting up so early?'

'I am trying to formulate a plan to send to Brother Andrew, to get his counsel.' He looked at his wife and smiled. 'Then I need to find financial support for my growing family, and I'm going to need some staff to help me do this work.'

Nadira turned to face her husband, tucking her feet under her. 'So what are you thinking?' she asked.

'The number one need is training for pastors. Most of them work alone, and they have had little or no seminary or Bible school training. I've talked with the bishops and denominational leaders. I want to organise a conference, a retreat maybe once or twice a year when pastors can come and be refreshed and encouraged and get some teaching. The leaders are encouraging me in this. I'm thinking of inviting Brother Andrew to be the first speaker.'

'That sounds like a good start.'

'There are many more needs and we can't address them all at once. But I'm particularly concerned about churches in rural areas. In some villages, churches have no pastor or priest. The conditions are just too severe for a young man to settle there with his family. The poverty means congregations can barely give even a small amount each month. Often there are no schools, or at best a mosque that only offers teaching of the Quran. For a man who wants to educate his children, the opportunities are in towns or cities. So I'm concerned about the state of churches in villages and I'm thinking about how lay leaders need to be raised up to help fill the gap. Also too many Christians are illiterate. They can't read their Bibles and they know very little about their faith. They are unable to get better jobs and improve their economic situation, which means the church is severely limited in its influence.'

'So my husband is going to change the social fabric of society,' Nadira chuckled. 'He's going to solve the problem of illiteracy and improve the financial health of the Christian community.'

Butros had to smile – his wife loved to tease him and her humour helped him keep a balanced perspective. 'We'll start small,' he said. 'I'd like to experiment with starting literacy centres in a couple of villages. Since many of the rural churches don't have pastors, perhaps we can help strengthen those churches by teaching adult Christians how to read and write. Maybe later we can provide job-training programmes as well.'

'You don't have any facilities or trainers . . .'

'I know. There are so many questions. That's why I'm up early. There is so much to pray about.'

Nadira set her empty teacup on the floor, reached out, and took her husband's hand in hers. 'Well, I'm here to help. We can begin by praying together about this.'

The support of a good wife was a precious gift, and Butros breathed a silent prayer of thanksgiving for Nadira. 'There's one other thing we need to pray about,' said Butros. 'The young convert Ahmed.'

5

Three months later

Ahmed had successfully faded into the vast maze of the capital city. The tiny flat that Butros had located provided him a safe house. He'd survived by doing odd jobs and receiving occasional meals and food bags from Butros. He had too much time on his hands and his mind churned over ways he could start a business. He'd decided not to continue university education for a while, since it would mean transferring from the college in Suq al Khamis and that would alert the family to his whereabouts. The only one from home he'd talked to was his sister, Farah, and they only had short conversations in which he provided no clue as to where he was living. While it was a lonely existence, Ahmed had used the time to read the Bible and some other materials Butros had provided. As he learned more about the Christian faith, he became increasingly eager to talk about it with Muslims.

Along with Zaki, Hassan had been one of Ahmed's best friends. Since Hassan was a university student in the capital city, it wasn't hard to find him. The campus was only a twenty-minute walk from Ahmed's home.

Today they sat in a bustling courtyard as students criss-crossed the campus or spread out their books to work on their assignments.

After settling into the safe house, Ahmed had immediately shaved off his closely cropped beard and decided to dress in jeans and T-shirts instead of the traditional white robe – the *jallabiya*. Butros, who often wore slacks and a dress shirt, had protested the transformation, saying, 'Christianity is not concerned with outward appearances.' But Ahmed had felt the change in dress was important – it was a reflection of what was happening in his beliefs.

Hassan had noticed immediately. When Ahmed first tracked down his friend on campus, Hassan had shouted, 'Ahmed, have you become a Christian?' Once, when they were back home in Suq al Khamis, Hassan had said to Ahmed, 'Christians kiss each other on New Year's Eve, eat pork, and believe in three gods and other false teachings. How can anyone believe those things?'

When Hassan had yelled his question on campus, Ahmed had told him to be quiet and guided Hassan to a corner of the student cafeteria. Ahmed was surprised that his friend hadn't immediately rejected him, but instead the two had started a series of intense discussions culminating in Hassan asking if he could borrow Ahmed's Bible.

'So what did you think?' Ahmed asked as Hassan pulled the New Testament out of his backpack and returned it. 'Did you read Matthew's Gospel?'

'I read the whole book.' Hassan grabbed the New Testament back and opened it to the Sermon on the Mount in Matthew 6. 'Listen to this. "When you pray, do not be like the hypocrites, for they love to pray standing in the synagogues and on the street corners to be seen by men . . . But when you pray, go into your room, close the door and pray to your Father, who is unseen. Then your Father, who sees what is done in secret, will reward you." This deeply touches me. I read this and feel a very intimate relationship between God and myself.'

'That's because you have a close relationship with your father,' Ahmed observed. 'That passage teaches something that is foreign to Islam.'

Hassan wasn't interested in talking about differences between Islam and the teachings of Jesus. He closed the New Testament and said, 'As I was reading this book, I had the feeling that my heart was getting washed, but I can't explain how. I read about Jesus and I feel I see Him walking and standing before me in a very special way. He's touched my soul.'

Ahmed was pleased at his friend's response but also knew that there was a necessary process that takes time. 'I want to ask you to think about three questions,' Ahmed said. 'First, what if you die now, where will you go?'

'Straight to hell,' Hassan laughed.

Ahmed didn't laugh with his friend. 'Second, do you think God loves all people to the same degree? Or does He love believers more?' Hassan nodded but said nothing. 'Third question, do you think that God loves you and knows you in a very intimate and personal way?'

Hassan seemed deeply moved by the last question and closed his eyes as Ahmed said, 'Ramadan begins next week. You should use the month of fasting, and pray honestly during this time.' Hassan opened his eyes, surprised that Ahmed had not pushed him toward Christianity. He wasn't sure that he wanted to remain a Muslim.

Ahmed concluded, 'If you seek God through prayer, He will reveal Himself, as long as you want sincerely to know Him.'

—◦∾◦—

Two weeks later

Butros and the refugee from Suq al Khamis were sitting in a coffee shop roughly halfway between their homes. It was late evening and everyone had broken the fast earlier, many with lavish meals. While most women stayed at home to watch the new soap operas that were wildly popular during Ramadan, many men were lounging in the coffee shop in their *jallabiya* with *kaffiyeh* on their heads. Some were puffing contentedly on their water pipes. There were several enthusiastic games of backgammon in progress, and the shop rang with the zing and rattle of dice being shaken and rolled over the boards.

Sometimes Butros felt self-conscious about wearing western-style clothing, and he admitted the native dress was comfortable, especially on scorching hot days. But he had got used to shirts and slacks in England and generally preferred such attire. Indeed in the capital city a lot of men wore western attire, though most women were still covered with the traditional *abeyya*, a full-length black coat, and a head scarf.

After the waiter brought the men small cups of Arab coffee flavoured with cardamon, Ahmed leaned forward, aware that curious ears might overhear if he spoke too loud, and almost in a whisper said, 'I want to start a business.'

Butros tried to hide his surprise. 'What kind of business?' he asked.

'You know I need some consistent work. I need a regular income so I'm not dependent on your generosity. I was thinking of starting a print shop.'

'Why a print shop?'

'I've seen what you do. You are developing study materials and they need to be printed. You are planning a conference and you'll need materials prepared. And you know pastors and priests; their churches have printing needs. I think we could meet that need.'

Butros sat back in his seat, grabbed his coffee, and downed it in a quick gulp. Then he said, 'You are right. We do need printing services. But you have no place to work. You have no equipment.'

A big smile came over Ahmed's face. He reached into the pocket of his jeans and pulled out a piece of paper. 'I found some open business space not far from here. Now I know you are looking for office space.' Butros nodded, acknowledging that soon he would have to move. 'Well, there is room for you to have your office, and there is space right next to it to set up the printing equipment. I've got some numbers to show you. Here's what it will cost for us to get started . . .'

For the next few minutes, Ahmed showed Butros his plan. He had the costs for renting the space, purchasing a small printing press, and paying for the initial stocks of paper and ink. Clearly he'd done some good research. But costs were only part of the business. Butros took a deep breath and replied, 'Well, you have thought through a lot of things. But that's a lot of money, and I don't have it.'

'But you have friends. Surely someone would like to invest in such a great venture.'

'Ahmed, you haven't shown me why this is a great venture. You have costs but no business plan. How much business do you think you can bring in? What will it take to break even? How will you pay back investors, and how much profit can they make on their money?'

'I trust you. You'll find business.'

Butros laughed. 'No, Ahmed. I have my hands full right now. I can introduce you to some people, but I don't have time to find you business. And I need to ask you, how much experience do you have in printing?'

'I learn fast.'

'Suppose I could raise the money and we set up a print shop, do you know how to run a printing press? Do you know how to maintain it and fix it when it breaks down?'

Ahmed's voice rose in pitch as he said, 'I can do this. I'm good with my hands.'

'Okay, calm down.'

'You should see me with my motorbike. I can take it apart and fix anything. No problem.'

'That's a motorbike, not a printing press.'

'So what's the difference?'

'Ahmed, if you're good with motorbikes, find a job repairing motorbikes. As you can see, there are plenty of them in this town.'

'So you aren't going to help me? I thought you were my friend. I bring you a good idea . . .'

'It is a good idea. But I don't have the money to set you up in this. And you don't have the experience. There is no business plan. Even if we had the money for the equipment, there's no assurance we could get enough business to make back our money.'

Ahmed slammed his hand on the table. 'I can't believe this.' He stood up and stormed out of the coffee shop. A couple of men looked up from their water pipes. One of them gave Butros a knowing smile.

Butros paid for the coffees and walked back to his flat. He had met only a few Muslim converts in the country, though he'd heard about others. Most he'd met were young men, unmarried, without jobs. They could be a burden on the Christian community. In some countries, he knew that foreign mission agencies supported these converts, but he didn't believe that was good for the men. They needed to find independence, for their own financial health but also for their spiritual maturity. It was one thing to help them in a transition, but it wasn't good for young men to become dependent. The good news was that Ahmed wasn't asking for charity. He seemed bright and willing to work hard. Still, Butros really knew little about him.

There was another concern. He thought of the Scripture: 'It isn't good for man to be alone.' Once he found steady employment, Ahmed needed a wife. But that problem was even harder to solve than finding a job. For one thing, in this culture, families usually arranged marriages, and these men were cut off from their families. Logically, the church ought to provide a place to meet eligible young women, but most Christian parents didn't want to see their daughters marrying 'Muslims'. Often traditional Christians did not trust Muslim-background believers in Christ (MBBs). The best solution was for these men to marry women who were also Muslim-background believers, but there weren't that many of them around.

Lord, I need Your help and wisdom. When he was stuck, the best thing Butros could do was pray. Ahmed had many needs. This certainly was a situation where the only solutions were ones that God could provide.

6

Six weeks later

Salima leaned back on a pile of pillows at the head of her bed and gazed at the television set where a man was teaching in Arabic from the Injil, the New Testament. She had first run across him three years earlier while surfing through the many channels beamed into her home via the family's satellite dish. At first, she had laughed at the strange preacher, but then she became intrigued. On the desk opposite her bed was a correspondence course she had ordered from the show. Each lesson she'd done had made her more interested in the Prophet Isa.

The teenager found it amazing that she would be watching such a programme. Salima's family was well-known in the country. Her father was a very successful businessman with close relationships to the royal family. She was the middle of seven children, four boys and three girls, and they lived in a rambling home on five acres of prime land at the edge of the capital city. Her large room had everything a girl could want – a wardrobe full of nice clothes, shelves full of great books, a collection of dolls that her father had started for her when she was just a toddler, and a first-rate stereo system.

Salima knew that many girls in her country received little or no education. However, she had loved school and her father had indulged her insatiable curiosity by paying tuition for a private education. Now she was even dreaming about the possibilities of college. Or she could sign up to take some computer courses and maybe get a job providing office support in the city. However, her father, proud as he was of her hard work, thought it would be better for her to marry, and he had told her that there were a couple of prospects he was checking out. Salima was in no hurry to get married, but she knew that while she had the right to refuse, it would be hard to go against her father's wishes.

It was curiosity that had caused Salima to send for the correspondence course. When a new lesson was expected, she kept an eye on the mail. So far, no one in her family had discovered what she was doing. Though they were very successful materially, religious expectations were also high. Her father and brothers went to the mosque every day. It wasn't as rigorous for the women – a place was reserved for them to pray in their home. But Salima knew that it would shame the family if it was discovered that she was exploring Christianity. So she was careful to hide her books and, if she had to, she would lie about her interest. No one must suspect what was going on in her heart.

There was something about the Prophet Isa that was irresistible. In Salima's understanding of Islam, Allah was far away and unapproachable. Certainly he didn't seem to care about the daily life of a woman. A Muslim man was allowed to have up to four wives, and Salima and many of her girlfriends considered that demeaning. She was glad her father had only one wife, but she knew other families where that was not the case.

The man Isa was so different from the men she knew. His life was astounding, beginning with the miracle of His birth. The way He healed people, the way He challenged hypocritical religious leaders, and most especially how He treated women – she almost wished she had been alive when He was living. Isa said God loved all people, and told His disciples to follow His example and love each other. She yearned to know real love, and something inside her seemed to say that she would find it in the Prophet Isa.

There was a knock on the door, and one of the housemaids announced that her older brother was ready to take her to the mall. She was wearing a blouse and skintight designer jeans, but she could never be seen like this away from her home. She grabbed the black *abeyya* that was hanging on the back of her door and threw it on over her clothes as she hurried to the foyer where her brother was waiting, impatiently jingling the car keys. Before passing through the front door, she made sure the *hijab* covered her head.

Salima's brother was a wild driver. He enjoyed weaving in and out of the city traffic. A couple of times she closed her eyes, sure they were about to crash. But they reached the mall safely in ten minutes, and she saw two of her friends waving to her as the car pulled up. Her brother said he would pick her up in three hours. She loved roaming the mall with her friends, especially looking at clothes and jewellery. Even though the girls couldn't display their clothes publicly, each of them had a wardrobe full of the latest western fashions.

The time spent with her friends flew past too quickly and soon her brother was recklessly driving her back home. As soon as Salima was inside the door, she tore off the *abeyya* and *hijab*, tossed them on a chair, and ran up the stairs to her room. She stopped in her tracks at the top of the stairs. Her mother was standing in the doorway of her room, staring furiously at her daughter. Suddenly Salima remembered that in her hurry to leave she had made a terrible mistake. Usually she cleared her desk before she left the house. Anything suspicious was locked in a drawer. How could she have done such a stupid thing? There, in her mother's hands, was the Bible correspondence course.

Butros always looked forward to his meetings with Pastor Yusef, the senior pastor of Al Waha Church. For more than twenty-five years, Pastor Yusef had been the pastor of the church and had seen it grow into the largest Protestant church in the country. Many other pastors recognised him as a spiritual leader and mentor. His passion was to make the Bible clear enough for anyone to understand, so his sermons were easy to follow. He had assisted in translating the New Testament into simple Arabic – the older Arabic Bible used for decades was archaic and difficult for many people to read.

Shortly after returning from England, Butros had visited Pastor Yusef, and he continued to meet regularly with this gentle man of God for counsel and encouragement. When Ahmed had fled to the capital city, Butros called Yusef who contacted a church member who managed some flats. Thus they were able to find a safe house for Ahmed.

Today Butros was reporting to Yusef about what he'd learned from visiting churches around the country and the plans he was developing. They were also discussing the need Butros had for office space and, eventually, staff.

'I would love for you to have your office next to me,' Pastor Yusef admitted, 'but I'm not sure it's a good idea. You are building relationships among all the denominations, so your office should be somewhere neutral. However, there may be several volunteers from the church who would like to help you.'

At this moment Yusef's secretary opened the door and announced, 'Pastor, there is a Mustafa here to see you.'

'Please excuse this interruption,' Yusef said to Butros. 'My secretary is instructed that whenever a seeker asks to see me, I will make that a priority.'

A lanky, bearded man entered the office, and Yusef and Butros rose to welcome him.

'I don't know why I'm here,' Mustafa said as they shook hands.

'Maybe you are here because God has brought you,' Yusef responded. He introduced Butros and said, 'Do you mind if he stays? Perhaps together we can help you.'

Mustafa looked at the two men and blurted out his frustration, 'This is the sixth church I've visited. The first five told me to go away.'

Yusef smiled and said, 'You are welcome here. Please sit down. May I get you a cold drink?'

While the three men drank bottles of cola, Mustafa told about his spiritual journey. 'I have written down more than three hundred questions,' said the member of Muslim Brotherhood. 'I'm confused and I have asked myself: *is the Quran God's words? If the Bible is true, then for whom do I live?*'

'Three hundred questions is a lot,' Yusef said gently with a smile. It was easy to understand why this man, who just turned sixty, had the confidence of so many people, and why Muslim visitors opened up to him. 'Have you found any answers?'

'I don't know. Maybe I believe the Bible is authentic. I certainly can't find any evidence that it's been altered.'

'Good. That's a start. So what is the question that troubles you the most?'

'How could God have a Son?' Mustafa became agitated and leaned forward as he repeated the questions he'd heard posed by Islamic scholars. 'How can God be a man? He is too holy, too great, sublime. He needs nothing.

You say Jesus was God. But He needed food. He went to the toilet. How can God go to the toilet? It is blasphemy to say this about God.' Mustafa sat back, pleased with his logical argument. 'And you say Jesus was crucified,' he continued. 'When He said He was thirsty, how come He allowed them to pour vinegar in His nose? How can God experience such a state of weakness? Also, if God needs nothing outside Himself, how come Jesus went to the temple to pray? That means He needed God, proving He Himself was only a prophet.'

Yusef smiled and said, 'These are good questions. And we have good answers. We believe Jesus was fully God *and* fully man. As a man, Jesus shared all the necessities of physical existence. As God, He can benefit those who accept His salvation and harm those who refuse Him. Christians find no problem with Jesus praying. This was His fellowship and communion with the Father. Also the Quran states that God prays. *Sura* 33:43 says, "He (Allah) it is who *yosalli* [literally: 'prays'] upon you [meaning Muslims] and His angels, that He may bring you forth from darkness into light." '

Mustafa looked momentarily confused that Pastor Yusef would quote the Quran. Then he leaned forward and said, 'But if Jesus is God's Son, that means Allah must have married and that the Son is not eternal." '

'The Quran describes Jesus as "a Word from God" and "the Spirit of God" '. The Injil calls Jesus the Son whom God loves and in whom He is well-pleased. All three phrases are saying that Isa comes from God. That is the intention of both books – to describe where Jesus comes from. Don't think of this in terms of God marrying Mary and having a son. That is not what the Quran or the Injil says.

'The fatherhood of God is not physical but spiritual,' Yusef continued with a twinkle in his eye. 'God is also our Father – same principle. And I am His child – same principle. That is really only an analogy to help us understand a little of what, in reality, lies far beyond our grasp. The biblical use of the words *Father* and *Son* is to explain the relationship between God the Father and Jesus, His eternal "Word". Both are beyond time. Both are united in the Holy Spirit . . .'

'What you call the Trinity,' Mustafa interrupted. 'You do believe in three Gods?'

'No, one God, but three persons.'

'One plus one plus one equals three,' Mustafa proclaimed.

'God is not a mathematical concept,' Yusef answered, not backing off at all from the confrontation. 'No scriptures, Christian or Muslim, interpret "oneness" as meaning that God has only one attribute or only one characteristic.' With this he stopped and opened his arms and said, 'My friend, we can't answer all your questions at once. But there are answers. I want to invite you to take your time and ask your wonderful questions.'

Mustafa listened and stroked his long beard. It was quiet for a moment in the office. Butros simply looked on. Then Mustafa admitted he was in trouble. 'About a month ago I had a vision. A man in a white robe appeared to me. He said, "I am the one you are looking for. Get up and read of Me in the Holy Book."'

'And who do you think that man was?' Yusef asked.

'Jesus.' Mustafa paused. 'I told you I belong to the Muslim Brotherhood on campus, but I've started to pull away. The sheikh has noticed, and a couple of days ago he came to my flat and accused me of disbelieving. I told him that *he* was behind this. He had encouraged me to read the Bible and to write a rebuttal. He tried to grab my papers, but I prevented him. Then he said, "You are an atheist. You will leave the group and you will stop teaching."'

'So what are you going to do?'

'I want to continue my study, but I don't think it's safe for me to do it in my flat.'

'Do you need a place to stay?' Yusef asked.

Mustafa nodded.

Yusef turned to Butros and asked, 'Do you think our friend Ahmed would like to have a roommate?'

When the heat wasn't too oppressive, Butros and Nadira enjoyed a stroll around their neighbourhood after sundown. Nadira was now eight months pregnant and two weeks earlier she had resigned from her teaching job. She moved awkwardly but looked forward to the walks. 'I have to get out of the flat,' she said.

This evening neither spoke for a while as they slowly walked past shops that sold cloth. Butros waited patiently while she examined several bolts of material. He understood that she was thinking about the baby clothes and curtains for the nursery she wanted to make – once they knew whether they would have a boy or a girl. Some colourful material caught Butros's eye and he pointed it out to Nadira. 'You should make a new dress for yourself.'

Nadira laughed and said, 'Don't be silly. Look at me – I'm great with child! Besides, we can't afford that just now.'

Butros blushed as his wife resumed her inspection of material for curtains. It was a dear older woman at his church who had gently noted Nadira's old clothes and reproved him for not taking better care of his wife. He desperately wanted to provide for her and decided that he would surprise her with the material for a new dress after the baby was born.

From the fabric shops they walked down the street to where there were several shops that sold spices. Nadira stopped to check with their favourite shopkeeper Abdul, who eagerly had her sniff and taste some cinnamon he'd just purchased. She bought an ounce, as well as some cumin and coriander. Another street over at her favourite fruit stand, she examined some dates.

'The sweetest dates in the country!' Hadi declared as he insisted Nadira and Butros each try one.

Nadira purchased half a kilo and as Hadi wrapped them up, he said to Butros with a smile, 'So when will I see you in the mosque?'

Butros laughed. This was an ongoing joke. Hadi had gone on the *hajj*, the pilgrimage to Mecca and Medina, and ever since had cheerfully invited any Christian who visited his stand to come and pray in his mosque.

The couple strolled down a few more streets. Nadira poked her husband playfully as she said, 'So, no witness for Hadi tonight?'

'He never misses a chance to try and bring me to Islam.'

'And when are you going to invite him to church?' she teased.

'Soon, Nadira, soon.'

Nadira noted that Butros wasn't engaging in the playful banter they often enjoyed. As they turned back toward their street, Nadira said quietly, 'You are tense, my husband.'

Butros smiled. 'You know me well,' he said, but he didn't answer her implied question. He knew Nadira was patient and would wait until he was ready to speak. She was a tremendous comfort to him. While he had developed a small network of pastors and Christian businessmen for his work, Nadira remained his closest advisor.

Just now his burden was for Ahmed and Mustafa, and there might be others moving into that tiny safe house. He was learning of more seekers and converts each week.

'I have an idea for a way the men we're helping might support themselves,' Butros said. 'You know the land we are currently renting to farmers. What if we used it instead to set up a little business on that land and the men could live there?'

Nadira grabbed her husband's arm to keep her balance on an uneven cobblestone pavement. 'Is there any danger, particularly for Ahmed, living so close to the town where his family lives?'

'I'm not sure. I'll need to think about it.'

'What kind of business are you considering?'

'I'm thinking of growing crops and also raising chickens. We could start them out with maybe fifty or one hundred birds. They could sell the eggs and meat.'

'Do they have any experience with growing crops and caring for chickens? They need to know what they're doing.' That was an important question. There was a part of the population that thought it was beneath them to get their hands dirty working on a farm.

Butros laughed, 'I don't know; I'm still getting to know them. I assumed since they have lived in the farming area that they would be comfortable with this idea. But no, I don't know if they'd be willing to live and work on a farm.'

'Speaking of living, we have only a shed on the property. You can't expect the men to live in that.'

Butros sighed. He had considered that the men could sleep in the shed or even under the stars for a short period. But they would need something more. Perhaps they could build a shelter, but he would also need to provide money for the building materials.

Back at their apartment building, Nadira let go of Butros's arm, grabbed the rail, and slowly climbed the stairs to their second-floor flat. After they closed the front door, Nadira said, 'You are a good man, Butros, a generous man. We should think about this and pray about it. But here's another thing we should consider. What is our mission? What has God called us to do?'

Butros looked into his wife's eyes. 'That concerns me too. Starting a business will take from the energy and resources we need for what we're already doing.'

'So let's think about how we might use our property to further those goals. God gave us that land for a reason. We must pray about how best to use it.'

Nadira took Butros's hand and placed it on her abdomen. 'Do you feel the baby kicking?'

Butros smiled.

'We must also think about our family,' Nadira continued. 'It's good that you think about the two converts. God entrusted them to us and we must do what we can to help them. But have you thought about how we will feed our child?'

'A lot,' he said. 'So far, God has provided for us everything that we need.'

'You and God are good providers,' Nadira said.

'But we are going to need more resources, and soon.'

7

One year later

Butros knew that it would be an hour and a half or more after the arrival of the Qatar Airways flight from Doha before Brother Andrew would emerge from his encounter with the chaotic passport control lines and battle to recover his luggage from a single creaking carousel built before the demands of massive 747s were anticipated. Still, Butros and twenty-five young people from his church crowded eagerly around the terminal exit to await their special guest.

Nearly three years had passed since Brother Andrew had challenged Butros to return home and serve God in his native country. They had stayed in touch, and in fact Andrew's letters often seemed to arrive at the perfect moment when Butros questioned whether he had heard correctly God's call. Sometimes there were exhortations from Scripture that seemed perfectly chosen for his circumstances. There was invaluable counsel based on years of going to the persecuted church, first behind the Iron Curtain and later to countries such as China, Vietnam and Cuba. That input gave Butros the confidence he needed to step out and trust God to reveal His plan for this ministry.

Now Butros sensed that Brother Andrew's visit, his first to the country, was perfect timing. Butros was eager to introduce Andrew to some of the church leaders and to talk about the growing vision to address the root issues that kept the churches in his country weak and ineffective. The highlight of the trip would be the first of what he hoped would be an annual conference for pastors. For five days these courageous men could come and rest and be refreshed as they received training from Brother Andrew and Pastor Yusef.

Stretching on tiptoe, Butros saw his friend pushing a trolley, loaded with two heavy suitcases and a couple of boxes, through customs to the exit. He turned to the group surrounding him and said, 'Everyone get ready.'

The Dutchman emerged and searched the crowd for a familiar face, ignoring an enthusiastic group of taxi drivers trying to sell him a trip into the city. Seeing Butros waving, Andrew burst into a smile and approached the group as the young people began to sing. After a verse in Arabic, they sang one in English:

> If my tongue is held in silence,
> My heart will sing and praise even unto death.
> I will sing that the Lord of glory has loved me
> And has given me His Holy Spirit.
> Hallelujah. Hallelujah. Hallelujah.

The men and women in their teens and twenties, dressed in western-style jeans and polo shirts, drew surprised stares. As the choir sang enthusiastically, Butros embraced his friend in a strong hug and kissed him on both cheeks in the traditional Arabic greeting. 'Welcome. You have finally made it to my country.'

Andrew listened to the powerful voices of the young choir, amazed that they would so boldly sing Christian songs in this Muslim nation. Already he realised he would be learning far more than he would be teaching on this trip. While this was a church living under persecution, at least one small group of Christians didn't appear intimidated by the Islamic culture.

It was past midnight by the time they reached the hotel, but Butros was eager to tell his guest about the plans for the next two weeks. He filled an electric kettle with bottled water and asked Andrew if he would like a cup of tea. 'I developed a taste for English tea during my years of study in England,' Butros said.

'Well, I'm Dutch, so that means I like coffee,' Andrew said with a laugh. 'But I'll gladly drink tea with you.'

They settled into two easy chairs, and Butros poured the tea, saying, 'I have so looked forward to your visit. There is much I want you to see.' He handed an itinerary to Brother Andrew and pointed out the highlights. He was most concerned about having Andrew speak twice a day at the conference. 'That will be eight times. I hope that's not too much.'

'Not at all. I'm here to serve you. But it would be a huge help if you could tell me a little about the men to whom I'll be speaking. How are their churches doing? What are the needs here?'

'We'll begin that briefing tomorrow. I want you to meet Pastor Yusef. You'll be preaching at his church on Sunday.' Then Butros leaned back in his chair, inhaled the steam from his tea, and quietly said, 'I think you'll discover that the Muslims would be very happy if there were no church at all in this country.'

―――∾∾∾―――

The next morning Butros picked Andrew up at 10.00 a.m. for the twenty-minute drive to Al Waha Church. He drove an older model German-made car that had accumulated many miles as he criss-crossed the country to visit churches and meet pastors. The city streets were bustling with several modes of transport. Wealthy sheikhs sped through the city in chauffeured Mercedes, throwing up dirt on the donkey carts plodding along the shoulder. Buses were crowded with young people. Men rode bicycles or motorcycles – one biker carried a stack of cages with live chickens; another had his veiled wife and daughter perched precariously on the rear bumper.

Dust also filled the air from the numerous construction projects in this sprawling city. Striking steel-and-glass high-rises were filling the city centre and construction cranes swung on top of several partially completed buildings – hotels, office buildings and residential flats. Andrew noted that on almost every street, next to each new building, was a shiny new mosque. In contrast Al Waha Church was a Gothic anomaly, the remnant of another era when colonialism ruled and a Protestant mission agency had tried to establish a beachhead for Christianity among the nomadic Arab tribes.

'At one time this area was a large walled compound with a school, a hospital and homes for the missionaries,' Butros explained as he parked behind the church building. 'The government nationalised the school and hospital many years ago and expelled the mission organisation that ran it. All that remains today is the church, and we are very grateful for its presence in the heart of the capital city.'

In the back of the church was a suite of offices, and even though it was Saturday, the place seemed full of activity – someone was making photocopies, an assistant pastor was counselling an older couple, and several young men were meeting in a conference room. Pastor Yusef's study was in a quiet corner. He welcomed his guests warmly and came round from behind his desk to sit with them as they talked.

'Has Butros told you about our church?' Yusef asked in perfect English. Then with a twinkle in his eyes, he asked, 'Did he tell you that the name Al Waha means "The Oasis"? I like that image. I like to think we are an oasis in the desert and we provide water for desperately thirsty people.'

'That is an excellent picture of what the church should be,' Brother Andrew said.

'So you will give fresh water to the congregation tomorrow,' Yusef said. 'We have a small service in the morning. Sunday is a workday, so many can't attend in the morning. Sunday evening is our big service. We will have more than five hundred people here.'

'Which makes this the biggest Protestant congregation in the country,' Butros added.

'My predecessor, the man who mentored me, always presented the gospel message in every sermon he preached. There was always an invitation to accept Christ. We like everyone to have a confrontation with Jesus,' Yusef said emphatically.

'Amen.' Andrew was drawn to this warm Arab man with a soft voice and exuberant passion. 'So anyone can come to this church. Muslims too?'

'Everyone is welcome. We never turn anyone away. We present Christ and people are like pigeons – they flock to the crumbs. We never present the church or a denomination. Our objective is for them to know Jesus.'

'I look forward to preaching tomorrow,' Andrew said. 'But isn't it dangerous to be so open, to let anyone come to hear you? Last night my friend Butros said that many people in this country would be happy if there were no church at all.'

Yusef looked sad as he answered, 'That is true. Yes.'

'In some Muslim countries there is no church, Afghanistan and Saudi Arabia to name two. At least here, you have an established church where you can meet legally.'

'Legally maybe, but under their control,' Butros answered. 'They certainly do not want to give us freedom to develop, to flourish, to grow.'

'So you are under the eye of government authorities?' Andrew asked for clarification.

'Worse than that. We live under constant societal pressure,' Yusef answered. 'We are always aware that we are being watched, and that some-one wants to prevent us from doing ministry.' He leaned forward to emphasise his next point. 'You need to understand that the church exists only as a permitted community in the midst of the great big majority of Islamic people.'

'So how strong is the church here?' Andrew asked. 'Is she having an effective witness to the culture?'

'We are weak and lukewarm,' Yusef answered. 'We are neglecting our first duty, which is missions. Christians act like the ten spies who returned to Moses from Canaan and declared that the proposed invasion should be called off.'

'So what can we do about it?' Andrew asked.

Yusef's kind eyes looked intently into Brother Andrew's. 'There is only one hope for the church to have any impact on the Muslim community.'

'What's that?'

'Love. After long years of war and persecution, Christians seldom see Muslims as people whom God loves and for whom Christ died. Christians need a new filling of the Holy Spirit to love those who disagree with them. And the greatest expression of love is to share with them the most precious thing a Christian has, which is the good news of the salvation of Jesus Christ.'

Andrew thought about that for a moment as Butros concluded by saying, 'So you see, an effective church is also the biggest threat to Islam. If we are truly being light and salt, we will be attacked.'

The scene before Brother Andrew was a serene contrast to the noisy clamour of the capital city just an hour's drive away. The rising sun painted hauntingly beautiful colours – red, teal, orange, and purple – over the rocky hills. He sipped a cup of instant coffee, having loaded it with two packages of sugar and another of creamer, and stepped out of his room on to a small patio to enjoy the desert scene. The pastors' conference was being held at a rustic retreat centre run by a foreign corporation. It had been an exciting four days as Andrew interacted with ministers from various Orthodox and Protestant denominations, as well as a priest from an Anglican church and another from a Catholic parish in the capital.

Early mornings provided the only quiet moments alone. Andrew strolled away from his room onto the rocky sand, enjoying the cool morning air that in less than an hour would become unbearably hot in its relentless climb well above 100 degrees Fahrenheit. It had been two weeks since his arrival in the Middle East, and later that afternoon, after a final message to the conference, Butros would drive him to the airport and send him back to his native Dutch culture. He wasn't eager to leave. The people here had captured his heart.

It is doubtful that Andrew and Butros could have done more in these two weeks. During the first few days, they had met with Christian leaders in the capital city, and Andrew had preached several times in their churches. On the second Sunday Butros drove Andrew to a village where there was one church, a Protestant mission that had many years ago built a simple stone chapel. The floor consisted of packed dirt covered with old faded carpets. The only furnishings were four chairs and a simple podium on a wooden platform. The pastor had warmly greeted Andrew, saying, 'This is the first time any foreigner has visited our mission in thirty years.'

Approximately one hundred people came and sat on the floor – men on the right, women on the left, with several children running freely between them – to hear this Dutch visitor. Andrew had looked over the crowd, most of them in traditional Arab dress, and felt awkward standing above them in his coat and tie. After speaking for a few minutes, he removed his coat jacket and went and sat on the floor in the midst of the congregation. Several children quickly gathered around him and two toddlers sat on his lap. As he 'preached' his sermon, Butros translated it into Arabic for the congregation.

Afterwards Andrew enjoyed a simple meal with the people and walked around the mission compound where several of the families lived. He was shocked to learn that the Christians were not allowed by the Muslim majority to draw water from the village well. The only water available to Christians was from a small well in the church compound, but it was not enough. Andrew offered to provide the money to dig a new well for the Christian community.

After that service Butros had brought Andrew to this conference centre. Some fifty men had participated in the meetings and they seemed hungry for the messages Andrew delivered. Now he wondered how to conclude the conference. What was the message God wanted him to leave with these dedicated men?

He was still praying about what to say when he heard the bell ring for breakfast. As he entered the dining room, he took a seat between Butros and Abuna Alexander, one of the few men he had yet to talk to during the conference. He spooned red beans on to his plate from a large bowl, mashed them with a fork and added some olive oil and salt, then ate the mixture with pieces of flat bread. 'Already you are becoming a good Arab,' Alexander said.

'*Shukran*,' Andrew replied. 'Thank you' was one of the few Arabic words he had learned.

'My English not so good,' Alexander said with a shy smile, indicating his desire to talk.

Butros leaned over and said he would be glad to translate and told Andrew, 'Father Alexander has served for many years in Suq al Khamis, a town in the farming region of this country.'

As Andrew poured a cup of strong tea from a pitcher in the middle of the table, Father Alexander told his story: 'I was born in a Christian family. My mother was faithful to attend the services, but my father attended only occasionally. When I was ten, my mother died. The local priest looked after me, and my father became more devout. As a teenager I felt called to the priesthood. I have been a priest now for thirty years.'

Andrew studied the face of the priest and thought he could see a weariness produced by years of hard, often thankless, labour. 'Please, would you tell me about your church?' Brother Andrew asked.

The priest explained that he served about seventy-five families, though many of them didn't attend regularly. 'We also run a school in co-operation with another church on the other side of town. We have two families that are relatively well-to-do. One is a gold dealer; the other sells televisions and other appliances. They are generous to the church and that helps us keep going.'

'What are the challenges you face?'

Alexander and Butros explained that many of the parishioners were Christian in name only and exhibited no passion for the services. Alexander also admitted that the congregation was slowly shrinking. Families with the means were moving to Europe or North America. 'The Muslims are glad to see them go,' Alexander said.

'It is not a healthy situation when a church is not growing,' Brother Andrew observed. 'You need new blood. The future of any church lies with the teenagers. Get them excited and the church will have life.'

The priest shook his head sadly. 'I'm afraid it's hard to get teenagers interested in church when their parents don't even attend. There is a Pentecostal church in town – they have a lot of teenagers. But no matter what I do, I can't seem to draw the youth into St Mark's.'

'Why do you think that is?'

'The other church has contemporary music. They don't respect the historical traditions of the church.'

Andrew knew that the priest wasn't about to change the style of worship to please a few kids. But he also had seen many vibrant liturgical churches and he thought he knew at least one reason for the difference. 'Have you encouraged them to read the Bible?'

'We read the Scriptures during liturgy. It is not our tradition for people to read the Bible at home. It is the priest's job to teach them.'

'But you can't teach them the Bible if they don't come to church.'

The priest spread out his hands and admitted, 'That is my problem.'

'In my experience there is nothing more exciting than young people studying the Bible together.' Andrew told about his own experience as a young man just out of the military and how the changed lives of him and several others caused a small revival in several churches. 'Many of us started reading through the Bible each year. As a result the entire youth group went to the mission field. What if you challenged the teenagers in St Mark's to read the New Testament this year and talk about it together – under your guidance?'

The priest stroked his beard as he thought about that idea.

Butros enquired, 'Alexander, do people have their own Bibles?' The priest shook his head. Butros continued, 'If we provided the Scriptures for you, maybe you could hold a rally, something fun to draw the teenagers, and there you could issue a challenge – you give each teen a personal copy of the New Testament if they agree to read it over the next twelve months.'

Alexander nodded and finally said, 'This could cause me new problems, if the youth get too much enthusiasm.'

Andrew responded, 'I've always said it's easier to cool down a fanatic than to warm up a corpse!'

Even with the language barrier, the priest understood the picture and started to laugh. 'Well, maybe I should welcome that kind of problem.'

'Butros will do whatever he can to help you. I have another question. Can everyone in your church read?'

'Maybe half the congregation reads. But with the teens, more do read. Their parents want them to have a chance to get ahead, and our church provides an opportunity for education.'

'But mostly only for the males,' Butros added.

'For those who can't read, you might consider a literacy training programme,' Andrew said.

'We are hoping to train some literacy teachers,' said Butros. 'Suq al Khamis would be an excellent place to start a programme.'

'And everyone who goes through the programme and learns to read would receive a Bible at graduation.'

'You give me much to think about,' said the priest. 'If we don't grow, we will die.'

Butros interjected, 'Father Alexander is also facing a new challenge. Please, tell Brother Andrew about it.'

'Last week a young Muslim man came to tell me he was now a follower of Christ. He's the fourth one this year. They tell me they want to convert and be baptised.'

'That's fantastic!' Andrew blurted.

'No, that's a problem,' said Butros. 'The situation in Suq al Khamis is tense just now. Muslim fundamentalism is on the rise. Young men are calling for a greater commitment to Islam. They are demanding that the government repeal western-style laws and submit only to Sharia law. The government is concerned about their influence. In some nearby villages there have been attacks against churches and Christian businesses.'

Father Alexander spoke and Butros translated: 'If we let Muslims into our church, we endanger the whole congregation. The police can close down the church. The extremists could gather a mob and burn the church down, and also our homes. It has happened. And the police will not stop them.' The priest opened his arms and turned his hands upward. 'So, what can I do?'

'Usually these young men who become followers of Jesus move to the capital city,' Butros continued. 'I have found a flat for three of them, a safe house. There are similar conversions happening in other parts of the country.'

'I hate to say this,' said Father Alexander, 'but my church doesn't want any converts. We simply don't know what to do with them.'

There was an uneasy silence among the three men. Then Brother Andrew said, perhaps to himself as much as to Butros and Father Alexander, 'How can there be a church where converts are not welcome?'

—◦◦◦—

For most of the drive to the airport, Brother Andrew and Butros were quiet. Part of it was weariness – they'd worked hard for more than two weeks. But also there was much to think about. Finally, Andrew broke the silence, saying, 'Muslims who become followers of Christ pay a high price.' Of all he'd seen and learned, his heart was most touched by the plight of converts. 'I do hope that next time I come, I will be able to meet some of these brothers.'

Butros nodded to acknowledge the request while driving through the chaotic traffic. A few moments later, as the airport came into view, he spoke. 'Yes, I want you to meet them. And I need your prayers about the situation. This has added a new complexity to the ministry.'

'I'm trying to understand why the church won't try to bring them into the body. I know there are risks . . .'

'Don't be too hard on the pastors. They have been deceived in the past by supposed converts. Wolves in sheep's clothing – I think you know that phrase? But even the genuine converts, they are considered infidels according to Islamic law. By helping them, the church commits a criminal act in the eyes of Islam. If it's discovered that a pastor baptised a former Muslim, that is considered deserving of death.'

Just outside the terminal parking lot, Butros pulled off the road and parked. He shut off the engine and turned to his friend. 'Andrew, I want you to understand the situation, because together maybe we can work out a way to help these brothers. I am taking the opportunity to disciple three of these men. They love Jesus, but they know very little about how to live the Christian life.'

'How old are they?'

'Two are in their early twenties; the third just turned thirty. That is part of the challenge. They don't have jobs. They aren't married. They have fled from their families. Right now, they are almost totally dependent on me. So you see if more Muslims convert, at the moment it would be very difficult to help them.'

'But if we don't help them, they could go right back to Islam.'

'Yes, and many converts do. It is well known that at least half of all Muslim converts return to Islam. The loneliness and the pressure from family and community and Islamic groups are simply too great. It takes great courage to leave your old life. They go to a church and are turned away. Often they are arrested and the police routinely torture prisoners. Everywhere they turn, they are intimidated and pressured to go back to Islam.'

Then Andrew said, mostly to himself, 'The old has passed away. Behold all things have become new.'

'But how does it become new?' Butros responded. 'Brother Andrew, I came home to help strengthen the church in my country so that the church will be a light, and that includes being a witness to Muslims. But the church is just trying to survive. It can't or won't reach out. And now we've got these converts . . .'

'Newborn babes.'

'Yes, spiritual babies who must be cared for. I didn't plan this. I'm one man. I have no staff. I have no infrastructure.'

'But you have the Spirit of God with you.' Andrew paused and lifted another quick, silent prayer heavenwards for his friend. He didn't want to suggest a formulaic solution that wouldn't apply here. In an hour or so he would board a plane for home. Butros had to carry on in the most challenging of circumstances.

'Butros, God hasn't made a mistake. And these Muslim converts aren't outside your calling. They are part of the church – we just don't see how they fit into the established body yet. Remember, you are God's chosen man for this time in this country. He will give you the wisdom you need. He will provide the resources you need. And by the way, my organisation is going to help. I have your latest plan and budget. You will hear from us soon, and it will be good news.'

Andrew withdrew his wallet, took out all of the local currency he had, and put it in his friend's hand. 'When I arrived I exchanged more money than I needed. Please take this and use it to help cover the costs for those men in the safe house.'

Butros was embarrassed to take the money. 'I can't accept this,' he said, trying to give it back.

'Yes, you can. Please don't deprive me of this small blessing.'

Butros fought his emotions. 'Brother Andrew, you are a great encourage-ment to me. I hope you will keep coming back. I need your prayers and counsel.'

'I will give you whatever help I can. Call on me. I'll come back as often as you need me.'

8

One week later

Two men in suits stood at the door of the flat. 'We are looking for Butros.'

'That would be me,' Butros said. He allowed the men to enter, and Nadira went to the master bedroom to nurse the baby, who now was nearly one year old. As Butros observed the men, he concluded immediately they were with the *Mukhabarat*, the country's secret police. They looked intently at the contents of the tiny living room, as though trying to memorise every detail.

'We have a few questions we need to ask you.'

'By all means. Please, come into my office. May I get you some coffee or tea?'

They were not interested in hospitality but quickly entered his study, shut the door, and indicated Butros should sit. The one who had spoken, wearing a blue shirt, said, 'We need to understand what you are doing in this country.'

'I don't understand,' Butros answered. 'This is my country. I was born here. I am a loyal citizen.'

'We're here for your protection,' the other man, who was wearing a white shirt, added. Neither had identified himself by name.

'I'm afraid I don't understand,' Butros said cautiously. 'Am I in some kind of danger?'

The men didn't answer, but blue shirt said, 'You'd better tell us what it is that you do.'

His senses on full alert, Butros silently prayed: *Lord, protect me. Give me the right words.* 'I work with churches. But you probably already know that.' The men gave no reaction. 'I help pastors to be more effective in their work.'

'What are these materials?' blue shirt said, picking up a stack of booklets Butros had received from the Bible Forum, a group of organisations that distributed Bibles and other resources in many countries.

'Bibles and teaching materials.'

'For churches?'

'Yes, for churches. So they can be more effective in teaching their congregations about the Christian faith.'

The man with the white shirt pulled out a notebook and made a few notes. He looked at Butros and said, 'You make a lot of money selling these materials.'

Butros shrugged his shoulders. 'No, not really. I give most of them away.'

Blue shirt put his hand on a Rolodex on Butros's desk, turned it, and began to thumb through the cards. Butros stiffened, then reminded himself that there were no names there that would cause any suspicions. Still, he didn't like this.

'So how do you fund your work?' asked white shirt. 'How do you make enough to pay for your conferences and your travels?'

'I have various sources of funding.'

'From where?'

'Several churches provide contributions.'

'Al Waha Church?'

'That is one of the churches. Yes.'

'Does any money come from Europe or America?'

'A little.'

Blue shirt closed the Rolodex and returned it to its original position. 'You haven't registered as an official NGO?' He was talking about a non-governmental organisation.

'Not yet. I plan to start the process soon.'

'You know you need to be an NGO to receive foreign funds.'

'I am aware that is required if you have over a certain amount of income from foreign sources.' Butros knew that he was pushing the limits of what was allowed without registering as an NGO, but he was also concerned about the government oversight that registering would attract and he wanted to avoid it for as long as possible.

White shirt changed tactics and said, 'So, who is this foreigner with white hair who visited you?'

'He is known as Brother Andrew.'

'He's a monk?'

'No, that's just the name by which he is known internationally.'

'He's from where?'

Butros resisted laughing, because they certainly knew where he was from. 'Holland.'

'Why did he come?'

'He came at my invitation. He spoke at several churches and at the pastors' conference.'

'Do you work with Muslims?'

This was a sudden switch. He would have to be careful. 'No, sir.'

'We've heard reports that you are proselytising Muslims. We will not tolerate that.'

'No, I do not proselytise.'

'Have you baptised any Muslims?' asked blue shirt.

'No, sir, I would never do that. I only baptise Christians.'

No one spoke for a moment. White shirt put his notebook away and looked at Butros. 'You seem like a decent man. You were educated in England, right?'

Butros assumed they knew all about his education. 'Yes, sir.'

'So why don't you leave this country and go back to England? It's safer there.'

The words were an implied threat. Butros was upset with the implication that he didn't belong here. 'Why should I leave? This is my country too. This is where God has placed us. It is His will that we should live here and work here. And that is our intention; as long as God allows us, we will live and work here.'

The two men headed to the living room. As they exited the flat, white shirt turned and looked at Butros. 'You should think about what I said. If you really love your family, your wife, and your son, leave while you can.'

—⁓—

One week later

There were three men living in the tiny flat. It consisted of two small rooms, and a cupboard-sized bathroom. In one room, the men slept on the floor on thin mattresses they rolled up during the day. In the other room, there were cushions against the wall and a small coffee table. On one side were a sink, refrigerator and stove.

Butros entered the flat bearing food his wife had prepared along with a stack of *khobz*, the local flat bread he'd picked up at the bakery around the corner, and bottles of soda he'd bought at the shop next door to the bakery. He spread his wife's packages on the small table. There was a plastic dish filled with hummus, and another of *baba ghannouge*, a tasty mash of eggplant mixed with tomato and onion. In addition there were appetizers of *mashi waraq ainab*, grape leaves stuffed with minced meat, and *fatayer*, small pastries filled with cheese or spinach.

The smells drew the men like bees to a sweet flower. Mustafa said, '*Bismillah* – in the name of God' and grabbed a circle of *khobz*, tore off a piece, and started to dip it into the hummus when Butros interrupted: 'Just a minute.'

Mustafa looked up, not sure what he'd done wrong.

'Before we eat, we give thanks to our heavenly Father for providing our daily food. So let's take a minute and pray together.'

After saying grace, Ahmed, Mustafa and Hassan sat on the floor by the table and ate eagerly. For a while, after their disagreement in the coffee shop, there had been a strain between Ahmed and Butros. Even after they had made peace, they had a couple more clashes. Clearly Ahmed was a bright man, full of ideas, eager to find his way in society and in his new faith. Butros understood the young man's struggle and was patient, praying for him, encouraging him, occasionally providing a little material aid, since Ahmed had not found a viable way to earn a consistent living.

Butros recognised that Ahmed had a gift for communication. After the meeting in Pastor Yusef's office, Mustafa had accepted the invitation to live with Ahmed, and the two had many long talks. Finally, Mustafa had an outlet for his questions, and Ahmed had been stimulated intellectually and spiritually by the discussions.

The change in the radical fundamentalist was gradual but dramatic. One day he'd blurted out to Ahmed, 'I can't believe the love I feel for all people. I want to kiss them all!' He had travelled home to his family and gone up to his mother, kissed her, and told her he loved her. She'd been astonished because he'd previously considered her an unbeliever. She asked why he now loved her.

'Because I now know a God who loves. He lives in my heart. And I know Him through Isa.'

She'd warned him not to tell anyone else in the family because he would surely be taken to the hospital and treated for mental illness.

'I'm not crazy!' Mustafa had protested to his mother. 'I've read the Injil. Jesus shows us what God is like, and He has brought me into peace with God.'

Hassan, clearly relishing the meal, looked up at Butros, who was sitting against the wall. 'Why don't you eat with us? This is wonderful food,' he said, then tipped his head back for a long drink of cola.

'This is what I eat all the time,' Butros said with a smile. 'As you can plainly see, I'm gaining some weight around the middle.'

'It's not Ramadan. You don't need to fast,' Hassan joked as he popped a *fatayer* in his mouth.

Hassan had moved into the flat a few weeks after Mustafa. Butros had met him shortly afterward, and Hassan spilled out the story of Ahmed's challenge to read the Quran during Ramadan. 'I asked God to reveal Himself to me as He had to Ahmed. I made a deal with Him – if He didn't reveal Himself to me, I would decide to abandon Him.'

'You mean Islam?' Butros had asked.

'Islam, Christianity, religion – all of it. I didn't want to play games. As I read the Quran, I felt nothing touched me personally – it was just a book of rules. It showed me a way. But when I read the Bible, it was the opposite experience. Jesus doesn't show me a way. He shows me *the* way. He is *siraat-e-mustaqeem* – the straight road. I saw that the Bible is a living book because the author who wrote it is living, and I felt God speaking to me through this book. The love of God touched me in a very personal way. As a result, I left Islam completely for a four-month period. And then my sister gave birth to a baby girl. Two days after her birth, the baby had a heart attack.

The doctors advised my sister to take the baby home because she would die very soon. Immediately I thought of Jesus the Healer and I began to pray: "Isa, when You were on earth You used to heal people. Now, I ask You to heal this sick baby." Immediately the baby opened her eyes and she had this beautiful smile. After that she closed her eyes and slept. My sister thought the baby had died, but God had healed her. She's completely healthy now, and the doctors can't believe it. That's why I came here to find Ahmed and to tell him the great news. I've been overwhelmed by the love of Jesus. I'm a new person. A new creature!'

Butros looked at the three men, astounded at what God had done in their lives, and more than a little concerned about the responsibility he felt not to leave them as orphans, to help them grow and mature and become healthy believers. He hardly knew where to start.

All of the food was gone, except for some of the bread, which would be saved for the next morning's breakfast.

'We have some important things to discuss,' Butros said as he removed the Bible from his satchel.

Hassan took a long swig of soda, then asked Butros, 'Sir, can you tell us what a real follower of Christ looks like? I want to be the best Christian possible. We all want that. How do we do that?'

'That's a good question, Hassan,' Butros answered. 'I've been thinking about how you can use your time most productively, and your question is a good lead into that. Let me ask if any of you have memorised the Quran.'

Mustafa raised his hand.

Hassan said, 'Ahmed and I memorised much of it as boys.'

'The Bible is a very different book from the Quran,' Butros said. 'It is actually a collection of sixty-six different books written by many authors over fifteen hundred years in three different languages. It consists of poetry, history, wisdom and more. Like the Quran it has rules, *sharia*, but it has much more than that. As Hassan has discovered, everything in the Bible points to the One who claims to be the way, the truth, and the life. Muslims believe the Quran can only be truly understood in Arabic, the original language. But the Bible is a living document. It has been translated into many languages so people can read in their own languages what God has to say to them. As long as the translations convey the spirit of the message, which is close to the original text, then God's Spirit speaks to us through it. The Bible is much longer than the Quran, so few people are able to memorise all of it. However, I believe it is valuable to memorise portions. The Scriptures say that a man is blessed if his delight is in the Word of God and if he meditates on it day and night. So I would like to propose a passage for you to memorise.'

Butros had the men turn in their Bibles to Philippians, chapter 2. After reading the first eighteen verses, he said, 'Hassan, this passage talks about the attitude we are to have as followers of Christ. This attitude is very different from the culture where we live. The writer of this letter urges us to think and act like Jesus. Now let me ask you what Jesus had before He left heaven and became a man.'

The three young men studied the passage; then Ahmed, who seemed to come alive when studying the Scriptures, spoke. 'He had everything. He had all wealth, all power, all glory. He was honoured, worshipped, praised.'

'And what did He give up to come and live among us?'

'Everything,' said Hassan.

'Except His position. He was still God,' said Ahmed.

'But He gave up all His honour as God. All His power and glory – He surrendered them to become human.'

Butros was impressed with how quickly his students grasped the truths they read in Scripture.

Mustafa asked quietly, 'It says here He was obedient to death, even death on the cross. I was wondering – the Gospels say they took His clothes. Does that mean He was naked?'

'It does.'

Mustafa's eyes became moist as he said, 'Can there be any greater shame than God, naked before the world, enduring a public execution?'

The words hung in the air for a moment. Arab culture was based on shame and honour, and so it was inconceivable to most Arab minds that God would allow Himself to be so humiliated. Finally, Butros broke the silence: 'Does this have anything to say to us today? As Arabs? As those who have come out of Islam?'

Ahmed answered solemnly, 'This is very different from the attitude of men in our culture.'

'What do you mean?'

'We're proud to be Arabs. We are obsessed with honour. Yet God gave up His honour by surrendering His glory to become a human being. And when He should have been honoured as a king, He was betrayed, beaten, spat on, insulted . . . killed. I wonder . . . does that mean we are supposed to be shamed by our family, by our culture, for Christ?'

The implications of that thought hung in the room. Finally, Butros said, 'I suggest you memorise this passage and think about it as you go to sleep at night, as you wake up in the morning, as you're sitting around the flat or walking on the streets. We'll talk more about this in a few days.

'Now I have a proposition to discuss with you.' Butros opened a box he had brought with him. He had set it on the floor while the men were eating. He pulled out three small books and gave them to the men. 'This is a study I want you to do on the Gospel of John. I received them from the Bible Forum. That's a group of organisations that publishes and distributes Bibles and study materials. They have suggested I open a stationery store and book-shop here in the city, and I would like the three of you to help me run this shop.'

Simultaneously the three men looked up in surprise.

'I've been thinking and praying about your situation,' Butros continued. 'It turns out maybe God wants to meet your need and my need together. The Bible Forum feels it is time to open a shop in our country. They have offered to pay the rent on a small retail shop. Ahmed, there is an excellent space near the one that you looked at. The Bible Forum will provide the inventory. They will also purchase a photocopy machine, so we will be able to provide a copy service as well. I will move my office there. Right now my son Thomas is sleeping with my wife and me. My wife has told me it is time to convert my study into a room for him.

'My proposal is this. Hassan, you are still at college. You are welcome to work with us when you have time. Mustafa and Ahmed, I would like to ask if you would run the shop and distribute Bibles and other Christian materials, like this study, to churches in the city.'

At the end of their time together, Ahmed walked downstairs with Butros. 'I want to thank you,' he said sheepishly. 'I know sometimes I get a little excited.'

'I accept your apology,' Butros said with a smile. 'Actually you have good ideas. But they aren't all practical, or sometimes they take time. I called my friends at the Bible Forum and told them about your idea for a print shop. They said that someday they might need a printing press here. But right now, because of my work with churches, they feel the time has come to have an office and warehouse to distribute materials.'

At the street, Butros turned and added, 'So you see, God used you. Maybe it's not what you envisioned, but God honoured your idea and this is the result.'

Ahmed burst into a smile. Butros gave the young man a hug and before he walked away, added, 'Ahmed, God has big plans for you.'

9

Three months later

Butros handed in his applications and sat next to a short man in a rumpled suit with an open-collared shirt. This was the first of what Butros knew would be several long days waiting in government offices so bureaucrats could tell him he needed to fill out another form or provide them with another document. Sometimes the process was legitimate. More often the official wanted *bakshish*, a bribe to speed the process along. He detested the system, and refused to pay bribes. He needed to register as a non-governmental organization (NGO) to operate legally in the country. The process would take at least two months – probably as long as six months without *bakshish* – and then he could open a bank account and receive funds from foreign sources. Butros was determined he would conduct all his business with honesty and that this was part of his Christian witness. If it meant certain processes took longer because he wouldn't compromise his integrity, then that was his cost of doing business.

'I've heard that time is money,' said the man sitting next to him. 'So, how much do you think it's costing us to sit here today?'

Butros glanced at his neighbour and saw he had a twinkle in his eyes. He stuck out his hand and said, '*Ahlan wa sahlan*. My name is Professor Kamal. I teach at the university.'

'*Ahlan bik*. I am Butros. What brings you here to spend so much money waiting?'

'Oh, I received a nice invitation. I run a little organisation that helps distribute Qurans to poor African schoolchildren. There were some questions about my annual report. Nothing serious. Just a mere formality.' He leaned a little closer, and whispered, 'Just a way to keep us honest, and . . .' He rubbed his thumb over his fingers. 'I guess someone needs a little help paying for his wife's shopping bills.'

Butros laughed. 'Well, since I won't play that game, I'd better get used to waiting here. I'm starting an NGO.'

'And what is the purpose of your organisation?'

'Several things. Primarily literacy programmes in towns and villages.' Butros didn't want to entertain too many questions about his work, so he quickly asked, 'What subject do you teach at the university?'

'Islamic studies,' the professor answered. 'I see you have a Christian name. Peter, I believe, is the English form.'

'That's correct.'

'May I ask what you do?'

'I'm a minister. I help pastors to be more effective church leaders.'

'Fascinating. I've always wanted to understand more about Christianity.'

'Really?' Butros looked sceptically at the man. 'Most Muslims have no interest in what we think.'

'No, I truly am curious. Since the Prophet Muhammad, peace be upon him, gave us the final revelation, I've often wondered why Christians don't embrace it. So I love to talk to Christians, to try and understand what they believe . . .'

'And to try to convert them to Islam.'

Kamal chuckled. 'Yes, that too. I know many of my brothers would force Christians to convert at the point of a sword, but I think that's the very last resort. A winsome approach is so much more effective.'

'Well, I must say you don't hide your intentions.'

'Not at all.' A door to the waiting room opened and an announcement was made. 'That's me.' Kamal stood and handed Butros a business card. 'I would be honoured if you would come and visit me sometime for some coffee and stimulating conversation.'

Butros stood and shook the man's hand. 'I look forward to that very much.'

The dining area in Butros's apartment was cramped to begin with. Add to that three hungry men plus a one-year-old boy in a high chair, and the room was bursting. While Nadira finished preparing the main meal in the tiny kitchen, Ahmed and his friends tore pieces of *khobz* and dipped them into hummus.

When Butros heard his wife grunt while removing a dish from the oven, he rose and went in to help, while noting the surprised look on his guests' faces. He returned a few moments later carrying a pot of stew, and Nadira followed with a platter of *kofta*. That was always a favourite with guests; her recipe consisted of seasoned ground lamb moulded into the shape of small sausages and cooked over rice.

Butros and Nadira considered hospitality an important part of their work. While Arab culture highly valued hospitality, Butros felt it had diminished, as people moved to the capital city, were busy with work, and had more entertainment options, such as movies and satellite television. There were fewer opportunities to just drop in, sit together, sip coffee or tea and talk. Butros and Nadira had decided that their home was one of the best places for ministry, and even though their flat was small, rarely a week passed in which they didn't have guests.

Half an hour later, when everyone sat back in their chairs with a satisfied, stuffed feeling, Butros rose and cleared the dishes. The three men noted that Nadira relaxed and didn't rise in embarrassment to take over those duties. This was something Butros enjoyed doing, to give his wife a small reprieve after the work of preparing the meal and to allow her more time to enjoy conversation with the guests. After Butros had rinsed and stacked the plates and put the leftovers in the fridge, Nadira returned to the kitchen to prepare tea.

As everyone drank tea and enjoyed a plate of *baklava*, Butros took the opportunity to talk about an important Christian truth. Butros had determined that if he were going to disciple and mentor Muslim-background believers, it would include teaching about and modelling a Christian marriage and family. These men had come from Islamic families and so were naturally unaware that in some areas Christians had significantly different thoughts about behaviour. That was especially true in the area of male–female dynamics.

'Nadira and I have been praying for you,' he began, glancing warmly at his wife as he spoke. 'There is a proverb in the Bible that says, "A wife of noble character is her husband's crown." I think you've noticed tonight that I have a precious crown.'

Nadira blushed as the three men stopped eating, wondering what Butros was doing.

'Don't be embarrassed,' he responded. 'I want you to notice that a Christian man should place a very high value on his wife. She is more than just the one who bears his children. And she is precious beyond measure, whether she bears a son or daughter – or no children at all! She is his partner in life and work. She is his spiritual mate. The Bible says that husband and wife need each other to be complete, that the two shall become one.'

Butros looked at Ahmed and saw that he was listening intently, yet his face showed confusion. Perhaps he struggled to understand why this was even being discussed. 'One of the things we are praying for you is that God will give you godly women for wives,' Butros continued. 'Of course, marriage and family are very important in our culture. But they have special meaning for us as Christians. I know you have been drawn to Jesus by His love. For Christians, marriage is one way in which we express that love. The Bible tells husbands to love their wives just as Christ loves His church. Jesus showed His love for the church by sacrificing Himself – by suffering death on a cross for her. One way we can show our love for Christ is by sacrificing our selfish desires and giving ourselves to meet the needs of our wife. The reason for that is very important. The church is called the bride of Christ. Our marriages are to be a reflection of that truth.'

There was an awkward silence. The men didn't know how to respond. Hassan finally said, 'You have a wonderful wife.' Looking at Nadira, he added, 'This was a wonderful meal. I hope someday to have a wife who can cook as well as you.'

Nadira and everyone at the table laughed. Then Ahmed blurted out, 'So how do I find a wife? My family is shamed because of me. None of our friends will allow their daughters to marry an infidel. Is there a church that will arrange my marriage? Will you find a family and provide the dowry for the girl's parents? What hope do the three of us have of finding wives?'

It was an impassioned outburst, and Nadira looked sympathetically at Ahmed as she answered all three men, saying, 'God will provide. We don't know how. Right now, we can't see any human answer, but God knows your feelings, your questions, your longings. We must wait and pray. Meanwhile God will use this time to prepare you. And if God has a wife for you, He will prepare her as well.'

Butros added, 'Hassan, Nadira does much more than cook. She is a wonderful mother to our son, but Nadira will always be more to me than the mother of our children. This work I do is also her work. We are partners in the work of Christ. I tell her what I am thinking. She listens to my dreams. She gives me advice and counsel. She works alongside me. We pray together. Without her, I couldn't do what I do.'

'Don't forget, I have dreams too,' Nadira said, nudging her husband.

'That's true. My wife would someday like to provide a place for battered women. That is part of *our* vision.'

Ahmed nodded in agreement, but Butros understood that the young man was trying to process this information. It would take time. That was okay. His purpose was to plant a truth in his disciples' hearts, one that someday would blossom when they had their own families.

—◦◦◦—

A loud banging on the door jolted Nadira out of a quiet reflection. When Thomas was napping, she often took a moment to just sit on the sofa bed in the nursery and close her eyes. Several weeks earlier Butros had finally moved his office into the shop provided by the Bible Forum, so that the child now had his own room. Nadira hurried to the front door, hoping that whoever was there wouldn't knock again and wake the child. She opened the door to find a woman dressed in *abeyya* and *hijab*. She said in a very low voice, 'Please, can you help me?'

Though nervous about the woman's intentions, Nadira opened the door wider so she could slip inside. As soon as the door closed, Salima removed her veil and *abeyya*. Nadira hung them up and escorted her to a seat at the dining room table. The girl burst into tears and for a few moments she was unable to say anything. After the tears, she just shook and Nadira wrapped her arms around her, saying, 'It's okay. You're safe here.' Nadira hoped she was right.

A box of tissues was brought out and set on the table. Tea was prepared. Thomas cried, so Nadira went and brought him back, cuddled against her chest. She sat opposite her guest and as she gently rocked the boy back to sleep, she said, 'Whatever your problems, please consider this your refuge.'

Salima already had a small pile of used tissues on the table in front of her. She blew her nose one more time, took a sip of tea, and apologised. 'I'm sorry. You don't even know who I am. My name is Salima. As soon as you let me in, I just fell apart. It's like everything was bottled up, waiting to come out.'

Nadira reached across the table and held the girl's hand. 'You don't need to apologise. Do you want to rest for a while? Or would you like to talk?'

Salima took a couple of deep breaths. 'I think I'd like to talk, if that's okay.'

'First, let me put Thomas back in his cot.'

Salima sat back in the chair and felt the tears coming again.

Nadira returned and sat next to her, took her hands, and looked into her eyes. 'Now tell me.'

Slowly, Salima revealed her story, how she'd learned about Isa and Christianity through a satellite television programme and the correspondence course, and then the awful day when her mother discovered the evidence.

'My brother was furious,' Salima said. 'He was horrible. He told me he would kill me for the honour of Islam rather than have me ruin the family's reputation. I tried to explain that I hadn't done anything against Islam, that the Quran talks about Isa, and I just wanted to learn more about this Prophet. But he wouldn't listen.

'When my father came home, he and my brother searched my room. They found a Bible and a couple of other books about Christianity, and with the correspondence course, they burned them in the backyard and made me watch. They tore the Bible apart page by page and threw it in the fire. "This is what we think of Christianity," my brother said as he tore the pages and burned them. "We don't want this in our house. This is vulgar, immoral." '

Salima started to cry again, and Nadira pulled a couple of tissues from the box and placed them in the girl's hand. Salima went on to tell about the terrible months that followed. Her father beat her. Her brother removed the television, stereo and books from her room, and for many weeks she was locked in her room, not permitted to leave.

'They said, "Now see if your God will rescue for you." The strange thing is I don't even know if I am a Christian.' She paused, then added, 'I just want to be loved like in the Bible.' She looked into Nadira's eyes and asked, 'Is that so bad? What's wrong with wanting to be loved?'

'That is the heart of Christianity,' Nadira said gently. 'God is love.'

Salima gave a mirthless laugh as she continued her story. 'Once I discovered the love of Isa, from that time on nobody in my family loved me any more. I should show you how they beat me.'

'Do you need a doctor?'

'I don't know. I don't think so. I would have given up except for one thing. One time after my father had beaten me, I was alone in my room and I heard this voice say, "Why are you worried?" I saw this man, dressed in the brightest white – He lit up the room. And He said, "You are not alone. You are a lovely person. Now be strong in your faith." '

She started to cry again. 'It took me a while to realise I'd seen a vision. He was so beautiful. That's what kept me going the next few weeks. Then my father decided the best thing for me was to get married so I would forget all about Christianity. He told me the man he had chosen, and he was not a good man. He was very critical of me and very strict about Islam. So I told my father: "I cannot marry him." He told me the invitations were sent and the engagement hall was booked. So I said, "Okay, you say I'm a Christian. So if he's also a Christian, I will marry him." And that made him very angry. He said I was shaming him, that I had no respect for his reputation. I'm afraid I said some things I shouldn't have.'

Salima was crying again. Nadira hugged her and encouraged her to continue talking. 'I told him, "You only think of your own reputation. I have already suffered so much because you insisted I was a Christian when I said I was not a Christian. So if you are right, my husband should also be a Christian." That was two weeks ago. He beat me terribly.' The memory brought a fresh round of tears. 'He hit me with a wooden chair. He beat me with his shoes. He hit me with his hands, kicked me with his feet. He locked me in my room. My body was bleeding and injured; I could hardly think for several days.'

'How did you escape?' Nadira asked.

'I had never thought of leaving my family before. I didn't think I could live without my family. But suddenly yesterday afternoon, I heard someone say to me, "Get up and leave this place." I think maybe it was the same voice I heard in the vision. So I thought if God wants me somewhere else, I will go. I got up, changed my clothes. I found there was still some money in my little purse. Somehow I pried open the door. And this was the amazing thing – we have a full and busy house, but there was no one there. I just walked out and found a taxi to take me to the bus station. That was two days ago. I found a public guest-house and said I had just arrived from out of town and needed to stay for one night. It was a very bad place, smelly and dirty. It was mostly village women there. This morning I walked until I found a church. The pastor thought I wanted money. I told him I was looking for a job. Anyway, I think he saw I was in pretty bad shape. He suggested I come here.'

'I'm so glad you came,' Nadira said. 'You must be exhausted after all you've been through. So here's what we're going to do. I'm going to get some hot water and I want to wash your cuts and bruises. I'll get you something to eat, and then you are going to sleep.'

At that moment Butros entered the flat, and for a moment Salima was filled with fear. Nadira saw it on her face and reached over to squeeze her hand. 'It's okay. This is my husband, and you can trust him. We're both here to help you.'

―∽∾∿∾∽―

Salima was sound asleep. The sofa bed had been pulled out, and the young woman had fallen immediately into a deep sleep. Butros had moved Thomas's cot into the living room and the child was also sleeping soundly. Nadira and Butros consulted in hushed voices. 'She's so afraid, but also she wants desperately to know God,' Nadira said. 'She has no idea what to do. She asked me if there is some ritual she has to go through at church to be a Christian. I told her it's not about rituals or church but about Jesus.'

'She needs time,' Butros said. 'And that's a problem. If she is from such a wealthy family, we can be sure they are searching the city for her. Maybe she can stay here for a day or two at most. Then we need to find a better, safer place.'

'Are you thinking of getting another flat, like you did for Ahmed and the others?'

Butros considered that for a few moments before answering. 'I don't think she should live alone. It would look suspicious. She needs a male escort. And she needs counselling and spiritual discipleship.'

'I wish we could have a refuge. A safe place to take care of ten or twelve girls like her.'

'That would be ideal,' Butros agreed. 'But right now there is no such place.'

'She's very tender-hearted,' Nadira said. 'She doesn't even know if she is a Christian, but she is drawn by the love of God.'

'I've got an idea.' Butros went into the kitchen and made a phone call to Abuna Alexander.

10

Four months later

Butros invited Brother Andrew to return to his country to see the progress of the work and to provide input to the growing concern of how to serve the needs of Muslim-background believers.

The day after Andrew arrived, they travelled across town to the university campus. 'I want you to meet Dr Kamal,' Butros said as they drove, explaining how he had met the professor on several occasions to talk about religious themes. 'His English is quite good, so you won't need me to translate.' They entered a four-storey, white stone building that was next to an old mosque and featured two ornate minarets framing a small dome.

The office was on the top floor. Professor Kamal was wearing the same suit he wore the first time Butros met him in the government office. He was clearly excited to meet Brother Andrew.

'I would like to welcome you with this Islamic greeting: May Allah's peace, mercy and blessing be upon you.'

'Thank you. I come to you and your country in the name of Jesus Christ, the Prince of Peace,' Andrew responded.

The professor offered refreshments but apologised for not participating. 'I am fasting,' he explained.

'I thought Ramadan ended four days ago,' Andrew said.

'Yes, but some Muslims fast for another six days.'

'If you are fasting, I will also decline refreshments. However, I am not familiar with this extension of Ramadan. Could you explain it to me?'

'Some Muslims fast every Monday and Thursday. But every day you fast during Ramadan is worth ten days of fasting any other time of the year. Ramadan lasts thirty days and so is worth three hundred days. The Muslim calendar is 354 days. So if we add six more days to Ramadan, that gives us more than a full year, 360 days of fasting.'

The professor led them down the stairs and through a hall that connected to the mosque. As they walked, Brother Andrew asked the professor about the purpose of Islamic fasts.

'Fasting in Islam is not only to prevent from eating and drinking. No, it means also to not do any bad thing to others. Your eyes should also fast – not to look to others with envy. A good person is one who does not hurt others with his tongue – he does not curse his fellow man. And he does not hurt others with his hands – for example, he does not steal. All these things are the meaning of fasting. It is spiritual. It is about how you treat others. It is meant to prevent yourself from doing any bad things.'

They stopped at the door of the mosque, and Brother Andrew replied, 'I wish I knew Arabic and could sit in class under your teaching.'

The three men removed their shoes and entered the mosque. The main room was much larger than Brother Andrew expected, judging from the outside of the building. Kamal said that two to three thousand could pray there and sometimes more prayed in the courtyard outside. In their stockinged feet the three men walked on the bright red carpet on which were printed individual prayer rugs pointed towards Mecca.

The room was dimly lit by hanging electric lamps spaced between marble pillars. The best light was near the front where shiny marble walls and alcoves topped with gold calligraphy reflected the light from the lamps. To one side two students knelt and bowed, apparently making up for the noon prayer time they had missed. In front of the intricately carved dark wood pulpit, a young man sat cross-legged with an open Quran resting on a wooden *rehal*. Around him were half a dozen teenage boys.

'He's one of my students,' said the professor. 'As part of his programme he teaches Quran to local secondary-school students.'

Brother Andrew observed the building as Kamal explained that this mosque was similar in design to the famous Al-Azhar University Mosque in Cairo. 'I earned my PhD at Al-Azhar,' he said. 'It is the centre of Islamic learning and a degree from there is the most prestigious in the world. My vision is that someday this university will have that same kind of reputation.'

'That is a big vision,' said Andrew.

'*Inshallah*. God willing, it can happen.'

As they collected their shoes and strolled across the campus, Andrew took advantage of the opportunity to say how glad he was that the professor was open to a discussion with Christians. 'You are so knowledgeable about Islam. I would really be interested to hear your vision of the ideal Islamic society.'

'Yes, Islam is an integrated system,' the professor answered. He locked his hands behind his back and seemed to switch into a lecture mode, as though Brother Andrew and Butros were two students in his very popular classes. 'It not only prepares one for a happy life in the hereafter, but it also deals with all problems and the probable solutions that help in eradicating them. That can only be achieved by establishing the Islamic society and by strengthening its main foundations.'

'And what are those foundations?'

'First, all believers are brothers. God said, "Believers are brothers, so make peace between your brothers." This brotherhood was a new kind of relationship, not known to Arab society before the advent of Islam. From a sociological point of view, this principle of brotherhood eliminates social defects, imposes social sensitivity among Muslims, and enables them to sustain a high level of social relationships and avoid any kind of fragmentation.'

Andrew decided for now not to ask the obvious question about why Muslim societies so often failed to achieve this ideal. Instead, he said, 'That's for Muslims. What about the minority in the country who are not Muslims?'

'The principle of brotherhood in Islamic society is not limited to Muslims only. A similar friendship should be realised with non-Muslims. God says, "Allah does not forbid you to be kind and to act equitably towards those who have not driven you from your homes. Surely Allah loves those who are equitable."'

'So does Islam believe that all people are equal, whether Muslims or Christians or Jews?'

'Yes, that is another distinguishing foundation of Islam – its call for complete human equality. Every individual, irrespective of origin, colour, language or wealth, enjoys the same social, political and economic status and privileges. In the Quran *Sura* 49:13 God said, "O mankind, we have created you from a male and a female and made you into nations and tribes, that ye may know each other. Verily, the most honoured among you in the sight of Allah is he who is the most righteous among you." There is no distinction between peoples whether Arabs, Persians, English, Africans, Australians, etc., except in the degree of piety.'

'Professor, I hope this will not offend you, but I can't help observing that there doesn't seem to be a lot of brotherhood and equality in the Muslim world. As you know, I work among the Christian community, and they feel intimidated and are often persecuted.'

'The Prophet, peace be upon him, said, "A true Muslim is he from whose tongue and hand others are safe." This means that anyone who injures or hurts his fellow brother by word or deed cannot be regarded as a true Muslim.'

'So members of the Muslim Brotherhood who attack Christians and burn down churches are not true Muslims?'

'They are not real Islam. Islam is about peace and brotherhood.'

'Would you say that in a true Islamic society no one is forced to believe in God or in a particular religious practice?'

'No one believes without conviction,' said the professor, 'and there is no conviction without evidence. People are free in choosing their religion and whatever doctrine they want. God said, "Proclaim. This is the truth from your Lord, then. Let him who will believe and let him who will disbelieve." The question of freedom with regard to belief and worship is of paramount importance in Islam. Every person is entitled to exercise freedom of belief and worship.'

The three men walked without talking for a while; then Andrew commented that the professor's vision of Islam was indeed appealing. 'I wish others saw it the same way you do. But honestly there are many Christians who suffer under Islam – in this country, in Egypt, in Pakistan, and in many other Islamic countries.'

'You are right. This is not good.'

'So what can we do about it?'

The professor didn't answer for a moment; then he said, 'I think talks like this are helpful.'

'Yes,' Andrew agreed. 'But we need more than talk. We need some doing as well.'

The men had walked in a circle and were now back at the mosque and adjoining academic building where they had started. Before they parted, Andrew said, 'Professor, this has been a very encouraging discussion. I want to thank you for taking the time to see us.'

'The pleasure is mine. Please come and visit me anytime you are in the country.'

'I will do that. May I ask you one more rather personal question?' The professor nodded. 'I admire your dedication to Islam. You are a truly good man. I was intrigued by your fasting six extra days after Ramadan. I'm sure you are faithful in praying five times a day and giving to the poor, and you've probably been on the *hajj*.'

'Several times. I lead groups on pilgrimage to Mecca.'

'You faithfully practise the five pillars of Islam. Does this guarantee you will go to heaven?'

'No, there is no guarantee of paradise.'

'So how can you be sure you will be saved? Apart from dying in a jihad, isn't there any way to have assurance that you are going to paradise?'

The professor looked down at the pavement for a moment. 'Do more good works,' he answered, looking up at Andrew. 'That's all you can hope for. The question of paradise belongs to God Himself, not to a man. We are trying to do our best. If you want to reach paradise, you have to do many good things.'

As they left the professor and walked to the parking lot, Andrew said to Butros, 'How sad! There is such a good, pious, dedicated Muslim, and he has no certainty at all that he will ever see paradise or heaven.'

—∾—

That night the two men drove to Al Waha Church and parked behind the building.

'We are going to visit a meeting for Muslim-background believers. I rarely attend, and you will be the first outsider to observe this meeting,' Butros said. He explained that Pastor Yusef was very sympathetic to the plight of MBBs, and several of them attended the church. But because of their unique needs, they also benefited from a chance to meet with other MBBs in a separate setting. The pastor had offered a room for that purpose. They walked downstairs to the basement and passed through a social hall to a smaller room in the back. At the door a young man smiled and shook Andrew's hand but stayed outside as they entered.

Inside there were about fifteen people plus several children. They all stood to honour the guests. Butros introduced Ahmed, Mustafa, Hassan, and a young man named Samir to Andrew.

'Samir has joined me as my first full-time team member,' Butros explained.

An older man handed out a stapled booklet consisting of a few photocopied pages with words for various psalms and hymns. There was no accompaniment; the man started singing, and the rest joined in.

Butros explained to Andrew: 'They are singing Psalm 24.'

Andrew opened his Bible to the Psalms and slowly read the words being sung in Arabic: 'The earth is the Lord's, and everything in it.' The voices of the tiny congregation seemed to swell until they sounded like one hundred voices. 'Lift up your heads, O you gates; be lifted up, you ancient doors, that the King of glory may come in. Who is this King of glory? The Lord strong and mighty, the Lord mighty in battle.' The chorus was sung with such conviction that Andrew almost expected the Lord Jesus to physically enter the room and declare His rule over the Middle East and the whole world. Andrew looked at the faces – everyone, even the children, sang with enthusiasm and joy. One of the women had her eyes closed, tears streaming down her face.

During the next song, Butros whispered to Andrew: 'This is a hymn one of them wrote. It's about the blood of Christ that saves us. One of the lines says, "We who love You are willing to die for You. No sacrifice is too great."'

Tears welled up in Andrew's eyes as he wondered how many back home in Holland would so enthusiastically sing such words, knowing that they could be fulfilled at any moment.

Between songs one of the men in the group was invited to pray. Of course

Andrew didn't understand the words, but he sensed a deep yearning and felt confident he could agree in his heart with the spirit of this prayer.

Then Butros invited the people to tell Andrew about themselves, as Butros translated. The first to speak was Samir, who introduced his mother and two younger sisters. 'We have been believers in Jesus for several years, but our father is still a Muslim. Please pray for him.'

A husband and wife with three small children told about their experience with discrimination. The wife worked at a hospital. She said, 'I was denied a promotion because of my husband's conversion. They threatened to have him arrested if I protested.'

Another man held his son on his lap as he told how he had been a Christian for three years. 'My wife is still a Muslim and her parents are putting pressure on her to leave me and take the children and go back home. She's very confused. Please pray.'

Butros prayed for the families.

When Brother Andrew was asked to say a few words, he began: 'I bring greetings from the church in Holland. This is a very moving service, and I am honoured to be here. You pay a great price to worship our Lord Jesus Christ. And while few will ever know of your existence, you are a precious part of the body of Christ.' Andrew read to them from 1 Corinthians 12: 'The body is not made up of one part but of many.'

Butros read from his Arabic Bible, ending with: '. . . those parts of the body that seem to be weaker are indispensable, and the parts that we think are less honourable we treat with special honour. And the parts that are unpresentable are treated with special modesty.'

Then Andrew said, 'The world may not know about this little part of the body. But because of your love for Christ, you are treated with special honour in the kingdom of God. It is my desire that we also move on in our experience to the following verses. If any part of this body suffers, we all should be able to feel that pain. There is nothing wrong with you when you feel the pain of persecution. But if we fail to identify with you in your pain, there is something fundamentally wrong with us. That is why we make every effort to get to know you. As far as your security allows, we visit you and fellowship with you. That is today my greatest privilege.'

Ahmed delivered a short message, and Butros whispered a translation for

Andrew. Ahmed stood and said, 'Recently, Butros challenged some of us to memorise Philippians 2.' After reciting from memory the passage slowly for the congregation, he picked up a well-used journal and said he had written a meditation, which he proceeded to read: '"I am your great Lord." One day man uttered this expression through the lips of pharaohs and caesars. He has reaffirmed it consistently through actions of kings, princes, presidents and lords. In moments of inebriation from the cup of his own egotism, man, in his historic arrogance, has asserted that he is god. How has mankind deceived himself to such an extreme?

'In the fullness of time, the one true God, who has no earthly likeness, the holy, eternal and omnipotent God, chose to become a human being. He chose to come down to us from His high place. He came down from His high heaven to become one with us, to share in our pain and dreams. It's what any truly great king would do to express solidarity with his people. He could not withdraw to his ivory tower. This God of love, filled with compassion and mercy, came down to us. He did not just descend to the atmosphere, no, He came down to our dirt. He walked among us as He still does, doing good. He heals those bound by the devil, whose egotism has overpowered them, blinding them lest they see the light that came into the world. They did not realise the darkness of their own selfishness. Selfishness is a most repugnant death. It leads down a false path causing one to gain the world and all things while losing the greatest thing – his own soul and the Saviour.

'Imagine it. Man asserts his deity and rejects God's becoming man. Where's the logic in that?'

Where indeed? Brother Andrew was moved by the depth of the young believer's insight. Here was a man who understood the gospel. How he wished the church around the world could hear this message and learn about these wonderful believers! He thought again of the passage he'd just read. Clearly this part of the body was weaker than some, yet indispensable. They had to be protected.

11

Brother Andrew stood just inside the entrance to the shop-front business and looked around. Butros stood behind him, allowing Andrew to absorb the scene. There were several racks with stationery and note cards for various occasions. 'We are meeting a need,' Butros explained. 'Christians don't have many places to obtain cards for Christmas, Easter, baptisms, funerals and other occasions.' There was a group of chairs on one side, with a coffee table displaying several pamphlets. Against one wall of the room, a set of bookshelves held various Arabic books and Bibles. 'Those are materials from the Bible Forum,' Butros said. 'Several Christian publishers provide resources, and this is the only place in the country where they are sold.'

Opposite that wall was an office with a window that looked into the shop. 'This is where I work,' Butros explained. There were two desks in the office, and Samir was sitting at one. He stood to welcome Andrew and they talked briefly before Butros led Andrew back into the shop and pointed to a door in the back wall. 'This leads into the warehouse. Let me show you.'

They walked into a room that was about the same size as the store. Mustafa and Hassan were bent over a copying machine, trying to fix something. Most of the room was filled with several rows of shelves holding boxes of books and stationery. In the opposite corner Ahmed sat at a desk and talked on the phone. He waved to them, finished his conversation, and stood to welcome Brother Andrew with a hug. The other two men wiped off their hands and came over to join them.

'We must celebrate,' Ahmed announced in English. 'I will get for you, Brother Andrew, some very good Arab fast food.' To Butros he added in Arabic, 'Leave everything to us.'

For the next thirty minutes Butros reported on the progress of his work with the Bible Forum. The partnership was proving beneficial for all – Butros had gained access to much-needed materials, the rent for the shop and office space was paid, and the Bible Forum had expanded its sphere of ministry. While Andrew and Butros talked in the office, Samir cleared the coffee table in the shop and covered it with newspaper. As Andrew and Butros emerged from the office, Ahmed and Hassan were opening several packages of food. 'We have *falafel*, really good,' said Ahmed, holding up a deep-fried ball of spiced chickpeas.

After Butros had prayed a blessing and Andrew had enjoyed some *falafel*, Ahmed handed Andrew a *shawarma*. He took a bite, leaning over the table, so the juice dripping down his chin would not fall on his clothes. 'This is delicious. What's in it?'

Butros answered, 'Lamb, tomatoes, and other vegetables and a special yogurt sauce that the restaurant owner mixes – it's his secret recipe.'

There was no more talking as the six men enjoyed the food. While Samir cleaned off the table, Andrew asked the MBBs if they could tell him about their spiritual journeys. Since Ahmed spoke only a little English and Mustafa and Hassan none at all, Butros translated.

Ahmed spoke first and told about his journey to belief in Isa. 'But my friend Mustafa, his journey is much more interesting,' Ahmed said. 'He comes from the same town as me, but he was far deeper into radical Islam.'

Andrew noted for the first time that Mustafa appeared several years older than Ahmed, and there was a tired look in his eyes. Mustafa bowed his head, as if embarrassed about what he was to say, and spoke so softly that Andrew was glad that Butros understood the language and was translating. The story Mustafa had to tell was electric. Of course he grew up in a strong Islamic family in a village near Suq al Khamis.

'I am ashamed to admit that my friends and I burned down the church in our village. We also stole from Christians – we didn't call it stealing but jihad.

However, if a Christian embraced Islam, our group helped him and brought customers to his shop.'

'Were you ever caught?' Brother Andrew asked, shocked at this open admission by a former persecutor.

'No, the police surely knew who did these things, but they left us alone. The Christians have no rights. What can they do?'

'And yet now you are a believer in Jesus Christ.'

'I am not the person I once was.'

'The Bible says you are a new creature.'

'Yes, I am changed. I used to be filled with hate for Christians and for Muslims who were not devout. Now that hate is gone.'

Ahmed spoke to Butros in Arabic. Butros addressed Andrew: 'These three men have asked to be baptised. As you can hear from their testimonies, they have given their lives completely to Jesus Christ. They feel the time has come for them to declare their faith in baptism.'

'And you agree?'

'Yes, I agree.'

'And we want new names,' said Ahmed in English. Butros looked at him in surprise. 'The Bible says we are new people, so we should have new names.'

Hassan spoke rapidly in Arabic. Butros translated. 'He says Abram was renamed Abraham. Saul became Paul. Simon became Peter, the rock.'

'But you can't use the names,' Butros protested. 'You can't put a new name on your government identity card. And it would be dangerous to use a Christian name around Muslims.'

'Yes, we understand,' said Ahmed. 'But *my brothers* would know my new name. We would use it with each other. It would be a constant reminder of how God has changed our lives.'

Andrew turned to Butros and said, 'Then they should do it. You should make a list of biblical names to give them at the end of the baptism service.'

'There is one more request I have,' Butros added. 'Would *you* please baptise these men?'

—⟨∾⟩—

Butros sat back in his office chair and closed his eyes, searching for the right words. 'Brother Andrew, I personally now know of more than fifty MBBs.

You've met some in the capital, but there are others scattered around the country. And there are many more Muslims enquiring. It happens quietly, of course. We need to work out what to do.'

'Do you have any ideas?'

'I'm thinking that the fellowship you saw could be a model for other communities. Some MBBs are attending an established church, but they come to these meetings because they need to meet with fellow MBBs who understand them. It's hard for Christian-background believers to understand the huge change in culture and religious thinking that happens when Muslims become followers of Jesus.'

'So you think that MBBs need to worship separately?'

'I am coming to that conclusion, yes. I know the church is one body, and I believe we need to keep trying to find ways to bring MBBs and CBBs together. But the fact is that the two groups are so different. It would be like bringing together Dutch Christians and Chinese Christians. They worship the same Christ but they speak different languages and have different cultures. Sure they can try to worship together, but the fact is they'll probably end up in separate congregations. And with the resistance many churches have to accepting MBBs, well, I think it might be better to find a way for MBBs to worship separately.'

Brother Andrew considered his friend's statement. He agreed that the Muslim converts needed a safe way to come together. But there were so many questions, such as who would lead these groups? 'The apostle Paul when he established a church made sure there were strong leaders.'

'Yes, he established elders in each church. It is essential that leaders emerge and be trained from among the MBBs, so that they are not dependent on outsiders. There are several men – Ahmed, Mustafa and Hassan are among them, also Samir – who are potential leaders. They are already witnessing. Ahmed and Mustafa have led several people to Christ. But they need guidance. They need ongoing discipleship.'

'They've asked to be baptised. It seems it has taken you a while to determine that they were ready.'

'This is a huge step. They are saying that they have decided to live totally for Jesus and are ready, if need be, to die for Him as well. They are turning away from their old life in Islam. Before they are baptised, they could go back to Islam. After baptism there is no going back. It's a death sentence. Any Muslim can kill them. That's why I don't think we can ever rush this decision.'

'Clearly they have counted the cost. So what is the next step?'

'Once we have MBBs trained and leading fellowships, one of their responsibilities will be to baptise. But someone needs to baptise these first leaders.'

'Why don't you do it?'

'Andrew, I'm willing. But I don't think it's wise. If the *Mukhabarat*, the secret police, discover that I have baptised Muslims, my work here will be finished.'

'Do you think they would find out?'

'Andrew, they are watching me. My work is unusual. I don't pastor a church, but I work with churches, with pastors. Government officials don't understand – it doesn't fit their perceptions of Christian work. They wonder how I am funded. They want to know if any western agencies support me. Of course, they know about Ahmed, Mustafa and Hassan. I'm sure they keep an eye on them, and so we need to be very careful. But if they found out I had baptised them, they would certainly crack down. That would be intolerable to them.'

'I assume that's the case for all ministers in the country.'

'Yes. There was an old pastor in his late seventies who would baptise Muslim converts, but he died last year. Yusef has probably baptised individuals, but it wouldn't be safe for him to do so many at one time.'

'So you want me to do it?'

'You told me that you were ordained, so this is part of your ministerial duties.'

'What right do I have to baptise these men?'

'Your right as a minister, as one who is committed to strengthening a church that struggles for its very survival.' Butros was passionate and leaned forward as he spoke: 'You have white hair, so you are respected as an elder by the young men you will baptise. You are anointed by God with a heart for our people. I don't want to bring in just any foreigner who doesn't know us, who doesn't know our hearts. And it's not as dangerous for you. If you are discovered, the worst that can happen is that you will be deported. Then I can honestly say, "I didn't do this." This will protect me. It will protect the church.'

Andrew closed his eyes for a moment, as though praying. He looked at his friend and with a determined voice said, 'This must be a temporary solution. In time, when leaders are trained and ordained, they should baptise their own people.'

'As soon as possible – eventually they must do it themselves.'

'Then with that understanding, you know that I am here to help you and the church. We're part of one body, and if you need this old body of mine, I'm available. I will do what you ask.'

Butros seemed relieved. 'The next time you come, we will plan a baptism service. Meanwhile, I will make a list of Christian names for them.' He stood up, came around the desk, and hugged his friend and mentor. 'Now, let's go for a drive. Nadira and I want to show you something.'

Butros drove by his flat, and Nadira was waiting for them at the kerb, with Thomas standing next to her, holding her hand. Andrew got out of the car to greet Nadira and admire the healthy boy.

'Hello, Thomas,' Andrew said. The child said nothing and stared curiously at the blue-eyed man with white hair.

Andrew offered to sit in the back, but Nadira insisted he stay in front; she put Thomas in a car seat and sat next to him. They drove out of town along a small river.

'Brother Andrew, we are going into the farming area of our country. Much of the country is desert. There you'll find sheep and goats and lots of date palms but not much else. The majority of our produce is grown in this region.'

'It doesn't look like there is enough water here.'

'On the surface, no. But there are deep wells throughout this area, and canals from the wells provide irrigation to the fields.'

Andrew looked at the farmland. For a few miles there were many orchards of oranges. Then the land opened up and he saw numerous people working in the fields. Every two miles or so there was a village and each had a mosque with one or more minarets that dominated the skyline. 'What is grown here?' he asked.

'Eggplants, leeks, tomatoes – you name it.'

'So where are we going?'

'To see a piece of land we own. If we stay on this road, we will come to Suq al Khamis, where Ahmed, Mustafa and Hassan grew up.' A few minutes later they left the main road and turned down a paved one-lane road that soon became a packed dirt path. There were men and boys going to and from fields, some with a tool slung over the shoulder, others driving a donkey cart or leading a water buffalo. They had to stop for a few minutes as a small herd of cattle lingered in the road while a boy beat them, trying to get them to move.

A couple of minutes later Butros announced they had arrived. He switched off the engine, and they got out of the car. Nadira carried Thomas as they walked a short distance.

Pointing to his left towards a small canal that distributed water to the surrounding fields, Butros said, 'From the canal this way is our property.' He pointed to posts in four corners. 'In total we have five acres.'

They walked into the field. In a far corner a man looked up from his work, and Butros waved to him.

'Brother Andrew, Nadira and I have been praying about how to use this property. We receive a small income by renting it out to farmers, but we think God has something else He wants us to do with this land.' He waved his arms over the property. 'I told you about the need to train leaders for MBB fellowships. We also need a place for conferences, like the one for pastors last year. Nadira and I envision a campus here. In the far corner, by the canal, would be a building that could sleep twenty people, with a kitchen and a classroom. That would be a place for rural pastors and church lay leaders to come for training – two to four weeks, maybe longer. It's a huge need.'

Butros turned to the opposite corner. 'Over there, we see another building for different kinds of training. For instance, if we could obtain some computers, we might train Christian young people to use computers. Also we could train teachers to run literacy programmes in the villages.'

'We would continue to farm a portion of the land,' added Nadira. 'We want to be as self-sufficient as possible.'

Brother Andrew started walking towards the canal. Away from the noise of traffic and the hustle and bustle of city life, he could hear birds chirping.

In the distance a man talked with a neighbour. There was a slight gurgle of water running down the little canal. Fields stretched into the distance until interrupted by a village. This was a serene setting. *Yes, this made sense. A refuge was needed for ministers. Butros could be so much more effective if he had a place, a campus, where he could bring people for extended training.* Andrew felt his pulse quicken. *The church would surely benefit from such a place. Of course this was beyond Butros's ability, beyond his own ability to make happen. But if God was pleased, He could surely provide the resources.*

Andrew turned and looked back at Butros and Nadira. 'This is a wonderful vision.'

'We are thinking to name it the Logos Training Centre,' Nadira said.

'Would you dedicate this land for that purpose?' Butros asked.

Andrew pulled out his little New Testament from his pocket. He opened to John 12:24–25 and read, 'Unless a kernel of wheat falls to the ground and dies, it remains only a single seed. But if it dies, it produces many seeds. The man who loves his life will lose it, while the man who hates his life in this world will keep it for eternal life.' Andrew explained: 'In one very literal translation, the passage says, "He who has no concern for his life in this world will keep it." We want this to be a place where people become fruitful. And we do that by expressing that they have no concern for this life but their concern is for the kingdom of God.'

Turning to look over the field, Andrew continued: 'Here we see plants and mud and footsteps of animals. But we see beyond that – we see buildings, we see people with needs, we see people studying the Bible. And we see these people saying, "I will not cling to my old life but I will invest it in the kingdom of God." This country needs a church where its members have denied themselves so they can live for Jesus. I see this place as a campus where church leaders come to deny themselves so they can invest their lives for the future of the church in their country.'

Lifting up his arms Andrew prayed: 'Lord, You have created all things, and therefore all things have value. Physical things have value when they are sanctified by Your word and by prayer. Set apart this piece of land as a beachhead for Your kingdom. May this land be used to train people who will go throughout the country and beyond, to the Middle East, to North Africa, to all of the Muslim world and beyond, teaching Your word. Sanctify this part of Your creation. By faith we can see church leaders from villages all over the country coming here for training. Dedicate this land for Your glory. May everything done here, the preparation of the land, the blueprints, the construction of the buildings, be for the kingdom of heaven. May there be no physical accidents during construction. Lord Jesus, You reign here. From now on this is Your place. We dedicate the staff who will eventually serve here. We claim the financial resources that will be needed. We pray this in faith, that this campus will be built and used for Your glory.'

Butros and Nadira joined in the 'Amen'. Both had tears in their eyes. Their faith, shaky as they dreamed, was now affirmed and strengthened by their friend from Holland. Surely God was going to do something wonderful here.

12

Three months later

Salima brought a tray of tea and biscuits to the living room where Butros and Abuna Alexander had settled. '*Shukran*,' Butros said as he took a cup, poured in milk and a teaspoon of sugar, and slipped a butter biscuit on to the saucer. 'Are you doing okay here?' he asked the woman.

'Yes, *shukran*. The priest and his wife have been very kind.'

When Salima returned to the kitchen, Butros asked Father Alexander for a report. 'She has suffered a lot,' he answered as he sipped his tea. 'She sometimes screams in her sleep, and my wife, Nour, has to go and comfort her. She breaks into tears without warning. And yet she has a toughness. She is in love with Jesus. She reads the Bible for hours every day. She is the first one in church for services. She asks me many questions. Frankly I have never seen such spiritual hunger in any of my parishioners.'

The priest had hesitated at first when Butros asked him to give refuge to the girl. Butros understood that Father Alexander couldn't take in local converts, but he had started calling on church leaders to temporarily house MBBs from other parts of the country, and the priest had agreed to give refuge to Salima. He had created a cover story for Salima and introduced her to his congregation as a relative who wanted to learn more about Christianity. Butros thanked the priest for his help. 'I really appreciate what you have done.'

'You are doing *me* an honour,' Father Alexander said. Butros registered surprise. 'I mean that sincerely. In all my years as a priest, I have never seen a more powerful conversion. God has used this woman's life to touch Nour and me. I was always sceptical that Muslims could ever really become Christians.'

'Now you see what God can do. What God is doing.'

'I am ashamed to say that I didn't believe it was really possible. By the way, I have been thinking about her future. I have a cousin living in England. Maybe she should move there, you know, to get a fresh start.'

'Why should she leave the country? Why should any Muslim convert leave the country?'

The priest put his teacup and saucer down and started to finger the wooden cross he wore over his cassock. 'Isn't it obvious? Salima has no future here. She could worship freely in England, or anywhere in the West for that matter.'

'Does she want to leave?'

Alexander sighed. 'No, that's the problem. I've mentioned it a couple of times, and she starts to cry. But I don't see what else we can do for her and for others like her. Say, how is Ahmed doing?'

'He is growing. He and his two friends have a hunger to learn about their faith. In fact that is why I have come to you today. I need your counsel.'

The priest combed his beard with his fingers while Butros explained his concerns.

'With many more Muslims exploring Christianity and making the decision to follow Christ, I think we need a structured plan for disciple-ship. Take the three men from this area. They need to channel their spiritual energies. I have them memorising portions of the Bible. But they need more. They are used to a structure – prayer five times a day, the Muslim feasts, the month of fasting. Now they are drifting. I see it when I'm with them and the call to prayer begins. There is a part of them that wants to stop and pray, and another part that realises they are free of the legalistic burdens of Islam.'

Alexander nodded and thought about what Butros had said. 'We have only the ancient liturgical practices. I know that you, as a Protestant, have very different worship practices.'

'That is why I seek your advice. In some respects, they might be more comfortable in a liturgical church tradition. But then there are problems incorporating them into existing congregations.'

'For my congregation it's not possible. You know the dangers if local Muslims start attending any church. Maybe it's possible in a large city. But if this movement grows and if we see more converts in villages and towns, you understand, the church is not ready for them.'

'So what do we do? Do we send them all to another country?'

The priest shrugged. 'I don't know the answer. What future do they have here?'

'They need to stay and be a witness in their communities. I'm observing that Ahmed and Mustafa and Hassan miss their homes – they miss the family gatherings, the religious holidays, spending time with brothers and sisters and cousins. They would like to go home. I think it's a mistake to take them away from their homes and families.'

'But if they stay, they are killed.'

'Perhaps we need to teach converts how to live their faith while still honouring their families. That's why I'm seeking your counsel. If more and more start enquiring about Christianity and believing in Jesus, we can't remove them all from their homes and families. Certainly sending them to the West is totally impractical. There must be a way for them to honour their families and yet practise their faith – without drawing unnecessary attention.'

'Then they need to remain Muslims. Otherwise, there will be problems.'

'You know what that means. A Muslim, by definition, submits to Muhammad and the Quran. How can they do that? Can they remain Muslims and also love our Lord Jesus?'

Alexander shook his head. 'They need to keep quiet about their belief in our Lord or we all will suffer.'

'I've considered that maybe, for a time, it is necessary for them to remain in their community. If their lives are truly transformed, well, that will be a witness to the family.'

The priest nodded, thinking. 'Can they truly grow apart from the church?'

'That's the dilemma. These men and women need to be discipled. They need to meet together. I've thought maybe they could have small gatherings after the Friday sermon in the mosque. But they also can't be bound by the legalism of Islam. I have told Ahmed and his friends that they can pray anytime, anywhere, twenty-four hours a day. That's true, but that's not enough. They need a community. They need a structure . . .'

'A daily pattern?'

'Yes.'

'You know the monastic traditions have a lot to offer.'

'I don't think these men are going to take monastic vows.'

The priest burst out laughing. 'No, I don't think they will.' He laughed again and said, 'I wasn't proposing that, but they can borrow from the tradition of daily prayer.'

'Could you suggest some things for me to give them, something Christian but that doesn't disrupt from the daily rhythm of Islamic society and culture? Maybe something that could become a model for others?'

'Okay. Let's begin with a simple pattern – morning prayer, afternoon prayer and evening prayer – three times a day instead of five, to break the cycle.'

'That makes sense.' Butros pulled out a small pad of paper and a pen from his pocket and started to make some notes.

'Morning prayer – early, when the cock crows. Ahmed and his two friends are from this area, so they're used to hearing the roosters. Here in Suq al Khamis the roosters start crowing just before the *muezzin* begins his first call to prayer. Have them read in Matthew's Gospel, chapter 26, about how Peter denied to the slave girl that he knew Jesus. They might pray something like this: "Lord, may I have the strength to be faithful to You today. May I not be like Peter who denied You. May I live out today the new life You have given me." I'm thinking this off the top of my head. I could write something out for you.'

'No, this is excellent,' Butros said, writing quickly on his pad.

'The afternoon prayer. I would suggest at three o'clock, at the time our Lord died. That would be a good time every day to remember our Lord's sacrifice for us, His death for our salvation, and that this is the reason for our love and commitment to Him. And at night, before they go to sleep, they could remember how our Lord taught us to pray: "Our Father, who art in heaven . . ." It is a perfect model for prayer.'

'Yes, this is what I need.' Butros finished writing and looked up. 'I can develop this further with them, but it gives them a daily discipline.'

'Butros, may I also propose that you teach them about the liturgical year? They need something to replace the feasts of Islam. Or – I'll have to think about this – maybe there is a way for them to remember key events in the life of our Lord during the Islamic calendar.'

'Like Lent during Ramadan?'

'No, Lent always leads up to Easter in spring. The dates of Ramadan are different each year. But Ramadan could be a time for Muslim converts to meditate on the fact that our Lord fasted forty days in the wilderness and that He was tested by the devil. What I have in mind are two six-month cycles. For six months they would concentrate on key events in the life of Christ – His birth, certain miracles, His teaching, His death, resurrection and ascension. The second half begins with Pentecost, when the promised Holy Spirit was sent, so Christ could be seen through us. They could remember the first martyr, Stephen. I would recommend you teach them about some of the heroes of the faith – the saints and martyrs who have shown us how to live, and how to die, for our faith.'

'Yes, that would be helpful. This gives me a lot to think about. Now I have one more request. Several men have requested baptism. Would you help me plan a service?'

—❧—

Layla was an attractive fifteen-year-old girl who regularly attended St Mark's on Sunday with her parents. It had been a surprise when Abuna Alexander announced a special evening for teenagers consisting of fun activities and ice cream. Thirty teens had attended the event, enjoyed the time together, and responded positively when the priest issued his challenge to read through the New Testament. All of them had accepted the book, and fifteen to twenty were coming each week for a time of discussion about the Gospels. A few of them had even started attending Sunday service. Layla had always had a spiritual interest, but she found her faith increasing as she spent time with others her age who were seeking to know more about the Christian faith.

This was a time when a group of young Muslim men seemed to enjoy prowling the marketplace, jostling and taunting young women who didn't wear the veil. Over the last three weeks, a number of boys had been standing across the street on Sunday afternoons after school. They particularly focused on Layla, leering at her and laughing and yelling across the street about how beautiful she was and how she should marry a nice Muslim man.

Layla's situation was complicated because an uncle, her mother's brother, had converted to Islam. He had never been a particularly committed Christian and when his business struggled, some Muslim businessmen made him an offer – they would send him a lot of customers if he converted to Islam. He had told Layla's parents that it was an offer he couldn't refuse, and since religion wasn't that important to him anyway, why not be a rich Muslim rather than a poor Christian? Naturally, his wife and children were required to follow him and become Muslims. Layla suspected that one of her cousins was encouraging this harassment of her.

As her family prepared to enter the church this Sunday afternoon, Layla complained, 'Abuna Alexander, I don't like the way those boys are staring at me.'

As Alexander observed the scene across the street, Layla's father told the priest: 'This week my daughter was accosted in the market.'

The priest's gaze quickly left the boys and focused on Layla. 'Did they hurt you?'

'I was very uncomfortable. There were four of them around me. They pushed me a couple of times, made threats.'

Layla's father added, 'Abuna, we don't know what to do.'

A parishioner overhearing the conversation said, 'I'll gather up several men and we'll go and talk to the boys right now.'

'No, that's not a good idea,' the priest said. 'This is tense enough. We don't need to raise emotions any higher.'

'Well, I'm not going to stand for this,' said Layla's father. 'I've told my daughter not to go to the market alone. And if those men approach her, someone is going to pay.'

Father Alexander looked again at the boys laughing at his congregation and quietly told the group, 'I think we need to go inside and worship.'

—◁◦◦◦▷—

It was after ten o'clock at night, and Butros and Nadira were finishing a cup of tea and preparing to go to bed when there was a soft knock on the door. Butros and Nadira looked at each other, then back at the door as the knock was repeated. Butros hurried to the door and opened it a crack. He saw a very familiar face – a man with a goatee whose picture was often on the front page of the national papers. Butros opened the door to allow the man inside and closed it quickly, hoping that none of the neighbours noticed.

The two men stared at each other for a moment. Then the visitor extended his hand. 'My name is Kareem.'

Butros was stunned. This man was dressed in a very expensive European suit. He held a very high position in the government. *What is he doing in here?* 'Nadira, would you please fix us some coffee?' Butros asked, regaining his composure.

Nadira, who had stood frozen when the famous man entered the apartment, hurried into the kitchen to prepare refreshments.

'You are welcome,' Butros said. 'I'm afraid this is a very humble home, but please, come in.' He gestured toward the one easy chair, inviting his guest to sit down, and he sat on the small couch adjacent to it.

'I apologise for startling you but I thought this was the best way to come to you. You understand that I couldn't come to your office.'

Butros didn't understand but answered, 'Of course.' What could this government official want with him? His senses were on high alert. Was the government about to clamp down on him? Was this a trap? But certainly they would delegate that to the *Mukhabarat*.

Kareem read the confusion on Butros's face and said, 'I will explain. I need to speak with you, but this is in utmost confidence. You are a pastor, right?'

Butros nodded in acknowledgement.

'I believe there is a thing called clergy confidence?'

'Yes, this can be considered privileged communication.'

'So you cannot repeat it to anyone else?'

'That is correct.'

Kareem smiled and sat back for a moment, closed his eyes, and took a deep breath.

Nadira used the opportunity to place a tray on the coffee table. There were two cups of coffee and a plate of pastries. She quietly stepped back to the kitchen. Catching her husband's eye, she put her hands together, indicating that she would intercede; then she disappeared from view.

When Kareem opened his eyes, he took a cup of coffee, sipped it and set it back down. He looked intently at his host. 'I got the idea for this meeting from the Bible.'

Butros said nothing.

'The Gospel of John. Nicodemus, a ruler of the Jews, came to see Jesus late at night. Right?'

Butros nodded.

'Well, it seemed like a good approach. I can't exactly show up in church, now, can I? But I need to talk to someone and I have had my eye on you.'

Butros lowered his eyes and squirmed. He never intended to draw attention to himself or his work.

'Please don't worry,' Kareem said, clearly trying to ease Butros's fears. 'I have ways of doing this so you won't get into trouble.' Kareem grabbed a slice of *baklava*, drank the rest of his coffee, and announced, 'I have become what I think you would call a follower of Jesus Christ.'

The news stunned Butros. This evening was getting more and more bizarre.

'Now of course no one knows but you. I can't exactly announce this, for obvious reasons. I would lose everything if I did that. My family would be dishonoured. It would cause a scandal to the royal family. So you see that I can't tell anyone, but I must tell someone. So I am trusting you.'

'Of course, sir. I will not tell anyone. But please tell me how you have reached such a decision.'

'Like you, I studied in England. And while I was there, someone gave me a Bible. Over many years I have read the Bible several times, and I have quietly bought Christian books when I travel in Europe and brought them into the country. It helps that I have diplomatic immunity – no one would dare to search my luggage. I keep these books in a safe place and I have spent hours studying until I am convinced that the final revelation of God's plan for mankind was made through Jesus Christ.'

'How did you reach this conclusion?'

'The Quran has numerous very short references to Jesus. But the Injil has the complete stories. The Quran says only that He healed the lepers and gave sight to the blind, but the four Gospels give numerous and detailed accounts of Him healing lepers and giving sight to the blind. The Quran says Jesus raised the dead. But in John's Gospel I can read the complete story of Jesus raising Lazarus from the dead. Tell me, my friend, do you believe that Muhammad gave us the final revelation of God?'

Butros smiled and spread his hands. 'You know I'm a Christian. I'm a follower of Jesus Christ.'

'Of course. And Muslims believe Jesus is a great prophet. Second only to Muhammad. When Jesus comes back, what will He do?'

'He will judge the living and the dead.'

'So He will speak again. He is in God's presence now, and when He returns, He will reveal more of Allah's will. So Muhammad is *not* the final revelation of God. The final revelation rests with Jesus. I have come to the conclusion that Jesus is alive and He is coming back to dispense justice.'

'All Muslims believe that Jesus is coming back,' Butros said.

'True. But Muslims don't believe He died on the cross and rose again from the dead. As you know, they think He was replaced on the cross, probably by the traitor Judas, and God removed Him from earth until the revelation of the *Mahdi*. But I'm convinced Jesus was executed. And God raised Him back to life after three days. Forty days later He ascended into heaven where He sits at the right hand of God the Father. And when He returns to earth, it will not be to declare that He is a Muslim.'

The pair talked for an hour as Kareem revealed more details of his spiritual journey. 'To everyone around me, I remain a good Muslim,' he said. 'But when I go to the mosque to pray, I am praying to Jesus. I have reached the point where I need to talk with someone who understands. If I have one friend who knows the truth and can keep this a secret, I believe I can go on.'

'How can I help?' Butros asked.

'Occasionally, I would like to talk with you'

'Any time.'

'But you must not contact me. I may come here to your home, late at night. Or I may ask you to meet in some other safe location. I will be the one who contacts you.'

Kareem stood and said, 'Please, thank your wife for the coffee and pastries.' He opened the door and looked to be sure no one was looking, then quickly ran down the stairs and slipped away into the night.

13

Two months later

A short distance from his hotel, Brother Andrew waited at the street corner. He held a plastic bag containing a change of clothes. Taxis, buses, motor scooters and lorries roared past, belching black smoke that seared his lungs.

Butros had informed him that someone would pick him up at this spot and take him to 'the Dip'. Thankfully, the wait was only five minutes before a white saloon pulled up to the kerb and Andrew jumped in. Instantly the driver merged with the mass of vehicles honking and weaving, drove 270 degrees around a traffic circle, and headed towards the airport.

After five minutes the driver made a sudden U-turn, doubled back several streets, then turned down a side-street and pulled into a walled compound.

'Quick, grab your bag,' said the guard at the gate. He opened the door of a black SUV with tinted windows. Butros was the driver and had already warmed up the engine. The guard reopened the gate. Butros drove through and headed back into town.

The crackle of a radio caught Andrew's attention. Butros picked up a walkie-talkie and spoke some words in Arabic. He kept looking in his rearview mirror, and his look of deep concentration kept Andrew from asking any questions.

As they neared the edge of the city, Butros pulled into what looked like a newly developed community. The road was rocky and bumpy. Few of the homes were occupied yet, but there didn't appear to be any construction crews. Butros continued to look in his rearview mirror. Andrew glanced back and could see no one following them. 'We're clean,' Butros said with a straight face. He pulled into one of the building sites and parked in front of a house that looked finished but unoccupied. All of the windows were covered with black plastic.

As they entered the house, a single candle was burning on the floor just inside the door. In a far corner of the front room, Andrew saw movement – three or four men were resting on the floor. Butros took Andrew to a small room where he put on the white cassock Butros handed him.

A few minutes later Butros led Andrew to the living room. A dozen men, dressed in *jallabiya*, rested against the wall. They quickly rose to their feet, grinning, eager to shake Andrew's hand.

On the opposite side of the room, a coffee table was draped with a tablecloth. Two candles on the table were the only light. Butros and Andrew sat cross-legged on thin cushions on the floor behind the table. The men seated opposite them were mostly in their twenties or thirties. Andrew recognised Ahmed, Mustafa and Hassan, and also another of the men from the secret church service he'd visited a few months before.

Butros welcomed the men. Then Ahmed started singing a hymn, and the men quickly joined in with beautiful baritone voices. Several of them turned their palms upward in a traditional posture for prayer and worship.

After the hymn Butros introduced Andrew, saying, 'Now Brother Andrew will bring a short message.'

Andrew spoke and Butros translated: 'This is a very special day because you are going to do something with your faith that you will remember for the rest of your life. To become a follower of Jesus Christ is the greatest privilege anyone can have.'

He proceeded to speak about the uniqueness of Christianity. 'It is not following a religion; it is becoming a follower of Jesus Christ. There is one book that tells us about that and it's the Injil. In this book we find out that Jesus Christ, when He was a full-grown man, came to John the Baptist to be baptised. Now many people were coming to John; they were confessing their sins and he was baptising them, symbolising their repentance. But Jesus was sinless. He didn't need baptism. So why did He go to John? Because Jesus was becoming the Lamb of God. In His submission to God the Father, He took our sins on Himself. His baptism was not a baptism of forgiveness for sins but rather of identification with us. You see, even Jesus had to obey the laws of God. That's why it is so important that we be obedient followers of Jesus according to this book.'

Then Brother Andrew got to the heart of his message. Before reading from Romans 6:4, he said, 'Jesus teaches us that, as new creatures, we have to bury the old person. "We were therefore buried with him through baptism into death." This is a definite experience in our Christian life. We make the decision, as we made the decision to follow Jesus Christ. Now we have decided to bury the old man. However, I won't leave you underwater. I will pull you up again. As the rest of the verse says, "just as Christ was raised from the dead through the glory of the Father, we too may live a new life".'

Even as he spoke, Andrew sensed the deeper significance of these words to the men in front of him. 'Baptism means being buried in a grave with Jesus Christ. In a way, what we are going to do in a few minutes is put ourselves and everything that belongs to us in the grave. Everything of the old life, before we were followers of Jesus Christ, we bury forever. This will remind us that for the rest of our lives we now live in a new kingdom. That also means that everything has become new. Our sinful past is completely gone forever.

'In 1 Peter 3:21 we have the promise, through baptism, of a good conscience. Many people do not have a good conscience because they know they have not done enough good deeds to earn heaven. That's why, in every religion, people are so afraid of the day of judgement. But we are not afraid of the day of judgement because we have put our trust in Jesus Christ. As you step out of the water, you can say, "I am a new person." '

Butros and Andrew were struck by the intensity of these men, their eyes boring into them, trying to catch every one of Andrew's inflections, even while waiting for the translation.

When Andrew finished his message, it was their turn to respond. Using questions Abuna Alexander had helped him write, Butros examined the men to make sure they understood the Christian faith and what they were about to do. 'Do you renounce the devil and all his works, the vain pomp and glory of this world, the covetous and sinful desires of the flesh?' he asked.

Through the prompting of Butros, the men answered, 'We renounce them all, and by God's help we will no longer follow nor be led by them.'

'Do you believe in Jesus the Christ, the Son of the living God?'

Enthusiastically the men answered, 'We do!'

'Do you accept Jesus Christ and desire to follow Him as your Saviour and Lord?'

'Yes, we do.'

'Will you be baptised in this faith?'

'Yes, that is our desire.'

'Will you obediently keep God's holy will and commandments all the days of your life?'

'By God's help, we will.'

They now proceeded to the room adjoining the one where Andrew had changed. There, an inflatable swimming pool Andrew had purchased in Holland was set up. Fully inflated, it was nearly nine feet long – much longer than Andrew had anticipated – but only about a foot deep. Clearly he had misread the dimensions on the package and he couldn't help chuckling – this had to be one of the most unusual baptisteries in the world, more suitable for little children splashing about on a hot summer day. But to the little congregation, this was holy ground. These men had counted the cost. They had understood the explanation that baptism symbolised burial of their past. They also knew that if their baptism was discovered, it could lead to a real and early grave.

One at a time, each man stepped into the pool with Andrew and sat down in the water. Andrew proclaimed, 'I baptise you into Jesus in the name of the Father, and of the Son, and of the Holy Spirit,' and lowered the man under the water. Then, raising the man out of the water, Andrew said, 'We welcome you into the family of God.'

As each man emerged from the pool, he was greeted with a hearty '*Mabruk*!' – 'Congratulations!' – from his brothers.

The last man to enter the pool was Ahmed. As Andrew plunged him under the water and pulled him up to his feet, a huge grin spread over his face. Impulsively Ahmed grabbed Andrew and embraced him in a dripping wet hug.

A few minutes later, having changed into dry clothes, everyone reassembled in the room with the coffee table altar. Several in the room wanted to tell their stories. One said, 'I took my children to a Christian doctor. He wrote a prescription and under it wrote the words of Jesus: "Come to me and I will give you rest." I asked him, "How do you find this rest?" He said he had spiritual medicine also, and he gave me a copy of Luke's Gospel in Arabic. I found the teaching of Jesus Christ was very strange. In our culture when someone hits us, we hit him twice. But Jesus says if someone slaps you, you turn the other cheek. That spoke to me. I wanted to follow the Master who says this unusual teaching rather than doing what naturally comes out of man's heart.'

Another man told about how several months ago he had a dream. In that dream he saw a pile of books floating in dirty water. He tried to clean up the mess and when he had pulled out all of the muddy, soiled books, there remained one book that was perfectly clean and pure. Three days later he met a man who gave him a Bible. In that book he learned about God becoming a man. 'Both my wife and I are now followers of Jesus Christ,' he said, his face beaming.

As soon as he had finished, another man spoke eagerly: 'I had difficulty with the legalistic aspect of Islam. It was like slavery. I was doing the daily prayers as a duty, not from the heart, so I started to search for another way. I studied other religions. In my search I also studied Injil. I now follow Jesus because I can do it from my heart and with love, not because I am forced. I believe the love of Christ binds us all together.' The other men responded with 'Amen' to that declaration.

Near the end of their time together, Andrew was asked to give each man his new Christian name. Butros had prepared for Andrew a list of names, each with a verse from the Bible. The first man was Ahmed. 'Your new name is Timothy,' Andrew told him. 'Timothy was a disciple of Paul. And the verse we have chosen for you is from Paul's final letter to Timothy: "I have fought the good jihad, I have finished the race, I have kept the faith."'

Then Butros and Andrew laid hands on Timothy's shoulders, and Andrew prayed, 'Lord, we lift up our brother Timothy to You. May he faithfully follow You all the rest of the days of his life. May he, like Your servant Paul, fight the good jihad, finish the race You have laid out for him, and keep the faith. Amen.'

From Timothy, they went down the line, giving each man his new name and praying for his walk of faith. When they had finished, the men asked for a picture to commemorate the occasion. Of course Butros obliged, though he wondered where they could ever use such a photo. These men could never be found with this photograph. It was too dangerous.

Andrew was astounded by the passionate faith of these men. 'I have a question for all of you,' he said. 'Do you think there are many men in this country who want to follow Jesus Christ?'

Almost as one, they replied, 'Yes, many.'

Andrew and Butros drank fresh orange juice and debriefed in Butros's flat as Nadira prepared a light supper for them. Young Thomas babbled contentedly in his high chair, playing with tiny pieces of flat bread. Earlier, Nadira had taken care of the wet clothes Butros had collected from several of the men who said they couldn't take wet clothing home without providing an explanation to an enquiring mother or sister. Butros promised to have them dried and returned.

'I meant to ask you,' Brother Andrew said, 'where did you learn the evasive driving manoeuvres you used today?'

Butros laughed. 'You think I've watched too many spy movies?'

'You have!' Nadira shouted from the kitchen.

'Actually, God is the source of creativity. It's not hard for the Holy Spirit to guide you in taking reasonable precautions.'

'And how did you find our meeting place today?'

'Obviously we couldn't meet in a church. We couldn't rent a hotel meeting room. It had to be a private residence, but somewhere we wouldn't attract attention. As you know, I now have several volunteers who help me out. One of them told me about this building site where construction was halted because the developer has financial problems.'

'Well, that was an amazing service. This is a day I will never forget.'

'It was an amazing day, but there is much more that must be done. This is really only the beginning. These men need teaching, Brother Andrew. With the help of Pastor Yusef, I've been working on developing a discipleship course for MBBs.'

'That is essential, but you can't do it alone. You will need trainers.'

'Yes, that is part of my challenge. I'm thinking of teaching the men you baptised today and a few others, and to train them to teach MBBs in the areas where they live.'

The phone rang, interrupting their talk. Nadira asked her husband to answer it. As Butros talked on the phone, Andrew sat back and enjoyed the rest of his orange juice.

There was a long silence, and then Butros appeared back at the table, his face ashen. 'We have a problem,' he said.

Nadira came out of the kitchen, wiping her hands on a towel, and with a worried voice asked, 'What's wrong?'

'Ahmed, Mustafa and Hassan have been arrested.'

14

Ahmed groaned as he gained consciousness. The cold of the cement floor added to the growing pain and stiffness he felt throughout his body. He tried to open his eyes, but one of them was swollen shut. Out of his left eye he could see a crack of light under a door. He started to roll over, but a cement wall prevented him from doing so. He reached out in the other direction and immediately felt another slab of cement. To turn over, he would need to lift himself up and twist, but when he tried to push up on his arms, he immediately felt arrows of pain in his arms and ribs. He surrendered to the cement floor and wondered how he had landed in such a hole.

Gradually the memories of the previous day began to emerge. The baptism service in the secret location – it had been the highlight of his life. He had never known such joy as that moment when Brother Andrew had pushed him under the water and pronounced, 'I baptise you into Jesus in the name of the Father, and of the Son, and of the Holy Spirit.' For the first time he had sensed he was part of the great body of Christ as he stepped out of the pool to greetings of '*mabruk*!' from his brothers. For an instant it seemed that he saw a throng of millions, all in white robes, singing praise to Jesus, and he knew he had glimpsed how he was part of a glorious company of believers around the world and throughout two thousand years of history. *The only choice before us is rejecting You or fully embracing You*, he had thought. He had gladly, totally, joyfully embraced his Lord.

He was a new person with a new name – Timothy. That was the name of the apostle Paul's protégé, trained to evangelise and make disciples. He intended to follow that example.

After returning home, he had left his friends in the flat and walked around the city for several hours, too excited to sit still and too burdened for the people he saw. How he wanted to be used by God to bring more Muslims to Jesus! He had walked back home as the sun was setting and as he rounded the corner, he'd seen police cars blocking the street. Immediately he'd turned and walked quickly in the opposite direction, past the stationery shop, past coffee shops and grocery stores, not knowing where to go, until his heart stopped racing. *How stupid – I should have known.* There had been evidence they were being watched. All three of them had made remarks of seeing suspicious individuals who seemed to linger too long around them. But they had taken extra care for the baptism, to be sure that no one knew where they were going. Still, the police had decided to raid their flat on this day. *What shall I do?*

He stopped and prayed. He thought of Mustafa and Hassan and wondered if they were being held until he returned home. He wouldn't be surprised if the police beat his friends to try to find out where he was. What should he do? Should he run and hide? They would surely search for him. No doubt they would go to Butros. They would hunt down anyone who had any contact with him. He could not put that burden on his friends, so he turned and walked back to the flat. But it was deserted when he arrived.

Soon the landlord knocked on the door and said, 'The police want to talk to you. I am supposed to call them as soon as you get here.'

'Then please call. I will wait for them.'

The landlord looked shocked.

'Please, you will get in trouble if you don't phone them,' Ahmed said.

Ahmed managed to push himself up again and this time was able to twist and turn himself over so he could lie on his back. But his body screamed in pain. He tried taking several deep breaths but that triggered pain in his ribs and he started to cough, which made it all worse.

They had beaten him as soon as he'd arrived at the police station, raining down blows with their fists and sticks. They'd cursed him for being an infidel and punished him some more. He'd passed out twice. When he'd regained consciousness, they had dragged him back to his feet and beat him again. He didn't remember being put in this tiny cell that felt like a coffin – he could reach out with his hands and feel the cold cement on both sides.

What have I done to deserve such harsh treatment? I didn't kill or steal or trade in drugs. Whom have I offended by believing in the Christ?

The sound of metal – a key turning a lock – jarred him out of his reflection. A pair of hands dragged him by his armpits into the light. Two policemen reached down and yanked him to his feet. He nearly fell over but they caught him and, pushing and pulling him, got him to a room where an interrogator was seated at a table. The two men who had brought him in stepped back. He wobbled for a moment and then spread his feet so he could remain upright.

The questioner let him stand there for a few minutes as he read from a file. Then he looked up and said, 'You have been conducting illegal religious meetings.'

Ahmed had trouble shifting his concentration away from his pain and understanding the words being spoken.

'I said, Why are you holding these illegal religious meetings?'

'I don't know what you mean. What meetings?'

He hadn't anticipated the blows coming from behind. The two men struck him and he fell on the cement floor. One of the men, wearing heavy boots, kicked him, then jumped on his ribs. He screamed as he felt what seemed like bones breaking. The two thugs backed away as he rolled on the ground.

'So are you going to co-operate?' He could hear the voice of the interrogator. 'Tell me the names of the people in your meeting.'

Ahmed struggled to understand the question. *What meeting was he talking about?*

'Al Waha Church. Does that ring a bell or do we need to provide you with some more motivation?' He sensed the two policemen moving toward him again. They seemed eager to inflict a lot more punishment.

Now he understood. 'I don't attend that church.' That was the truth, though the basement was used for the little meetings organised for fellow believers. As the police attacked him, he wondered how they had learned of these meetings. While the blows rained down on him again, he determined he would not give them the names of his brothers and sisters. They could abuse *him* all they wanted but not the others.

'Your memory isn't very good. We know you and your two friends attend weekly meetings at the church. We want to know why Muslims attend church. We want to know how many attend. What are their names? What do you discuss?'

Had they followed him to the meetings? Ahmed wondered. Or was there an informant – perhaps someone had infiltrated the small group and betrayed them. But that was impossible. They had been extremely careful about who was invited. Only those who were totally convinced Jesus was Lord were allowed. Still, they could have tortured one or more to get names. Well, they would have to work harder for their information – he wasn't going to reveal anything.

Your attitude should be the same as that of Christ Jesus.

He humbled Himself and became obedient to death.

Jesus had suffered. And now as his body endured more excruciating blows, Ahmed was joining in the sufferings of his Lord.

Then he lost consciousness.

—◈◈◈—

Butros looked at Brother Andrew in frustration. For several hours they had tried to obtain information. All they had learned for sure was that Ahmed, Mustafa and Hassan had been arrested, but as they stood at the entrance to the Central Justice Building, they didn't know for sure where the three were being held. No one could tell them why they had been arrested.

As they walked into the cool pre-dawn air, Butros kicked a rock in anger and sent it flying against a parked car that already had several dents. 'We might as well go home and get some rest. We aren't going to learn any more tonight.' But, head down, he walked past his car, as though somehow by walking the streets he could think of a solution. Andrew followed him.

Now they were away from the building where prying ears might overhear them, Andrew asked, 'Do you think it was because of the baptism service?'

Butros shook his head. 'We took every precaution. And after we left, all the evidence was removed.'

'Could there have been a spy in our midst?'

'No, all of the men were very carefully questioned. All of them chose to be baptised, and they would only do that if they truly believed.'

They walked a little farther in silence. Then Andrew asked, 'So what are our options?'

'Those three – Ahmed in particular – have become bolder in their witness in recent months. I know they are careful to whom they witness. They always probe, looking for genuine interest – a frustration with Islam, perhaps. Still, they only had to offend one person, someone who learned they were MBBs . . .' Butros didn't finish his thought.

'What possible charges could they face?'

Butros blew out a puff of air, then stopped and looked up at the sky that was turning red in the east. 'They could be accused of insulting a heavenly religion. It's illegal to put down any religion, though it's interesting the law is only enforced when Islam is the religion attacked. They could be accused of threatening national security. They could be accused of blaspheming the Prophet. They could be accused of desecrating the Quran.'

'Obviously they haven't done any of those things.'

'It doesn't matter. All it takes is one angry Muslim to make the accusation, to say he saw them tear pages out of a Quran or something like that. Or they could be accused of proselytising, trying to convert Muslims to Christianity. They could accuse them of holding an illegal meeting. Or they could just hold them without any charges.'

'How long can they hold them without charges?'

'Sixty days. But sometimes they extend the incarceration for another sixty days. And then another. They may or may not ever appear in court. And you can be sure they'll be tortured. That's common practice.'

'Are their lives in danger?'

'Could they be killed while in prison? Yes. It has happened.'

'Then we must act. They must not be allowed to do these things in secret.'

A few days later the *Mukhabarat* paid a visit to Ahmed's family in Suq al Khamis. The men sat in the living room with Ahmed's father. The women were dismissed.

'Your son has been arrested,' blue shirt reported.

'On what charge?' asked Ahmed's father.

'We were hoping you could help us determine that,' white shirt answered.

The reply almost brought the father out of his chair. He didn't like the *Mukhabarat* and had determined over the years to avoid attracting their attention. 'That is a strange answer,' he said. 'People aren't generally arrested without a reason.'

'Oh, we have reasons,' said blue shirt.

'But we need your help,' said white shirt, pulling out his notebook and pen. 'When was the last time you saw your son?'

'About three years ago.'

'And where did he go?'

'I don't know. Apparently you do. Maybe you can enlighten me.'

Blue shirt smiled at the agitated man and said, 'Sir, we're on your side.'

'Well, it doesn't feel like it.'

'Please, tell us why he left.'

'You should ask him yourself. He's of legal age. You have him in custody. He should be able to answer your questions.'

White shirt interjected, 'Have you had any contact at all with your son since he left home?'

The father shook his head. 'None. He has phoned a few times. He's talked with his mother and sister. But I have not talked with him.'

'And why did he run away?'

'Who said he ran away?'

'Sir, we know this is difficult,' blue shirt said. 'We're just trying to understand, so we can help your son.'

By now the frustrated father was sure his son was being tortured, and that realisation made him angrier. It was one thing for him to beat his son – Ahmed had shamed the family. But what right did these thugs, the *Mukhabarat*, the police, the government, have to interfere in a family matter? If Ahmed was an apostate, let the family or tribe handle it.

'Can you give us any other information that might help us?' white shirt asked, pen poised over his notebook.

'Since you won't tell me what crime my son has committed, I don't see how I can help you.' The father stood up, hoping to bring an end to the interview. The two men took the hint and decided there was nothing more they could learn at the moment.

At the door blue shirt stopped and looked at the father with an expression of concern. 'It must hurt you terribly to be the father of an apostate. I have a son, just two years old. If my son turned away from Islam, I don't know what I'd do.'

White shirt said, 'I'd kill him.'

'Yes,' blue shirt agreed. 'That is all you can really do with an apostate. If he won't return to Islam, kill him.'

—⁓⁓⁓—

The torture sessions blurred together. Ahmed had no idea how many days the horror lasted. He could remember electric shocks, beatings all over his body with various implements, beatings on the soles of his feet that left him unable to walk for days, then being hanged by his clothes, beaten some more, and threatened with rape. It was so savage, so cruel his mind could hardly comprehend that such behaviour was possible by fellow citizens. There were days when he was left to rot in a cell that wasn't fit even for animals. Drain pipes leaked sewage. The smell caused him to retch. There was no place to sit or lie comfortably, but he had no strength to stand.

What had he done to deserve such treatment? He knew the warped answer of his persecutors. He had done the unthinkable and renounced adherence to Islam. No one did that – no one rejected the final revelation of God. But worse, he had embraced Jesus Christ. In his society that was unforgivable. He was a traitor, an enemy of the state. It didn't matter his country had signed the charter of the United Nations that says all citizens enjoy freedom of religion. The laws of Islam superseded all other legal systems. Not only did these officials not respect his freedom to choose what he believed, they treated him as subhuman because of his decision.

Suddenly the torture stopped – no more beatings, no more questioning about the group of converts at the church, no more screaming at him to come back to Islam. Several more days passed in a fog. He remembered being transferred to another prison, but when he entered his new cell, he had lain on a thin mattress and fallen into a deep sleep. For how long, he could not tell. Now as he woke, for the first time, he felt he could move some of his limbs without excruciating pain. He felt his face and then cautiously opened his eyes. He could see out of both. And in the periphery of one eye, he saw there were many others in the room with him.

Carefully he rolled on to his back and looked up at the ceiling. *Your attitude should be the same as that of Christ Jesus.* The passage from Philippians had been the last clear thought he could remember. Was it morning, afternoon or night? He didn't know. He would need to find out and resume his daily prayer routine.

Prayer seemed to emerge from the depths of his soul: *My Jesus, I know that You were tempted like me. You were hungry like me. You were naked like me. You were imprisoned like me. I know loneliness was Your companion like me. You were surrounded like an exile and You resisted face-to-face. You challenged the virulence of fear and uncovered its cowardice and lies. You transformed the curse of poverty, hunger, and oppression – You changed it from a curse to fertile faith – a true wealth that never fades. You changed the curse to honour, which no longer fears death.* Thinking of Mustafa and Hassan, he continued, *In the midst of the flames, we are men. It fuels within us the passion to change the world and a passion for the Holy of Holies. It teaches us how to take risks and how to bear the essence of valour in any peril.*

A few minutes later the cell door opened and the men were released to go outside into a yard. He followed the group outdoors, looked up to the sky, and breathed in a deep breath of fresh air. Then he heard his name called. 'Ahmed, you are here too.'

He turned and saw Mustafa and Hassan coming towards him. He gave both of the men a warm embrace, though he winced when they hugged him hard in return.

'Timothy, my brother,' Hassan said softly so as not to attract attention. 'They beat us, but we didn't tell them anything.'

'A week ago it stopped,' Mustafa added.

'We're together in the same cell.'

The three friends walked together for thirty minutes, comparing notes about their interrogations. Then a guard yelled, interrupting their conversation. 'Back in your cells.' He wielded a bamboo stick and any who were too slow felt the sting.

'Have the attitude of Christ,' Ahmed reminded his friends as they separated. Someone had commandeered his mattress – there were more men in the cell than beds or mattresses. As the door clanged shut behind him, he sat in the only available spot, near the toilet, and leaned back against the cement wall, exhausted yet somehow exhilarated. One of the men in the cell spoke: 'Hey, are you a Christian?'

For the first time Ahmed looked at the others. There were perhaps thirty men in a room meant to accommodate no more than ten. All stared at him. 'Why do you ask?' he said.

'Because we get a reward if we convert you back to Islam,' said the man lying on his mattress.

Ahmed studied the men in his cell. Prayer poured out from his heart: *You, my Jesus, are as You are, unchanging. You forgive. You love. You liberate. You bind up wounds, heal, rejoice, struggle, and hang on the cross alone as though it were Your song alone, Your will alone, Your revolution alone. My Jesus, before You, the wisdom of this world becomes deaf, dumb and blind. Who can overcome love? Who?*

Ahmed, now known to Jesus and his brothers as Timothy, grinned and said, 'Give it your best shot.'

～∞～

Back in Holland Brother Andrew looked over the drafts of two letters. As soon as he'd arrived home, he'd contacted a news service with the story of the arrests. Within twenty-four hours an article had been sent to newspapers, radio and television stations around the world. Then he'd asked a staff member, who co-ordinated campaigns on behalf of persecuted Christians, to write to the ruler of the country where Ahmed, Mustafa and Hassan were imprisoned. Butros had agreed that if the three men were in danger of being killed, publicity certainly couldn't hurt and might actually help. The ruler, who was trying to maintain beneficial relations with western democracies, would not want the negative backlash of a gross human rights violation. Towards that end, the letter to the ruler reminded him that, as his country was signatory to the United Nations Charter, Article 55 committed his country to 'universal respect for, and observance of, human rights and fundamental freedoms for all without distinction as to race, sex, language or religion'.

Before returning home Andrew had gone with Butros to meet a lawyer, a Muslim who was sympathetic to human rights issues.

'What can we do to help these three men?' Andrew had asked.

The lawyer had asked in return, 'Have any of these men ever spoken against Islam?'

'Sir, they only speak of their love for Isa,' Andrew had answered.

'Depending on what they said, some might consider that an attack against Islam.'

'So they have no right to speak about their love for one of the great prophets?'

The lawyer had smiled at the Dutchman's naïveté, but he had promised he would file a motion with the court to have the three men either charged or released. 'However,' he warned, 'the police can hold them for sixty days without charge. And then hold them for another sixty days, and so on. So it may not do any good.'

'Would a publicity campaign help them?'

The lawyer had concluded it was probably worth a try. So now the first letters to government officials were sent. And Andrew was determined to keep the pressure on, which was the purpose of a second letter, to churches around the world, urging them to pray for the three men and to take some action: 'Please send *appeals*, in English or your own language, to (and here he filled in the names and addresses). Please also send notes of *encouragement* to Ahmed, Mustafa and Hassan. (Again, an address was provided.) Colourful postcards or short, one-page letters would be best. Write words of encouragement saying that you are praying for them and their release, and perhaps give them a short Scripture verse.' In addition, Andrew had arranged extra meetings in churches throughout England and Holland to tell the story of these men and urge people to pray and write on behalf of their suffering brothers in the body of Christ.

Lord, what else can I do? Andrew was determined that these men would not be forgotten. They had paid a great price for declaring their faith in Jesus Christ. The least he could do was intercede on their behalf. If he was successful, and if hundreds or even thousands followed his lead, perhaps these three wouldn't suffer so much. But even more important, hopefully the struggling church would realise they were not alone, and that there were parts of the body around the world who wanted them to be a strong light in this Muslim land.

15

Six months later

For Abuna Alexander and the parishioners of St Mark's Church, Friday was often the most stressful day of the week. Most shops in Suq al Khamis closed their doors at noon, so faithful Muslims could gather at the nearest mosque for the weekly sermon. Some of the imams used their pulpits to provoke hatred of Christianity, the West and all things not Muslim. In some villages mobs had stormed out of Friday services and torched churches and the homes of Christians. To add to the anxiety, the local Muslim Brotherhood had recently started distributing cassette tapes that aggressively challenged young Muslim men to a more complete and dedicated practice of Islam. One especially passionate preacher frequently railed against Christians, insisting they should be isolated from the rest of society.

Fortunately, there had not been many incidents in the larger town, until last night when the priest and several members of St Mark's had received phone calls warning them to be careful. Other pastors in town had received similar threats. Father Alexander stood at the front window of his flat as the Friday prayer meetings ended when he heard a roar in the distance. He stepped outside his front door to see if he could determine the location. Then the phone in his home rang.

It was Bashir, the owner of a butcher shop that served Christians almost exclusively. 'They've attacked my store,' he shouted over the phone.

'I'll be right over,' said the priest.

'No, don't come. It's too dangerous. Oh no. They're . . .' There was a click and the phone line went dead.

Father Alexander froze, unsure what to do. He felt he should go and be with his parishioner, yet he knew that in his clerical robe his presence might make the situation worse. 'O God, our help and assistance, who art just and merciful,' he said quietly, reciting by memory from the daily prayer book as his wife, Nour, came alongside him. 'I acknowledge and believe, O Lord, that all trials of this life are given by Thee for our chastisement, when we drift away from Thee, and disobey Thy commandments. Deal not with us after our sins but according to Thy bountiful mercies. Thou knowest our misery and suffering and to Thee, our only hope and refuge, we flee for relief and comfort; trusting to Thine infinite love and compassion, that in due time, when Thou knowest best, Thou wilt deliver us from this trouble.'

His wife added simply: 'O Lord Jesus Christ, Son of God, have mercy upon us.'

The phone rang again. Another parishioner was calling to report that the crowd of mostly young Muslim men had destroyed the local video store. More calls followed rapidly. Bashir's market had been burned as well as a shop that sold wine and several other shops, all belonging to Christians.

'This seems co-ordinated,' said one caller. 'They targeted particular shops that sold pork or alcohol and had any connotations of western or Christian influence.'

The priest walked outside to the front of his church where he could see smoke rising from the centre of town. He wondered if the mob were satiated, or whether they would march on the churches. Should he stay put and try to protect the building? He wanted to go somewhere, to take action, to help his congregation, but he felt helpless. The best he could do was stay where he was and be ready to minister to all who came by the church.

The butcher arrived a few minutes later. He wept as he hugged his priest and revealed that he was ruined financially. 'I have a brother in Europe who for years has wanted me to move there. It's time to go . . .'

'Don't give up,' the priest interrupted. 'Give it a little time. You can rebuild.'

'No, it's over,' Bashir said, regaining his composure. 'This is no place for my wife and children.'

The priest couldn't deny that for those who had relatives overseas and the means to leave, their children faced a much better future. And yet, if all the Christians fled when times got hard, how would the light of Christ shine? He wanted to urge his friend to stay and yet he understood why he felt the need to escape.

As he tried to comfort Bashir, Alexander's wife came out to tell him of another call. 'The crowd is breaking up,' she reported. 'I think the worst is over.'

'For now,' said the butcher.

So the mob wouldn't attack the churches. At least not this time. But what was worse? A crumbling building with a leaky roof and a terrified congregation seeking to flee the country or a burned-out building and a congregation prepared to stay in the community and live for Christ? He had fought for years to have his church repaired. Now he recognised the real problem. The church was people, not a building, and his flock was terrified. To Bashir he said, 'Come with me and let's visit those who are suffering tonight.'

—⌇∿⌇—

The second time Butros met Kareem was in a private room of a very exclusive restaurant, one Butros never dreamed he would ever visit. He'd received a handwritten note giving him instructions, time and location. He arrived dressed in his best suit and was escorted to the private room where Kareem, dressed in a starched white *jallabiya* and *kaffiyeh*, rose to greet him.

'I am so glad you could come. I hope you don't mind my choice of location. I know the owner well, and we will have total privacy.'

A waiter named Salim entered the room and handed the men menus mounted on leather-covered boards. Butros noticed there were no prices on the page, and he couldn't make any sense of the names written in French.

'There is a different menu every night,' Kareem said with a big, winsome smile. 'The chef was designated "Maître Cuisinier", a master chef, by the French government. There are only two hundred of them in the world. Do you like caviar or *foie gras*?'

Butros looked dazed. He'd never had either.

'The *foie gras*,' Kareem ordered. 'It's outstanding.'

'I've always wondered what that is.'

'Goose liver pâté. Very good! You'll like it. Then you must have the *crème de truffe du désert* – cream of desert truffle soup, made with *zubaydi*. It's the best. Now, for the main course, I recommend the lamb – tender, cooked to perfection with garlic and olive oil. Superb.'

Butros blinked and nodded.

'Wonderful.' Kareem gave instructions to the waiter, who left and closed the door. 'Now, we can talk openly. When the food is ready, we will hear a bell, but Salim won't enter until I push the button.' The government minister laughed at the discomfort of his friend. 'You've never been in such a place, no? Well, relax. I come here often. Please enjoy the food. This is my pleasure.'

'Thank you.' It was hard for Butros not to laugh at the situation. If Nadira could see him now. He and his wife didn't live in poverty, but it was rare they ate at a restaurant. They were very careful with their budget, and Nadira carefully planned their meals before shopping at the local *suq*.

Clearly, his host lived in a different world of luxury. But he was also a man with needs, and Butros was alert, trying to sense whatever God intended for him to see or hear in the next couple of hours. He said, 'My wife and I have prayed for you since that night you visited us.'

Kareem turned serious. 'Thank you for your prayers. I apologise for the way I came to your home, but it was the only way I could think to approach you – for my safety and yours.'

'There is no need for apology,' Butros said. 'I understand. I am eager to hear how you are doing.'

'There is a part of me that wants to declare to everyone what I have discovered, but of course I cannot do that.'

'Do you still go to the mosque?'

'Yes, I am a good Muslim,' he said with a hearty laugh. 'The men around me have no idea what I'm really praying. But that raises questions.' Kareem paused and turned serious. 'I sometimes wonder. Am I a Christian now? Or am I a Muslim who loves Isa? How long can I keep this a secret? I will never shame my family or the royal family. I sometimes wonder if I'm a little like the Jewish prophet Daniel who served faithfully the king of Babylon without compromising his faith.'

'That may be a good comparison,' Butros answered. 'You seem to know the Bible.'

'I read it every day. There is a room in my house that no one can enter. That is where I keep the Bible and other Christian books I've collected. It is also the place I can be alone and pray.'

Over the meal Kareem talked mainly about the pressures of his work in the government.

Butros was astonished at the quality and flavour of the food. He thought this was perhaps the best meal he'd ever tasted.

Salim brought in a plate of tiny pastries for dessert along with the finest Arabic coffee.

When they were alone again, Kareem brought up the problem of Ahmed and the others who were in prison. 'I am very sorry about their situation. This is not good.'

'Are they going to be charged with a crime?'

'That is a dilemma,' Kareem said. 'There has been too much international attention brought on this case. Originally the government arrested them for organising an illegal meeting. We received information from someone who attended one of the meetings at Al Waha Church. Muslims were meeting in a church to plot a coup against the royal family and set up a new kingdom.'

'What?' Butros couldn't believe anyone could seriously believe that.

Kareem laughed and his big smile put Butros a little more at ease. 'You would agree, of course, that we do belong to a heavenly kingdom. You and I, we have sworn allegiance to King Jesus.' He laughed again and leaned forward to say, 'You can see how someone who doesn't believe in our Lord Isa might view this politically as an attempt to overthrow the government.'

'But we are loyal citizens. We pay our taxes, obey the laws, support the king.'

'Yes, of course we do. Christians make the best citizens. I know. But if the *Mukhabarat* came in right now, they would certainly interpret our conversation differently. They would say we are traitors to Islam and Sharia and so we can't possibly be loyal subjects. This is their thinking, but to the rest of the world looking at us, they see three men in prison in violation of their religious freedom. They see people of good conscience meeting in a church to worship and pray. What could be wrong with that? The West doesn't understand why a good Muslim considers that treason.'

'Yes, these three men are caught between two worlds.'

'I can tell you that the royal family wants the problem to go away. The authorities are trying to find a face-saving way to release them.'

The two men talked for nearly three hours. As they concluded their time, Butros felt convinced that he had to take a risk. What he felt compelled to say could end this relationship. He took a deep breath and spoke: 'Earlier this evening you compared your situation to that of Daniel, but there is one major difference.'

'What is that?'

'Daniel never compromised who he was in relation to God. He did a quality job in his position as a government official but he also recognised the situations in which he had to submit to a higher authority than the king.'

Kareem nodded and stroked his neatly trimmed goatee that helped make his face so recognisable in the country. Butros wondered if he had stepped over a line in their relationship.

Then the official said soberly, 'You are right. I do not know how long I can keep up this pretence. I will admit I am uncomfortable staying in Islam, but you know my circumstances. What would you recommend that I do?'

'I don't know,' Butros admitted. 'It may be, like Queen Esther, that God has put you in your position for a certain time. He may call on you someday to make a choice.'

'You must pray that I will make the right choice.'

'You can be sure that I will do that. Now, I do not want to presume on our friendship, but I have one request. I wonder if you would be willing to meet a friend of mine from Holland.'

'The man you call Brother Andrew?'

Surprise and fear suddenly welled up in Butros. 'You know of him?'

'Of course. We know all about his visits.'

'So you know that he is a mentor in my work. And maybe he can be an encouragement to you. You may also know he has met with Muslim leaders in several countries, including even leaders of fundamentalist groups like Hezbollah and Hamas.'

Kareem thought for a moment, pulled out a business card, wrote a number on it, and handed it to Butros. 'This phone number will connect you

to my personal assistant. Call him to arrange an appointment the next time
your Dutch friend is visiting.'

—–⁓⁓⁓—–

The situation in the sanctuary of St Mark's Church threatened to get out of
hand. The pews were filled. It appeared that every family in the church was
represented at this meeting. Several men were shouting at once. Abuna
Alexander raised his hands to urge calm and called on Salim to speak.

'We must take action. The Muslims will drive us all out of town if we don't
stand up to them.'

'What do you propose that we do?' Alexander asked.

Several men shouted at once. The priest recognised Adel.

'I say that we march through the streets. We get all the churches together
and we go right down the main street and let them know we are here.'

'And we're not going away. We won't be intimidated,' shouted Salim.

Several others in the congregation shouted, and Abuna Alexander again
urged calm. 'A march would be provocative,' he said. 'That would probably
make things worse.'

Bashir stood and said, 'But there are many Muslims in town who agree
that these attacks on us are wrong. Several of my neighbours were very
supportive when my shop was destroyed . . .'

'But they will not publicly support us. Two imams called me to say they
are sorry and what is happening is wrong. However, they also say they
cannot speak out. The fundamentalists are calling for a greater commitment
to Islam and no Muslim leader will say anything that appears to compromise
the superiority of Islam. A public protest would only force them more into
the other camp.'

'So what can we do?' shouted Salim. 'Are you saying we are helpless?'
Several others joined the chorus of protests.

'No!' The force of Father Alexander's exclamation brought a hush to the
room. 'We are *not* helpless. There is one thing we can do a lot more of. Pray!'
He paused, but no one interrupted him. 'We must ask God to step in and
defend us. How many times in the Scriptures did the people of God cry out
to God because they had no other hope? And God stepped in to defend them,
to fight for them.'

'That was thousands of years ago,' someone said.

'Has God changed? Have we really called on Him and admitted that if He doesn't defend us, we are lost? I'm not suggesting a prayer or two and then we go on with life. I am suggesting we pray and fast and call on God as though our lives depend on it. And I believe that is exactly the situation.'

Alexander looked over the room. He saw that in one corner all of the teens were sitting together. It appeared that everyone who had received a Bible and was participating in the challenge to read the Scriptures was in attendance. The sight of these young people listening to the discussion, knowing they were responding to the challenge to live out their Christian faith, filled him with encouragement. He turned back to the entire congregation and said, 'We are the church. Not this building but people. That includes us and that includes Muslims who are believing in Jesus. I want to tell you something I have never spoken about publicly before. God is drawing Muslims in Suq al Khamis to Jesus. I have met several of them. I can't tell you the details, but you should be encouraged. If He can change the heart of Muslims, He can defend us against the extremists. Remember that when we are living for Christ, He promises the world and the devil will counterattack. The world hates Christ and hates His church. But don't stop there. Jesus also said this: "Be of good cheer. I have overcome the world."'

—∞∞∞—

Layla usually walked home from school with several friends, but today she had stayed late for some tutoring by one of the teachers. Her friend Fanziah usually joined her in these sessions, but today she was ill and had stayed home. Lately Layla and her friend had been talking more about church and the Bible. The two girls had accepted Father Alexander's challenge. They faithfully read a chapter of the New Testament each night and on their walks home from school, along with discussing boys and school and their futures, they often talked about the Bible.

The sun was beginning to set, and Layla wanted to hurry home, so she cut through an alleyway that would save her five minutes. She felt fairly safe; this was primarily a Christian neighbourhood, and it had been several weeks since she had seen the boys who had harassed her at the market and ogled her outside the church.

At the end of the alley she noticed a boy talking on a cell phone. *Don't panic, Layla,* she told herself. *I'll just walk quickly past him and turn on the street and hurry home.*

But as she walked past the boy on the phone, a car suddenly screeched to a stop right in front of her, blocking the exit from the alley. She noticed the boy pocket his cell phone and move behind her as two doors of the car opened and two more teenage boys jumped out. She felt a hand cover her mouth. Strong hands grabbed her arms and pulled her into the back seat of the car. Before she could even think of struggling, the doors slammed shut and the tyres squealed as the car sped down the street, turned on the main street, and headed out of town.

Strong arms held her down, and a voice from the front seat – the same one she'd heard a few weeks before in the marketplace – said calmly, 'What a surprise! A nice Christian girl walking alone.'

'Without a headscarf,' added the voice of the boy pressing her down.

The hand came off her mouth and she tried not to yell as she said, 'You're hurting me.'

'Just a few minutes and you'll be safe,' said the boy in the front passenger seat.

'Where are you taking me?' Layla asked, trying to quell the panic rising inside her.

'You'll see,' said the boy in front.

'She's got spirit,' laughed one of the boys in the backseat. 'You should get a lot of work out of her.'

Layla felt the grip lessen on her arms and she lunged for the door handle. *I have to get out of here, even if the car is moving.* But even before her hands touched the handle, the two boys in the back seat grabbed her arms and twisted them behind her back. Her scream caused them to laugh, and the grip on her tightened. Someone put a blindfold over her eyes, and the other two boys pushed her on to the floor.

'Relax,' said the voice in the front seat. Layla was already hating the sound of that voice. 'I am going to make you very happy.'

'That's right,' laughed the others. 'You'll make our friend a good Muslim wife.'

16

One month later

By phone Abuna Alexander briefed Butros on the situation in Suq al Khamis. 'It's very tense,' he said. 'The girl's parents don't know what to do. The police act like they are helpless.'

'Does anyone know where she might have been taken?' Butros asked.

'She's almost certainly not in Suq al Khamis. She's probably in one of the villages. We think there may be a cousin involved – her mother's brother converted to Islam a few years ago. But the uncle claims he knows nothing. He says he would ask all his relatives if they've heard anything, but we've learned nothing more.'

'Have you ever faced a situation like this?'

'We haven't had this happen in Suq al Khamis, but there have been other parts of the country where Christian girls were kidnapped and forced to convert to Islam. Sometimes they are kept as slaves to the family. Sometimes they are given to a man as a wife and also forced to do slave labour. It's not good.'

'And it sounds like the authorities are no help.'

'Worse. They *refuse* to help. We've filed a complaint, but they won't act. One of them insulted the parents, saying the girl left of her own free will because she obviously wanted to marry a Muslim boy.'

'How are the girl's parents holding up?'

'Terrible. Several of the men in the church want to take revenge. But they don't even know who to attack. They've asked about these boys but no one will say who they are or where they are from.'

'Revenge isn't a solution,' Butros said.

'I know, but how do I deal with their anger? How do I channel their rage in a productive way?'

Butros sighed, feeling at a loss to know what to do to help his friend. 'I know it sounds like a cliché, but I promise I will pray.'

'That's not a cliché,' the priest replied.

'Recently we started a weekly interdenominational prayer meeting at Al Waha Church. May I bring this up at the prayer meeting?'

'By all means. Please also tell all the pastors you work with.'

'There are a growing number of people who feel we must pray for our country. God is moving, and they want to pray for many Muslims to come to Christ.'

'I'm afraid there aren't very many people in my church who have any charitable feelings toward Muslims. Probably most want them to go to hell.'

There was silence on both sides. Father Alexander apologised: 'I shouldn't have said that.'

'Don't apologise,' Butros answered. 'I know that many Christians feel that way.'

'But what is the heart of God?' the priest asked. 'I've seen the changes in Salima. I've seen the changes in Ahmed. We should rejoice when God does such work.'

'We must pray,' Butros said. 'There is no other answer. We can't solve the problem of Muslim extremism. We can't change the prevailing attitudes of our Muslim culture. But we can be faithful Christians. And if God is drawing Muslims to Jesus, we must be available for Him to use us.'

'I have challenged my congregation to pray,' said the priest. 'Maybe we need to do this with all the Christians in town. I think I'll contact the other pastors in Suq al Khamis about starting a prayer meeting.'

—∽∽∽—

Brother Andrew was thinking about his next trip to see Butros. It had been several years since his first contact with the graduate student, and now he regularly visited at least once and sometimes twice a year. It was late evening and Brother Andrew was about to turn on the evening news before heading to bed when the phone rang. It was Butros.

'Brother Andrew, I have news for you. Ahmed, Mustafa and Hassan have been released.'

For many months, Andrew, through letters from many friends, had kept pressure on the government to release the three men. He had also written the men personal letters to encourage them, though Butros said as far as he knew none were delivered. 'But don't stop sending them,' he'd said. 'The more letters that are sent to these men, the more the officials will realise that people around the world are watching this case.'

As the lawyer had predicted, the men had been held without charge for sixty days. Then legal procedures in the court system had resulted in their spending another six months in prison without formal charges being filed. When they'd finally appeared before a judge, he'd released them without any charge.

'Without formal charges,' the lawyer had explained to Butros, 'we may never learn the real reason for their arrest.' And that was apparently what the government wanted – they were releasing the men because they were attracting too much international attention. But no explanations were needed because no charges had ever been made.

'How are the men doing?' Andrew asked.

'Quite well, considering. They are all very thin, and Nadira is determined to fatten them up. But other than that they are in wonderful spirits. And they have asked to talk with you.'

'Me? Why would they want to talk to me?'

'Because they have some exciting ideas about ministry and they want your advice.'

'So, Butros, does all our pressure on the government mean MBBs will be safer now?'

'It may mean others are not arrested and imprisoned. However, I don't think it will be easier. The government will simply become more subtle. There are other ways to handle these situations.'

'What do you mean?'

'Well, for one thing they can lean on the families of MBBs.'

'So the families will pressure the MBBs to return to Islam?'

'Yes, and if they don't, the families will kill them.'

—⁘⁘—

Two weeks later Brother Andrew was back in the country to fulfil several speaking requests. During this visit, Butros arranged for him to meet Ahmed, Mustafa and Hassan, and Andrew delivered a large stack of letters sent to the three men by concerned Christians from around the world.

'We want to thank you for being our advocate,' Mustafa said, speaking for the three of them. 'We believe your work on our behalf kept us from suffering worse than we did. I know I could not have survived much more.'

'I would like to ask you men to tell me how God worked in your lives in prison.'

'There was one very special moment for me when I went into the prison yard and Mustafa saw me and called me "Timothy",' Ahmed said. 'That was incredibly important for me. Calling me by my Christian name was a reminder that I was a new person and, regardless of what they said or did to me, nothing could change that truth.'

Hassan opened several letters and his eyes filled with tears as he caught the gist of the messages. 'People were praying for us?' Hassan asked.

'Thousands were praying all over the world,' Andrew answered.

'That explains it. There were times when I felt I couldn't go on any more, and then I would feel a power beyond me as though there were others who were taking my suffering and carrying it for me.'

Andrew was moved by these words. 'Hassan, that is exactly what happens. The Scriptures say that when one part of the body suffers, all suffer. We are called to share in one another's suffering. When it is more than you can bear, there are others who, prompted by the Holy Spirit, pray for you and somehow remove some of that burden from you.'

'There is something I'd like to say,' said Mustafa. 'Something very unexpected happened to me in prison. I don't know quite how to express it, but I talked to a lot of the prisoners and I felt, how shall I say, how lost they were.'

'I felt the same thing!' Ahmed exclaimed.

'Naturally they wanted to know why I was in prison,' Mustafa continued.
'I told them that I was a follower of Jesus Christ and, since we had a lot of
time to talk, we discussed Islam and Christianity. There were even two men
who privately told me they were convinced that Isa was the real way to God.
Anyway, I realised that I want to reach out to more Muslims. And I was
wondering if you have any suggestions about how to do that.'

Brother Andrew bowed his head to think for a moment. 'Before you go
out and witness, you need time to heal. You need to spend some time with
Christians.'

'Pastor Yusef has offered to spend some time with them,' said Butros.

'That's good. He will give you some good input. My brothers, I can't tell
you how to proceed in ministry. God has to reveal that, and He promises to
do that through His Holy Spirit. When Jesus said, "I am the way", He did not
say, "I am the destination". You will find the solution in your culture, in your
situation, by walking with Jesus in the way. Walking with Jesus means
talking with Jesus. The more you walk, the more you talk. That's how you
learn from Him. I'm not talking about Bible school or seminary – you don't
have that option in this country. The answer is a relationship with Jesus. But
I also want to say that your desire pleases Him, and I want to be supporting
you and praying for you in your efforts.'

Ahmed stood up and started to walk around the room. Butros watched
him, puzzled.

'I thought about this a lot in prison,'Ahmed began. 'I think it's time to go
home.'

'Home?' Butros asked after translating for Andrew. 'Do you mean, to Suq
al Khamis?'

'Yes, yes. I want my family to know the truth. How will they know if I
don't go and tell them?'

After Butros had translated, Andrew commended Ahmed for his passion
but asked, 'You had to flee for your life. Have things changed?'

'I know I must be careful. But it's been several years, and as long as I don't
draw attention, I think it's okay. My sister is very close to believing, and there
are also a couple of cousins who are curious.'

'You would live with them?'

'No, I will start some kind of business, and I will find a flat. When there are enough believers, I want to start a fellowship, a place where those who love Isa can meet.'

Hassan said, 'Mustafa and I agree with this. We should bring the good news to our families.'

Andrew asked Butros for his reaction.

'I think in many respects this is the right approach. The most effective witness is usually to those who are closest to us. Of course, it is also the most dangerous. But we are a tribal culture. So the most logical place to take the gospel is to those in our family and tribe.'

'But we must be shrewd,' said Ahmed. 'I was too outspoken when I first discovered the truth. My sister, Farah, has been discreet about her questions and spiritual search. She hasn't caused any alarm in the family. I believe there are others like her, quietly seeking. We need to go back and let God make us aware of those who are interested, who are searching for answers to life's big questions.'

'Who are secretly struggling with Islam,' said Hassan.

'Yes, and there are many.'

Butros closed his eyes, as though praying. Finally, he said, 'I think I may have a way that can help you, that may provide you with a cover.' He opened his eyes and saw everyone staring at him. 'I have formed an official NGO. It's called Al Kalima and its purpose is to provide educational opportunities for Christians – literacy training, job skills. Maybe we can open an office in Suq al Khamis.'

'I like that,' said Ahmed. 'There is a need for that in the town, plus it would provide a base for outreach into the villages.'

'Then I will ask you to run it,' said Butros.

Mustafa asked to speak. 'I believe God has showed me something very important He wants me to do.'

There was a dramatic pause. Finally, Andrew said, 'What is that?'

'I believe God wants me to go on the *hajj*.'

It took a moment for the full impact of this statement to sink in. Mustafa was talking about going on the pilgrimage to Mecca that is required of every Muslim to complete once in his lifetime.

Andrew chuckled and said, 'I've always wanted to go to Mecca. I've tried. As you know, there are signs forbidding all non-Muslims from entering the city.'

A big grin spread over Mustafa's face. 'Well, my identity card still says I'm a Muslim. I had a dream that I was in Mecca at the time of the *hajj*. There were millions of people circling the *Kaaba*, and I was on top of the *Kaaba*, telling them about Jesus. Telling them that Jesus is the way!'

Ahmed and Hassan stared at their friend in stunned disbelief.

17

Three months later

Layla's father called Abuna Alexander late one night. The priest hurried to the home, which was packed with relatives.

'Layla called us an hour ago,' the father said. 'It was very brief. She said only that she wanted us to know she is alive and that she will be beaten if she is caught on the phone.'

'Why are we sitting here talking? Let's go and rescue her right now!' said Layla's older brother from one corner of the living room.

'We don't know where she is,' said Layla's father, clearly exasperated. 'I called my brother-in-law. He insists he knows nothing about this.'

'He's lying,' someone shouted, and everyone began talking.

Abuna Alexander raised his voice and shouted for calm. 'I want to say something and then I want to pray.' The room became very quiet. 'First, I know we are all very angry. Rightly so. But if we don't stay calm and respond appropriately, we cause more harm for Layla. And we could add to the problems we already have in this town. We don't want mobs burning down our homes and church. So let's think. And pray.'

'We can't let them get away with this,' said a male voice.

'They've made her a slave,' said another.

'They've forced her to convert to Islam,' said a third.

'Please, listen,' said the priest, raising his hands to urge calm. 'Let's not jump to conclusions. We don't *know* what her situation is.'

'We know how these people think,' someone protested. 'It happens all over the country – some lecherous Muslim boy kidnaps a Christian girl, makes her his slave, forces her to convert . . .'

'They can't force her to convert,' the older brother shouted. 'She would never shame our family that way.' Again everyone started talking.

'Please,' the priest shouted. 'Here is what we need to do.' The room quieted. 'First, we need to go to the police and report that she has contacted us.'

'We've gone to the police. They will do nothing . . .'

'We will follow the legally prescribed process. Second, I want you to arrange a meeting with Layla.' The priest addressed the girl's father. 'Call your brother-in-law tomorrow. Tell him you want to meet your daughter . . . to make sure she's okay.'

'He insists he doesn't know where she is,' said the father.

'I'm sure he can find out. Ask him to contact everyone he knows. Almost certainly Layla's kidnappers have some connection, however distant, with your family. Your brother-in-law can find out. Someone has heard about this or seen something unusual. If he persists, he can find out where she is.'

'Then we go and get her,' said the brother.

'Then her father and mother go. Only them. We must not escalate this situation into a violent confrontation,' Father Alexander insisted.

'You should come too,' said the father. 'You're her priest.'

Alexander shook his head. 'This could be a trap. The law says that before anyone can convert from Christianity to Islam, that person must meet with a priest. If Layla is intimidated and says under duress that she has become Muslim in front of me, they will claim she has fulfilled the law. No, it is better just for her parents to go and see her.'

'Suppose they refuse.'

'They probably will. But at least we will know where she is and who her captors are and we will try again to get the police to act on that information.'

'I don't like this,' said the brother.

'Suppose you be quiet and listen to our priest,' said the father.

Alexander continued. 'One more thing I will do is talk to a couple of the imams with whom I am on good terms and see if they can help. Now, let us pray.' The priest unfolded his stole, kissed it, and laid it across his shoulders and neck. The people in the room fell to their knees as the priest pleaded for the life and soul of Layla. 'Lord have mercy. Christ have mercy. Lord have mercy.'

The people repeated the prayer.

'O God of peace, who hast taught us that in returning and rest we shall be saved, in quietness and in confidence shall be our strength; by the might of Thy Spirit lift Thy daughter Layla, we pray Thee, to Thy presence, where she may be still and know that Thou art God; through Jesus Christ our Lord.'

Everyone responded, '*Amin.*'

—◦◦◦—

Almost everything looked the same as Butros and Andrew drove down the dirt path. Fields stretched out in every direction towards small villages a mile or two in the distance. The only interruption to this pastoral scene was a six-foot-high brick wall around the five-acre plot of land that Brother Andrew had prayed over several years before. A guard, with a rifle slung over his shoulder, opened the gate and gave a little salute as the car drove on to the campus. Immediately to his left Andrew saw some boys playing a lively pick-up game of football, while several girls watched and giggled. Beyond them was a two-storey brick building that stood near the canal. To his right Andrew saw that a significant portion of land was still being farmed, and in the far corner a flock of chickens foraged around a shed.

'Welcome to the Logos Training Centre,' Butros said as he and Brother Andrew emerged from the car. Andrew was here to formally dedicate the campus and participate in the conclusion of a retreat designed to strengthen the youth ministries of churches in the area. 'Rather different from the last time you were here, isn't it? The kids are taking a break while their leaders are in a training session.'

Slowly Andrew surveyed the scene. For more than a year he had helped Butros put out the word to friends on four continents that this would be a great investment in the church.

Butros gave him a tour of the new building. On the second floor were dormitory rooms that could sleep twenty people. At one end was a flat and a very pregnant Nadira, with Thomas clutching her dress, who welcomed Andrew. 'We stay here when there are programmes at the centre,' Butros explained. 'Eventually we will hire a caretaker for the campus who will live here with his family.'

Downstairs there was a kitchen and small dining room, a couple of classrooms, and a large meeting hall.

'This youth leadership event is our third conference,' Butros said. 'At the first one we trained eighteen rural lay leaders for four weeks. They received teaching on basic hermeneutics, how to prepare sermons, development of church leadership, and pastoral care of the congregation. At their graduation we gave each of them a beautiful Arabic study Bible. Then two weeks ago we graduated our first class of literacy teachers. Twelve people went through the programme, learning how to teach reading and writing. They will be our trainers as we begin to open Al Kalima centres around the country. Al Kalima is the name of our NGO. It means "The Word" in Arabic.'

'How are you finding these teachers?'

'They are recruited from churches. We look for volunteers – mostly older people who have been teachers and those with education who have a heart for this work. We used our pastors' network to help us identify them.'

A bell went off and about fifty sweaty and excited teenagers came into the assembly hall, joined by ten leaders. Andrew noticed the one hundred padded chairs in the room. 'This is nice quality furniture,' he said.

'Yes, we want this to be a place where people are comfortable,' Butros explained. 'The right environment is very important to the learning process. But also we feel it glorifies God to have quality workmanship and furnishings. We want people to come here and be lifted up as they worship and study.'

The first fifteen minutes of the meeting were spent in enthusiastic worship by the teenagers. Andrew was encouraged to see the passion on their faces and couldn't help but think, *They are the hope of the church and of their country.*

After Butros introduced his special guest, Andrew spoke to the assembly: 'The last time I was here, there was nothing but an open field. Now as I look at the transformation, I can't help but think that this is an appropriate metaphor. We come to God with nothing, and God begins to pour His resources into our lives.'

As his text, Andrew chose 2 Peter 1:4–7. Holding up his Bible, he asked, 'What is our primary resource? The apostle Peter says God has given us His very great and precious promises. My friend Butros and I agree that whatever is built here will have the Word of God as the basis for teaching and training.

Through Jesus and the Word you have inherited the divine nature. It is up to you to build your Christian character on that foundation. Add to your faith goodness; and to goodness, knowledge; and to knowledge, self-control; and so on, ending with love. All of these "adds" make you into a person who can be of great use to your society, your culture, your church, and indeed – why not? – to the whole world. The key is to realise that this is an act of your *will*. You were not born with habits; you will now form them – all new, but based on what Jesus did for you. That is indeed the great challenge you young people want – to live a life of great value to Jesus and to people. That is what keeps me going too.'

As the teenagers and their leaders listened intently, Andrew added one more challenge, inspired by the apostle Paul's exhortation to Timothy to pass on what he'd learned to faithful men. 'You have learned much. When you leave here, let me ask that each one of you teach another what you have learned. Each one teach one! Just the people here in this room are enough to start a chain reaction that sweeps the country and beyond, to all of the Middle East. I have often said, don't curse the darkness but light a candle. Each one of you is a candle. You may say, "I don't have much light." But I say the bigger the darkness, the easier it is to spot your little light. And if each one of you lights another candle, the light will grow and the light of Jesus will shine even brighter.'

After the service Abuna Alexander came forward to greet Andrew and give him a traditional Arab hug with a kiss on each cheek. 'Thank you for your encouragement,' he said.

'I remember when we first met and talked about the youth in your church.'

'There are about twenty teenagers at St Mark's reading through the Bible each year. I brought four of them with me to this retreat.'

Andrew sensed that, despite the good report, there was a deep sadness in the man. He probed: 'So how is your church today?'

'We are stronger but we are suffering. One of our teenagers, a lovely girl who should have been at this retreat, was abducted a few months ago. Please pray for her. Please pray for us.'

—⌇∿⌇—

Layla tried desperately to use her eyes to convey a message to her mother. She was covered completely, except for her eyes, by a black *abeyya*. Her mother tried to read the emotion her eyes revealed. Fear? Definitely. Sadness? Yes. Resistance? Perhaps some, but it was dwindling. How long could her daughter maintain any resolve under such conditions?

Her father controlled his rage. He had followed his priest's advice and through his brother-in-law tracked down the location of his daughter to a village twenty-five kilometres from Suq al Khamis. As he suspected, it was a distant cousin who had instigated the kidnapping. While he didn't trust his brother-in-law, he did believe the man had nothing to do with the abduction. When contact was made, the family holding Layla had said the girl didn't want to see her parents. But he had persisted, insisting that he just wanted to make sure his daughter was all right.

Now they were together in an awkward meeting inside a cramped farmhouse. Two young men stood on either side of his daughter, and another right behind her. More men stood nearby. There had been no offer of traditional Arab hospitality. No other women were visible in the cramped room.

'Layla, are you okay?' the father asked.

Layla had determined her only hope was to say nothing. She nodded her head. Besides, what could she say? That they had beaten her, forced her to work on the farm fourteen to sixteen hours a day, made her sleep locked in a shed? Her captors had issued terrible threats if she spoke up. Her parents would be killed. She would suffer unspeakable punishment. She had experienced enough to know she could not take the risk.

'I want to know why you have kidnapped my daughter,' the father said to the men surrounding Layla.

'You misunderstand,' said an older man. 'She came to us willingly. My son,' he pointed to the young man standing behind Layla, 'brought the girl here because she loves him. She told him she wants to become a Muslim. We are teaching her the way of Islam.'

Layla wanted to scream that this was all a lie. But when her father spoke to her, gently asking 'Is this true?' she felt a sharp object in her back. She knew this was when she had to speak her line. She felt detached from the situation, as though someone else spoke the words with a trembling voice: 'I have converted to Islam. I have found the straight path.'

18

Four months later

'Hallelujah to the Lamb of God.'

The sanctuary of St Mark's Church in Suq al Khamis was full and rocking to the beat of a four-piece band and six singers, who stood in front of the altar. The music was a curious mix of Arab sounds and western beat. The words in Arabic were projected on to a screen, but many of the young people had their eyes closed and their hands raised as they sang their heartfelt praises to God. Most of the two hundred-plus in attendance appeared to be under thirty. Some, rather than singing, were sitting or kneeling, hunched over in fervent prayer. Most were dressed in jeans and sweaters rather than the traditional Arab clothing. And they were pleading for the soul of their country.

Ahmed, Butros and Abuna Alexander stood at the back of the sanctuary and watched the scene. The priest had opened his church to the weekly three-hour prayer meeting after a smaller church in town had quickly filled to overflowing. Father Alexander admitted he was uncomfortable with the music and style of worship, and yet apart from Christmas, Easter and recent congregational meetings, he'd never seen St Mark's this packed. It appeared to him that about one-fifth of the people were from his congregation, and that all the churches in town were represented. He noticed Salima near the front, her eyes closed, head raised, tears streaming down her face.

The music transitioned to a western tune: 'Jesus, name above all names.'

There followed another Arab song that declared the defeat of Satan: 'We are victors. We are conquerors. Jesus, You are our King. We are the army of the Redeemer.' The singing continued for an hour as more people joined the service, having hurried there from work.

As the music began to die down, the worship leader held up his Bible and urged the congregation, 'Let us shout "Blessed is the One coming in the name of the Lord."' A roar came from the crowd, followed by rousing applause.

Abuna Alexander winced at the sound, hoping this enthusiasm wouldn't disturb the neighbours and bring unwanted attention. At the same time, as he and Butros walked to the platform, he felt a surge of gratitude for the seeming revival that was for the first time truly unifying Christians all over town, regardless of their denomination. And that was only part of the story. For similar prayer meetings were being held in towns and cities all over the country. There was even talk about a national gathering for prayer and fasting for the nation. Butros had offered to erect a huge tent at Logos Centre for that event.

The worship leader invited everyone to sit, and Abuna Alexander gave a brief greeting, then he introduced Butros, saying, 'I want you to meet a man who is a dear Christian brother. He was the one who had the vision for this meeting, and I am so glad that he can be with us tonight.'

Butros, dressed in slacks and a dark blue dress shirt, came on to the stage, gave the priest a hug, and transitioned to the main work of the evening.

'Jesus told His disciples a parable to show them that they should always pray and not give up.' He invited those who had Bibles to read with him the parable of the persistent widow from Luke 18. 'Why are we coming on Monday evenings, now for several months? Our persistence means we have no other solution. Our persistence means we love our friends, and we will keep on begging for our friends – for the people of this country and the whole Arab world. God says through the prophet Isaiah, "I will gather all nations and tongues, and they will come and see my glory." Do we believe that? Let us take *big* prayers to the Lord. Let us be bold. When God comes to the Middle East, may He find faith because we asked Him for big things.'

Butros asked the congregation to stand and gave them a few brief instructions: 'Ask the Lord to put the right prayers in our hearts – based on love and faith for our friends, for our families.' Seamlessly he transitioned into prayer. All over the building, people began to pray out loud. Their passion spoke louder than their words. After about ten minutes, the roar subsided, and Butros urged the participants to pray in groups of two or three.

After two hours of prayer, Butros invited Ahmed to join him on the platform. They had talked about this opportunity. Butros didn't want to reveal much about the MBB from Suq al Khamis, yet they also felt it would be beneficial for Ahmed's work to have some sort of a presence in the city and to solicit the prayers of the church. Both yearned for the day when there would be one body joining MBBs and Christian-background believers, but that time was yet to come.

Ahmed spoke briefly but passionately: 'Jesus Christ declared His divinity in word and deed. His birth was unique, removed from the arrogance of the palace, far from the humiliation of the hovel, distant from the hypocrisy of the temple. He is still the fountainhead of humanitarian values. He remains the essence of truth, justice and equality. He still causes His sun to rise on the poor, the mourner, the oppressed and the persecuted.'

Butros studied the crowd and saw in them an intensity he'd rarely seen in a regular church service. The people seemed to identify with every word this young man spoke. Out of the corner of his eye, he noticed Salima. She seemed to be studying the speaker with a deep spiritual yearning.

'Jesus says, "Go to all the world" – to man created in the image of God. God's image in man has been disfigured and man is responsible for the disfigurement. Man is responsible for wars, for poverty, for oppression, for licentiousness, for cultural and ethical backwardness. But Jesus never separated Himself from sinners or tax collectors or the poor. On the contrary, He loved them and forgave them. He set them free, fed them and healed them. As for us, as Arab Christians, we declare we are filled with hope, which motivates us to change the world, to heal the brokenhearted, to set the captive free in the freedom of the glory of the children of God. The love that has been poured out in our hearts is a gift and work of the Holy Spirit who is in us. Every bit of love for others and any forgiveness towards our enemies is the work of Christ within us. Christ changed us and made us a new creation, who respects the other and rejects servility and blind submission.'

Listening to his friend, Butros knew that God had indeed called Ahmed back to his home town. Though he hadn't mentioned his Muslim background, clearly he had articulated the transformation that Christ had made in his life and offered to make in all who were willing to follow Him.

Stepping forward, Butros suggested, 'Let's end our meeting tonight by praying for our families and friends and neighbours in Suq al Khamis.'

Ahmed visited his father late that night after the prayer meeting. His sister, Farah, had arranged the meeting, eliciting a promise from her father that he would not harm her brother. Inside the front door father and son embraced in a strong hug, then moved to the kitchen and sat at a tiny table to drink coffee while the older man smoked.

'Your mother is asleep,' the father said. 'Actually, she doesn't know you are here.'

Farah had assured Ahmed that their father had softened. 'He has some health issues,' she had said. 'Too many cigarettes.'

Ahmed had often tried to imagine this moment, but now that it had finally arrived, he struggled to know how to behave. Haltingly, he said, 'Farah said you've not been well.'

The father sucked deeply on a cigarette, then admitted, 'I'm paying the price for this dirty habit. Your mother and sister have wanted me to quit for years. Now the doctor says I have emphysema. But...' He shrugged his shoulders. 'I'm too old to change.'

'What does the doctor say you should do?'

'Quit smoking. But it won't make much difference. So what's the point?'

'Maybe you'd be with us a few more years.'

'*Inshallah*, if God wills, I'll live to see your children and grandchildren. If not...' He shrugged his shoulders again.

The fatalism of his father was maddening to Ahmed. It was so typical of many in the culture. If God wanted you to die, you died, and there was nothing you could do about it. So why go through the difficult challenge of changing a bad habit? He saw a different perspective as a believer in Jesus – one that made him free to change, free, that is, to allow the Holy Spirit to change him. As he looked at his father's sad face, he suddenly felt intense compassion. 'Father, I'm sorry.' He was sorry – not for leaving Islam and embracing Isa but for the way he had done it, for putting his father in a difficult, shameful situation. Now he would do it differently. Was it too late to start again, to make things right, to show his father the love of Jesus?

His father looked out of the kitchen window as he snuffed out the cigarette and drank his coffee in one gulp. Without looking into his son's eyes, he said, 'The *Mukhabarat* paid me a visit when you were in prison.'

Ahmed froze, wondering what this admission meant.

'The goons,' the father spat the words. 'Idiots! They think they can come in here and intimidate me. With a straight face they say they're doing this "so we can help your son".' He turned his head to look at his son. 'Did they hurt you in prison?'

'Yes, Father. It was not good.'

'Bastards.' He lit another cigarette and stared out of the window.

Ahmed felt a wash of emotions. Gratefulness that his father hadn't co-operated with the *Mukhabarat*. Fear, knowing that his father could still round up the uncles and cousins and have him killed. But most of all, love, more intense than he'd ever felt before, love that prayed his father might someday know what he knew. That would take time and prayer. But how much time was there?

'Father, I want to move back to Suq al Khamis.' He held his breath to see how his father would respond.

The man nodded. 'You want to move back home?'

'No, I have a chance to set up a small business here. I'd probably live in a flat above the business.'

'What kind of business?'

'A school, to teach adults to read and write.'

The father took a couple of puffs on another cigarette. 'You're not going to embarrass me?'

Ahmed couldn't tell if it was a question or a threat. Quickly he answered, 'No, sir, I will keep a low profile.'

'You always did love books. Can you make any money teaching people how to read?'

Ahmed laughed. 'Not really, but there's an NGO that funds it. So I'll get a salary. I'll be fine.'

The father snuffed out the cigarette and sat back in his chair. 'You need to get married.'

'Yes, sir.'

'I can arrange something, if you would like.'

Ahmed didn't want his father to arrange a marriage for him. But he didn't want to challenge him on this, either. So he kept quiet.

'Think about it,' the man said.

'Yes, sir, I will.'

'Will you come back and visit your mother?'

'Soon.'

'Good. I'm tired. I think I'll go to bed now.'

The man rose, and son embraced father again, silently rejoicing that the first step in reconciliation had been achieved.

The next day Ahmed and Butros walked the streets of Suq al Khamis for more than an hour, talking about the move Ahmed would be making soon. They had visited a nondescript building that was available for rent. Above the room was a small flat where Ahmed, Mustafa and Hassan could live.

Ahmed and Butros had already had several long talks about their vision for the school. Through churches, they would identify adults who were illiterate and encourage them to participate in an eight-month course. During that time, they would learn to read and write and learn basic maths skills. There would also be sessions on nutrition, health and hygiene. Through the classes they would identify those who, with some individual coaching and a small investment, might be able to start up a new business. Ahmed would serve as the team leader in Suq al Khamis and set up the programmes in town. Mustafa and Hassan would go to villages where there were Christian communities and establish satellite programmes.

'I talked with Abuna Alexander,' Butros said. 'He has identified several families that he will encourage to participate in classes. And he will talk with his fellow priests in the area and encourage other churches to participate.'

As Butros talked, Ahmed seemed distracted. He looked around the familiar streets and buildings and his heart ached. 'We should invite any who wish to come, not just from the churches,' he said.

'We've discussed that,' Butros replied patiently. 'You must be careful. The Muslims may not appreciate that this literacy curriculum is based on the

Bible. For the moment these courses must be only for Christians.'

'I know. I know. But they are so lost.' He thought of his father – the resignation on his face as he faced death. How many were there like him? How would these people learn of the hope that lay in the prophet Isa? The two men walked on in silence, covering their noses with their hands in an attempt to filter out the dust kicked up by traffic, including many donkey and horse-drawn carts.

Finally, Ahmed spoke again. 'I called my sister this morning. She wanted to know how the meeting with our father went. Here's the exciting thing. She says there are several family members and friends who are curious, who want to learn more about Jesus. And Mustafa and Hassan each have friends they also want to meet. I know God has brought us home. And He has prepared the soil here. We will sow seed and, God willing, we will reap a harvest.'

'Move cautiously,' Butros said.

'I've learned my lesson. We will be very careful. Still, we are hoping that we can start a small fellowship here soon.'

As they headed back to St Mark's Church and a final meeting with Abuna Alexander before driving back to the city, Butros brought up one more item. 'My friend, there is something very important we need to discuss.'

Ahmed turned quizzically to Butros but said nothing.

'The Bible says it is not good for man to be alone. Abuna Alexander and I have talked, and we agree you need help for your work here. You cannot do this alone.'

'What kind of help? I have Mustafa and Hassan.'

'I'm talking about the kind of help my wife Nadira gives me.'

'I would like that very much. Do you have someone in mind?'

'Alexander and I have talked. We think that Salima would make a good wife.'

'She's the woman living with the priest and his wife?'

'Yes.'

'I noticed her at the prayer service last night.'

'Then it is time you should meet her.'

—◦◦◦—

Ahmed was more nervous than he could remember being in years. Opposite him sat Salima, looking down at her hands folded in her lap. Butros had to control himself and not smile at their discomfort.

Alexander and Nour had prepared Salima for the meeting. Salima was hesitant. She had enjoyed Ahmed's message at church and he seemed like a good man, but she missed her family and longed for their involvement in this decision. And yet what choice did she have? She couldn't live with the priest forever, and the only other option in this culture was to marry. She felt trapped, but she also trusted this dear couple that they had her best interests in mind.

Now she sat looking at the young man. He looked handsome, but what was he really like? She knew he had paid a high price for following Jesus. That gave them something in common. But was that enough to hold them together as a couple? She knew so little about him. Of course, most marriages in this country were arranged and often the woman knew even less than she knew about Ahmed.

Carefully the priest explained the challenges the two would face if they married. 'In the eyes of the government, you are both Muslims. Neither of you have changed your identity cards, have you?' Both shook their heads. 'Of course not. It is almost impossible to do so – unless you are a Christian and become a Muslim. The good news is that means you won't have problems getting a marriage licence. It's a lot harder if you have different religions on your cards.

'There is another problem.' Both looked up at him. 'I don't know if this is the right time to bring it up, but you should think about this before you marry. Your children will be considered Muslims. You need to think about how you will handle that.'

They were silent as they thought about this; then Ahmed said, 'I want our children to grow up as Christians. That is very important.'

'In your home, fine, your children will be Christian. But what about when they go to school? If they have Christian names but their ID cards say Muslim, teachers will ask questions. And how will they relate to fellow students?'

Salima put her head down, fighting back tears.

'Look, I'm not trying to talk you out of this,' said Father Alexander. 'I'm in favour of this marriage. I just want you to know it will be difficult. I don't know the answers, but it's better to discuss these things now rather than be surprised later.'

Butros spoke to Salima: 'Have you had any contact with your family?'

She shook her head. She looked up and said, 'There is an aunt and an uncle. I have talked with them. They aren't really close to my parents. That's why I called them, to try to make some connection. They have been sympathetic.'

Butros addressed Ahmed: 'What about you?'

'I think marriage would make things easier for me now that I am moving back to Suq al Khamis. My father specifically asked about it.'

'This could solve several problems,' the priest said. 'It saves face for both families.'

Butros waited a few moments before asking gently, 'Ahmed, are you willing to marry Salima?'

Ahmed looked at the woman opposite him. She was quite attractive, he thought. But there were more important issues. She had paid a high price for declaring her faith in Jesus. He had noticed her at the prayer service, her emotion as she sang praises and as she prayed. 'If Salima is willing, yes, I would be honoured to be her husband.'

'Salima, are you willing to marry Ahmed?' Butros asked.

Not knowing the right decision, Salima said nothing. She felt terribly lonely and wanted to have a family, but she hardly knew Ahmed. She was trusting these two men, Butros and Alexander, to advise her well. If only her mother could be here. The priest's wife was kind, but she couldn't replace her mother, and Nour was deferential to Alexander's decisions, so Salima didn't really feel she could openly discuss this with Nour. She had to make a decision. She could say no, but then what? What future did she have without a husband?

Salima nodded her head to indicate her agreement.

'We should have a Christian ceremony,' said Ahmed.

The priest said, 'Ahmed, you have family here. Think about first having a traditional Muslim ceremony with your families. That would be officially recognised by the government. After that we will have a private Christian ceremony. Butros and I will work out the details.'

Butros looked again at Salima and noticed tears falling down her cheeks. 'Are you sure this is agreeable to you? No one is forcing you ...' He stopped, unsure what else to say.

The young woman wiped the tears with the back of her hand and said, 'Someone needs to contact my parents. That is all I ask.'

19

Two weeks later

Ahmed and his father arrived at the appointed time at a restaurant in the capital city. Ahmed was dressed in a suit and tie, his father in his best *jallabiya*, bleached and starched.

A few minutes later a man entered and introduced himself to them: 'I am Hussein, Salima's uncle.'

The two men were surprised. 'We were expecting to meet Salima's father,' Ahmed said.

'Please, be patient,' Hussein responded. 'My brother has asked me to represent him. It will make things easier.'

Hussein ordered coffee and a plate of dates and asked Ahmed to talk about himself. Cautiously Ahmed told him about his life, trying to avoid any details about his spiritual journey. He had no idea how Hussein would respond, and he didn't want to offend his father. Hussein listened impassively, as though already aware of far more than Ahmed cared to reveal.

Ahmed talked about the NGO Al Kalima. Hussein interrupted: 'How much does this job pay?' Ahmed revealed his salary and also that he was provided with a flat in Suq al Khamis above the NGO office. When he had finished his answer, Hussein stared at Ahmed for a long time, as though trying to evaluate the words but also to increase Ahmed's obvious discomfort.

Ahmed's father smoked his cigarettes nervously but said nothing.

Finally, Hussein addressed the older man. 'My brother thinks this marriage might relieve us both of a difficult situation.'

Ahmed's father nodded in agreement.

'Please understand, my brother does not wish to see his daughter again. He has authorised me to negotiate the details with you. I will represent the family at the wedding and sign the necessary papers. After that, Salima is on her own.'

'I understand,' Ahmed's father said.

'You are prepared to pay a dowry?'

'Of course,' his father replied. An amount was proposed.

Clearly this was far less than a woman from such a prominent family would expect. However, this was not a normal situation.

'My brother insists that in the contract Salima will keep this money if there is a divorce.'

'There will be no divorce,' Ahmed said.

'Nevertheless, that is one of his stipulations. The bride price is to be placed in a separate bank account and only Salima may access it.'

As the two men talked, Ahmed thought about his future bride and how her family was protecting her. He realised he hardly knew her. Clearly she came from a much wealthier family than he did – he would probably never have met her and certainly not have had the chance to marry her under normal circumstances. Yet God had brought them together – he was sure of that. He had heard of cases in which a girl had been killed for the honour of a family – certainly this could have been Salima's fate. He suddenly felt a sense of deep gratitude that she was alive, coupled with responsibility to love and protect her.

When the negotiations and other details of the marriage were decided, Hussein spoke again to Ahmed. 'I wish you and my niece a happy life. Please understand I do not approve of what is happening. I am following my brother's instructions. He loves his daughter and this whole situation has been very difficult for him. Her rejection of Islam shames him and the family. If she won't come home and be a good Muslim, there is nothing more to say. From now on you will please stay away from our family. You will make no attempt to contact my brother. Is that clear?'

Ahmed gulped and nodded. In this oblique way, he knew that apart from a miracle of God, Salima would never see her family again.

―∾∾―

One month later

Suq al Khamis had several small cafés where men in the town could relax and talk while they smoked a water pipe, drank tea or coffee, and played backgammon or dominoes. Ahmed had visited many of them, as well as the local library, as a way to find young men with whom he could talk. Most afternoons when he wasn't working in his office or running an errand in preparation for his wedding, he was seeking opportunities to witness to the Good News of Jesus. He knew the Holy Spirit was preparing many hearts – around the country people were seeing visions, dreaming dreams, experiencing healing, coming across foreign Christian radio and television broadcasts. But most of them, maybe all, needed to meet someone in whom Christ dwelt. They needed a human being to help them understand the uniqueness of Jesus and to introduce them to the wonderful book that told the story of God's work throughout history.

Are we waiting for Christ or is Christ waiting for us? Ahmed thought often about the needs of his fellow countrymen. As he prayed over this town where he had lived the first eighteen years of his life, his spirit was in turmoil. *It seems to me that the sight of it not only provokes me, it also provokes heaven who, one day, screamed in the face of it all through our Jesus. Heaven still screams through the voices of the seven thousand who have not bowed the knee and the calloused feet who carry the news of peace, freedom and love. The question floods my spirit from all sides: 'Who is waiting for whom?'*

Who were the ones God had prepared? *God, show me who is seeking You.* That was Ahmed's daily prayer as he found an empty table in a coffee shop. Often he felt like a dove among serpents. You said, *'Ask and it will be given to You.' I am asking You to give me someone who is seeking the truth, someone who is seeking You, even if he doesn't know it.* If someone was alone, reading the newspaper, Ahmed might ask if the man had read a certain article. Or he might mention a local event, such as a recent Islamic lecture, and ask, 'Did you attend that meeting?'

Some of the men made small talk and returned to their tea and newspaper, or said they had to leave and go to work or an appointment. But of others who seemed willing to talk, Ahmed would ask, 'Why do you think so many people don't believe in Islam?' Depending on the reply, Ahmed would then say, 'You have only read the Quran. But if we compare Quran and Injil, maybe we'll understand why Christians don't become Muslims.'

That was the point when the conversation either stopped or moved on to a deeper level. Many days Ahmed found someone willing to go deeper. Often he left them with a small Arabic booklet containing the Gospel of Luke with commentary designed for Muslims. He'd obtained a case of them from the Bible Forum. He was also encouraged by the response from members of his family. His sister, Farah, had made her commitment to Isa soon after he moved back to Suq al Khamis, and her husband was interested in knowing more. Farah had also pointed Ahmed to several cousins who wanted to talk.

Ahmed recognised the face of a man walking into the shop, and the man, as he turned to find a seat, recognised Ahmed. The two gave each other a warm greeting, and Ahmed invited his friend to sit at his table and ordered tea. 'Saeed, it is so good to see you. It's been many years.'

'I have often wondered what happened to you,' Saeed replied. 'There were rumours, you know.'

'What sort of rumours?'

'That you went crazy.' He pointed and twirled his index finger at his temple. 'They say you left Islam and that you now believe in three gods.'

'You should not believe everything you hear. I believe in one God.'

The waiter brought the tea, and after taking a sip Saeed looked at his old friend and said, 'So what *did* happen to you? Why did you leave Suq al Khamis?'

'I had to get away, to think, to make some decisions.' As he gave these vague answers, Ahmed studied the face of his friend. *Lord, what should I say? Is he seeking the truth?* His spirit seemed at peace, so he took the risk. 'Tell me, what do you think when you compare the Quran with the Bible? How do we answer the Christians?'

'With the edge of a sword. With the end of a gun.' Saeed roared with laughter.

Ahmed winced as he saw a couple of men look over at them. 'Why don't we win them?' he said quietly.

Just as quickly Saeed got serious. He leaned forward and asked, 'Have you read their book?'

'I have.'

'So what did you discover? The Jews and Christians corrupted it, right?'

Ahmed looked into the eyes of his old friend, trying to determine whether he was a seeker or potential betrayer. He made a decision. 'Let me try and explain with this picture. Islam is like a frog in a well.' Saeed looked confused yet curious. 'Suppose another frog falls into this well. He comes from a big, open sea. He says to the first frog, "What are you doing in such a small place?" The first frog is offended. He insists that nothing is bigger than this well. But the second frog knows better – he has seen the big sea.'

'So how is Islam like the frog in a well?'

Ahmed leaned closer to Saeed and practically whispered, 'Do you know that 90 per cent of the Quran is found in the Bible, but that the Bible has so much more? God is like the sea, and the Quran is taken from that sea.'

'But Christians say God had a son. God cannot have a son.'

'Saeed, do you have a son?'

'Not yet. I was married last year and my wife is pregnant. *Inshallah*, I will soon have a son.'

'But you have lots of cousins. What do you call a small boy in your family?'

Saeed frowned.

'Your older brother's boy, you call him "son". But he's not really your son, is he? My friend, I've studied both books. I've compared the teachings of the Quran and the Injil, and I learned that after God there is no one like Jesus. The only way you can explain Him is to say He is God.'

Saeed looked away, seeming to gaze at the passers-by on the street. Without looking back at Ahmed, he said, 'They were right. You *are* insane.' Then he rose and walked out of the shop.

―◦◦◦―

Six weeks later

It was late evening when Salima first saw her new home, the tiny flat above Ahmed's office. Mustafa and Hassan had vacated the premises, both having moved to nearby villages where they were establishing branches of Al Kalima. Ahmed was suddenly embarrassed as he thought of the life of wealth she had left. He said, 'I'm afraid this flat isn't much, but I hope you can make it a nice home for us.'

Salima said nothing, and Ahmed hung back so she could explore. It had been a strange day. Ahmed had dressed in a starched *jallabiya*, Salima in a beautiful white gown, and they'd gone to his father's mosque for a simple ceremony. Three times the imam had asked Ahmed, 'Are you willing to marry this woman?' Three times he had answered, 'Yes.' Ahmed signed the marriage licence. Salima's uncle acted as her *wali* or guardian and signed for her father. Two men added their signatures as witnesses, and the imam proclaimed, 'I now pronounce you husband and wife, in the name of God, the Most Gracious, the Most Merciful.'

Salima's uncle and aunt had expressed congratulations at the mosque and left quickly. Everyone else attended a reception at the home of Ahmed's parents, and all of his extended family had come and partied and warmly embraced Ahmed, as though he had never left home, and courteously congratulated Salima.

His sister, Farah, went further, attempting to make Salima feel a part of his family. He observed, when the two women hugged, that Salima fought back tears as Farah said, 'You have become a dear sister to me.' They had slipped away from the crowd to talk in a back room. Salima was smiling when they returned to the party fifteen minutes later.

Salima seemed relieved when the party ended. Now she explored their tiny bedroom, shyly looking in the closet. The women from St Mark's, under the direction of Abuna Alexander's wife, had hung up her clothes in the closet and arranged fresh flowers on the dresser. When she looked in the kitchen, she found cabinets fully stocked with staples; fresh vegetables, fruit and even two kilos of chicken were in the fridge.

'I will prepare for us a wedding meal,' she said.

'I'm not hungry,' Ahmed said.

'Neither am I,' Salima admitted.

Ahmed reached into the fridge and pulled out a carton of mango juice. 'Let's go on to the roof and drink to our future.' He grabbed two glasses and escorted his wife out of the door and up the stairs to a rooftop garden, where

Ahmed had planted some flowers in large pots and placed a small round table with two chairs. The sun had set hours ago and with no moon, there was a spectacular array of stars in the clear night sky.

Salima looked up and took a deep breath. The sweet fragrance of jasmine drifted over from the neighbour's garden. For the first time today Ahmed saw his wife relax. She closed her eyes as she said, 'We always had jasmine in our garden. Sometimes I would go and cut some and bring it to my room so I could smell it as I went to sleep at night.' She stopped speaking and tears welled up in her eyes as she thought that she would probably never see that garden again.

Ahmed pulled out one of the chairs so his wife could sit. He poured out two glasses of juice, sat opposite her, and said, 'Many waters cannot quench love; rivers cannot wash it away. If one were to give all the wealth of his house for love, it would be utterly scorned.'

'That's beautiful!' Salima said. 'Who wrote that?'

'It's from the Bible. From Solomon's wedding song. Do you like poetry?'

'I love good Arab poetry.'

'I have memorised a little poem for this evening,' he said. Salima gazed up at the stars as Ahmed took a deep breath and said, 'It's called "The Alchemy of Love" by the Sufi poet Rumi.

> You come to us from another world
> From beyond the stars and void of space.
> Transcendent, pure, of unimaginable beauty,
> Bringing with you the essence of love.
> You transform all who are touched by you.
> Mundane concerns, troubles and sorrows
> Dissolve in your presence,
> Bringing joy to ruler and ruled
> To peasant and king.
> You are the master alchemist.
> You light the fire of love in earth and sky
> In heart and soul of every being.
> Through your love
> Existence and non-existence merge.

All opposites unite.

All that is profane becomes sacred again.

Tears flowed down Salima's cheeks. 'That's very beautiful,' was all she could say.

Ahmed took his wife's hands in his. 'Salima, I love you.'

Salima stared at the tabletop as she said, 'You hardly know me. How can you say that you love me?'

'Because I *choose* to love you.' As she looked up in surprise, Ahmed continued, '"You have stolen my heart, my sister, my bride; you have stolen my heart with one glance of your eyes." Those words are also from the Song of Songs. I want our love to glorify the God who loves us and gave us to each other. What we did today was to get married in the eyes of the legal authorities. But in two days, we will have another ceremony, a Christian ceremony, where we will make a covenant before God. If it is okay with you, I want to wait and not consummate our marriage until after that ceremony. Is that okay?'

Salima nodded her head.

'I do this as a symbol of my love for God and my love for you.'

'Ahmed?'

There was a haunting plea in the way she spoke his name. With trepidation, Ahmed answered, 'Yes?'

Looking up at the glorious night sky, Salima said, 'As a little girl, I used to dream of my wedding day. I looked forward to having my mother and sisters and aunts and cousins at the wedding.' She fought back tears and continued. 'We always had such wonderful family celebrations. I was thinking about how when my nieces and nephews were born, my mother smothered them with love, and I looked forward to having my mother with me when my children were born . . .'

She stopped and Ahmed waited, not knowing what to say.

Salima looked into Ahmed's eyes and almost pleaded as she said, 'You are all I have. You are my entire family now.'

Ahmed squeezed her hands, trying to reassure her.

'Will you be my rock? Can I count on you in stormy times? Will you . . .' She bowed her head and cried.

'It's okay. I'm here for you. I *will* be your rock.' What else could he say? Besides, he meant those words with all his heart.

———◦◦◦———

The assembly hall at Logos Training Centre had been decorated with flowers and a white runner ran down the centre aisle. Hassan and Mustafa stood with Ahmed. Farah stood with Salima. Several families from St Mark's Church sat in the first few rows, with Nour, Father Alexander's wife, in the front row substituting as the proud mother of the bride. For several weeks she had prepared Salima for marriage, teaching her the things Salima's mother would have taught her at home.

Butros read from Ephesians 5:31–33: '"For this reason a man will leave his father and mother and be united to his wife, and the two will become one flesh." This is a profound mystery – but I am talking about Christ and the church. However, each one of you also must love his wife as he loves himself, and the wife must respect her husband.'

Butros looked at the couple standing before him and said, 'Christian marriage is a unique institution because it is a picture of the relationship we have with almighty God. Today you are not entering into a simple legal contract that can be easily severed. In the eyes of our society a husband can say three times to his wife, "I divorce you", and the contract is broken. But today you are entering into a covenant before God and it cannot be severed because it is sealed with blood – the blood of our Lord Jesus.

'Timothy, I charge you from Scripture to love Salima in the same way that Christ loves you. And how does He love you? By dying for you. He shed His blood so you may have eternal life with Him. You have a new name, Timothy, because you are a new person. One way you demonstrate your new life in Christ is by loving your wife as Christ loves you, so much that if need be you will die for her.

'Salima, I charge you from Scripture to submit to your husband and respect him. You are to submit to him as unto Jesus Christ, not because he is perfect but because he has the responsibility to love you following the example of Jesus Christ. You are to respect him, because your respect will be for him as the air he breathes. He has big dreams and heavy responsibilities, and God has given you to him as a helper to encourage him and support him.'

Butros and Father Alexander had talked several times about this ceremony and agreed they were establishing a model for MBBs. There would be others like Ahmed and Salima. This couple needed to understand the covenant of marriage because they would be an example for others. The two leaders had carefully scripted the service to reinforce these truths. When Butros finished his charge to the couple, Abuna Alexander took over.

Addressing the congregation, Alexander read: 'We are gathered here in the sight of God to join together this man and this woman in holy matrimony, which is an honourable estate instituted by God, signifying unto us the mystical union between Christ and His church. It may not be entered into unadvisedly or lightly but reverently, discreetly, advisedly, soberly and in the fear of God.'

Speaking to the couple, he continued. 'Timothy, have you a good, free and unconstrained will and firm intention to take unto yourself Salima as your wife?'

'I have,' Ahmed answered.

'Salima, have you a good, free and unconstrained will and firm intention to take unto yourself Timothy as your husband?'

'I have,' Salima answered.

After the couple exchanged vows, the priest prayed, 'O holy God who did create man out of the dust and fashion his wife and join her unto him as a helpmate, for it seemed good to Thy majesty that man should not be alone upon the earth, extend Thy hand from Thy holy dwelling place and join Thy servant Timothy and this Thy handmaid Salima. Unite them in one mind and one flesh and grant unto them fair children for education in the faith, for Thine is the majesty, and Thine is the kingdom and the power and the glory.'

'*Amin!*' The congregation responded.

20

Six months later

The first worship service for MBBs in Suq al Khamis occurred on a Friday in Ahmed and Salima's home. They had cleared out all the furniture from the living room, so that everyone could sit on the floor. The windows were closed and covered. There were seven men including Hassan on one side of the room, and four women including Farah and Salima on the other side. Three of the women and two men, including Farah's husband, were from Ahmed's extended family. The others were there because of long conversations with Ahmed that had led them to become convinced that Jesus was indeed God come in flesh, that He had died on the cross for their sins – despite what Islam taught, no one had taken His place in death – and that He had risen from the dead three days later. Mustafa was also in the building but remained downstairs in the office. If unexpected visitors arrived, he would push a button. Salima had tea and sandwiches prepared, and the congregation could immediately transform the meeting from worship service to tea party.

Ahmed was thrilled with the congregation. He had carefully considered all who were invited, knowing that one person who wasn't sure of his faith could betray the entire group. He thought sadly of Saeed and how he had reacted to Ahmed's good news. Their paths had not crossed again, and Ahmed had not returned to the café where they had met. He only hoped his former friend had kept their conversation to himself.

The service had been planned in consultations with Butros and Abuna Alexander. The priest had struggled with the fact that Ahmed and his small flock could not participate fully in the liturgical tradition. Of course Ahmed was not ordained, and Alexander knew he could not personally get involved – it would endanger this little flock as well as St Mark's Church. There could be no outward evidence of a Christian gathering. There would be no church building with a cross on top and no vestments or incense or other liturgical elements. In fact it was felt that the group should probably vary the meeting location and perhaps even the day they met each week. Abuna Alexander had suggested Scripture readings that fit into the liturgical church year, so that the young believers learned systematically the basic stories and teachings of the Bible. Also he proposed a simple model for prayer: a psalm of praise, a prayer of confession, sharing and praying for various personal needs, and concluding with a prayer of thanksgiving.

Abuna Alexander was uncomfortable when they discussed the celebration of Holy Communion, which the priest called the Eucharist. Still, he worked with Butros and Ahmed to provide his counsel. Ahmed would teach and prepare the flock over several weeks before they would celebrate the Lord's feast. They had agreed that Ahmed should lead the meeting with no outside guests. Muslims didn't sing in their meetings, but the two mentors felt that Ahmed needed to teach the congregation psalms and hymns. Ahmed had collected several from the fellowship that had once met in the capital city. They would be handed out for each meeting and returned and put in hiding afterwards.

The service started with the singing of two hymns. They were sung a cappella and in soft voices so as not to attract outside attention. Then they read together in unison John 1:1–18. Ahmed had made a copy of the passage for everyone because no one would openly carry their Injil to the meeting. 'We will be studying John's Gospel for the first few months we are together,' Ahmed explained. 'I will give you the passage each week so you can read it before I teach on it the following week. You may want to memorise as much of it as you can so that the Scriptures, the Word of God, may grow deep inside you and guide your life.'

Before Ahmed's teaching, one of the men gave a testimony. Nadir owned a candy store in Suq al Khamis and his wife and five children lived in cramped quarters behind the shop. Ahmed had entered the shop one day and bought a generous amount of candy for the children in his neighbourhood. As he paid for his purchase, Nadir had grumbled, 'It's nice to have a customer who doesn't ask for credit.'

Ahmed, always alert for opportunities to strike up conversations, had asked, 'Do you have trouble collecting?'

'It's ridiculous,' Nadir had said as he handed Ahmed change. 'Everyone wants to pay me later. When I go to collect, they make excuses. I don't know how much longer I can stay in business.'

For some reason, Ahmed had asked, 'Doesn't anyone pay you?'

'Strange you should ask. Yesterday a man did come in to pay me. A Christian. He paid me back, with interest.'

That was the start of a friendship and extended talks between the two men. 'I was not a devout Muslim,' Nadir admitted to the gathering. 'I struggled with alcohol, and when I drank too much, I got into arguments and fights. Several times my wife called Ahmed to come and talk with me. He gave me a Bible, and I have been reading it for several months. The message of the gospel has transformed me. So much that my wife last week begged me to tell her what was changing me so dramatically.'

Nadir ended his testimony by asking for prayer for his wife and children. 'They don't know I'm here. I have started to tell them stories from the Bible. My wife is hungry to know more. Please pray I will know how to lead her into faith. Her father is a devout Muslim, and so I feel I need to be careful.'

After Nadir had finished, Ahmed led the prayers. He sat in front, facing the group. As a sign of respect for the Scriptures, his Bible rested on a small wooden pedestal. He had prayed long about what to say to this small flock and had chosen as his Bible text the words of Jesus from John's Gospel: 'A new command I give you: Love one another. As I have loved you, so you must love one another' (13:34). His words were carefully written in his journal, along with his poetry.

'True love is what saves,' he began his message. 'The One who causes love to dwell in our hearts, causing us to love enemies and sinners, He alone saves. He who makes us His sons and not His slaves, He it is who saves.

'How do we explain the change in the life of our brother Nadir? Only love can explain it. Jesus is the true and only God who is able to save. He is the only one who never fears your sincere search, your just doubts, and your bold questions. He alone mystifies the world. He alone mystifies you and me. And He alone is able to change us.

'The religion of love accepts only those who follow voluntarily. Whoever approaches it by commandment will never attain it. We see that in the passage we just read. The law was given through Moses; grace and truth came through Jesus Christ. The Quran can only reveal law. God is revealed to us through Jesus Christ. Whoever is forced to believe has lost his way, for the God of love does not force us to believe. The God of love delights in nothing save love. He wants to make us like Him. Ideologies command murder. Christ answers, "But I tell you that anyone who is angry with his brother will be subject to judgement. I tell you, Do not resist an evil person. Love your enemies and pray for those who persecute you."

'It is love that must characterise our fellowship. Jesus has granted all who accept Him, both good and bad, both Jew and Gentile, to become children of God – the apple of His eye, His joy and delight, from every tribe and people and tongue. It is inclusive, revolutionary, untamed. It has no spot or wrinkle. No divisions, pollution or bloodshed. It embraces all. It is the true people of God who reflect His love. They liberate others. They bring justice. This is His glorious church, which the whole world awaits.'

Ahmed, in speaking to that little flock, felt for the first time his real calling in life. He wanted to shepherd these souls. He wanted to guide them, to see them grow and mature, to become a light in the darkness of Suq al Khamis. These eleven people – with Mustafa, there were twelve, the same number Jesus had for His disciples – they could change this town. They could go into the surrounding villages – Mustafa and Hassan had already started. They would sow, and they would reap. And the result would be a harvest greater than any this country had known, not a harvest of corn or wheat but of souls. Yes, this was his heart's desire. He would do everything possible to learn and train so he could feed these sheep.

⤙∾∾⤚

Layla picked up a bucket of feed and scattered it among the chickens. Her stomach recoiled from the smells of the barnyard. Suddenly she dropped the bucket, hurried behind the shed, and lost the tea and stale bread she'd eaten for breakfast. She stood for a moment, hands on her knees, to catch her breath. Then slowly she stood up and headed over to the two goats she had to milk. At least for that chore she could sit on a little stool. This was one of the few jobs she didn't really mind.

The nearest village was a kilometre away, but Layla was never allowed to leave the farm. She felt trapped. It was the length of days that wore her down. Rarely did she get more than six hours of sleep, and that was preceded by the nightmare she had to endure from Abdul-Qawi. How she hated him! After her kidnapper had tired of her, she'd been transferred like an old cart, no, like a donkey that pulled the cart, to his friend who then performed a sham of a ceremony and made her his wife. She was ordered to keep silent as three times the village imam had asked Abdul-Qawi, 'Are you willing to marry this woman?' How she wished he would exercise his right for divorce, saying three times, 'I divorce you', and send her back to Suq al Khamis.

Every night the monster had his way with her, then left her in her tiny room in the family farmhouse and locked the door. Many times he'd warned her of dire consequences if she ever tried to escape. Since he thought nothing of taking a bamboo rod and beating her for the least perceived infraction, she had no doubt that he was capable of carrying out his more vicious threats.

Usually Abdul-Qawi's younger sister unlocked her door just before sunrise, and her mornings were fairly routine – feed the animals, clean the stalls, care for the vegetable gardens. Then she spent long hours in the fields toiling under the hot sun. She never ate with the family. Usually she was tossed scraps as though she were one of the barnyard animals.

Hate fuelled her days, giving her the energy she needed to do all of the work and avoid more serious beatings – that and hope that she would somehow find a way to escape. But hope was fading. It had been more than a year since she'd been abducted from Suq al Khamis. For a moment she had thought, after her parents' visit, that she would be rescued. But that idea had faded when 'ownership' was transferred to Abdul-Qawi. Did her parents even know where she was? And what would they think of her when they learned that she had 'married'? Her brother would surely take that personally – how could she shame the family? As if she had any choice!

She simply couldn't give up hope. If she did, there was no reason to go on living. There had to be a way of escape. She would try to steal the key from

Abdul-Qawi or his sister. With the key she would escape in the middle of the night. She needed to be alert. An opportunity would arise and she would be ready. Meanwhile, she drew comfort from the New Testament readings she remembered. And she prayed fervently that God would rescue her from this nightmare.

―∞―

Threatening calls to Butros began coming fairly regularly. Sometimes they called his office, sometimes his home. Nadira said when she was home alone with their two children, the caller said nothing, but she could hear someone breathing and occasionally talking in the background.

When Butros answered, there was a message. 'We know what you are doing.' The voice seemed to belong to a man who was educated and articulate. 'We don't like western organisations interfering with our country.'

'I'm not sure I understand what this has to do with me.'

'You understand perfectly. We know about your foreign visitors. We know you receive money from the West and that you are a front for western missions. You work with enemies of Islam. You have a conference coming up soon. I am warning you – you should cancel it.'

'I think you are making a mistake,' Butros said one time. 'This conference is for Christian leaders.'

'You convert people to Christianity. We will not tolerate that.'

'No, that is not the purpose of the conference. And besides, we have freedom of religion. I'm not involved in anything illegal.'

'We're not concerned with anything legal or illegal,' the man responded. 'We are just warning you. What you are doing is not good. You must stop or there will be consequences.'

One evening Butros came home and found his wife weeping at the dining table and Thomas and their baby girl screaming. After Butros calmed the children with some food and held his wife, trying to comfort her, he learned that she had received another phone call.

'We're watching you.' The voice on the phone was sinister.

'Who is calling, please?' Nadira asked, trying hard not to betray any anxiety in her voice.

'This is a warning. Tell your husband that he will stop what he is doing or we will kidnap your children.'

———✦———

Butros lay staring at the ceiling. The clock by his bed told him it was after three o'clock in the morning. His wife, her head resting on his shoulder, had finally slipped into a fitful sleep, but Butros was nowhere near sleep as he wrestled with God. He had arrived home seven hours ago to find Nadira in a panic. Butros had told her about the phone threats, but until now they had been vague, meant only to intimidate. This was different. He didn't mind putting his own life on the line, but threats to his family were another matter.

What should he do? He hardly knew how to pray. If he ran, the extremists would believe they had won, and that would encourage an expansion of their campaign of fear. How could he expect pastors to remain at their posts if he fled at the first serious threat? All churches in the country lived with threats and persecution. As a minority consisting of only 5 per cent of the population, it was expected that Christians would be repressed by the Muslim majority. But lately the threats had become more overt. Imams were preaching more provocative sermons, calling Christians infidels and the West enemies of Islam. Local cells of the Muslim Brotherhood were taking a higher profile, and though the government publicly advocated a moderate position, allowing that Christians had historically always been part of the region, local police authorities were generally letting the radicals have their way. Fundamentalists were insisting that women cover their heads, closing down theatres and stores that sold alcohol and pork, and in some cases attacking churches. Young women seemed to face the greatest danger – there were increasing incidents of kidnapping and forced conversions to Islam. There were also cases, especially in larger cities, of inducements to convert to Islam – promises of a better job or free housing were attractive incentives to a poor Christian man. However, until recently, overt physical threats against Christians were rare.

So what should he do? Should he ignore the threat to his family? That didn't seem prudent. He could add locks to his flat for security, but anyone who was determined could get in. He could make sure Nadira and the children didn't go anywhere without him or another male escort. He could take them to Logos Training Centre and live away from the city – but would that protect them? If anything, they might be more vulnerable out in the countryside.

Recently Nadira had talked about taking the children home to see her parents. Maybe this would be a good time to do that. It would allow Butros to think and find a way to protect his loved ones. It mustn't seem like they were fleeing, but they couldn't just wait in fear either.

Nadira rolled over in her sleep and mumbled some words. Butros leaned over and kissed her head, laid his hand on her shoulder, and whispered, 'Lord, I beg You to protect my family. Give my wife Your peace instead of fear. Keep my children hidden in Your arms, far from any enemies who would harm them.' He paused as his wife sighed in her sleep. 'Heavenly Father, I need Your wisdom more than ever. You called us to this work. Show us what we should do.'

For the first time in many hours, a peace washed over him.

21

Two months later

Brother Andrew was scheduled to speak at a pastors' conference at the Logos Training Centre. At the last moment, Butros, because of the escalation of threats to him and several other pastors, decided to cancel the event, and he sent his family for an extended stay with Nadira's parents. But he urged his mentor to visit the country. This time they would meet with individual pastors who were feeling the increasing pressure of hostility in their communities. 'Let's listen to them and pray with them,' Butros requested. 'Your presence here will mean a lot to them.'

It had been a busy time. Each day was filled with several meetings with pastors and also the growing team for the NGO Al Kalima. Andrew also found time one afternoon to visit Professor Kamal at the university. He waited in the professor's cramped office while Kamal talked with students after a lecture. Behind his desk and on two walls, floor-to-ceiling shelves sagged under the weight of academic books on Islam. As the professor entered the room, Andrew rose and gave his friend a traditional Arabic greeting: '*Assalaam Aleikum*', meaning 'Peace be upon you.'

The professor smiled, shook hands with his guest, and replied in Arabic: '*Walaikum assalaam wa rahmatullahi wa barakuatuhu.*' Then he translated: 'That means "God's peace and mercy and blessings be on you."' As the two men sat down, the professor explained: 'Whatever greeting you are offered, you should give back more.'

'I like that,' Brother Andrew replied. They chatted for a few moments before Andrew said, 'In our greetings to each other we speak about peace. When I say "*Assalaam Aleikum*", I mean it from my heart. I want peace. I bring peace. I want *you* to have peace – God's peace. And you respond beautifully by giving back more. But what if a Muslim doesn't accept my peace? What if he says, "No!"?'

'If you say no, it means there is enmity between us,' said the professor.

'I say this because some in the West say Islam is a religion of peace. But others see the attacks by some Muslims and say that Islam hates Christians and Jews. Not everyone in Islam wishes us peace.'

Kamal stood up and looked for a moment at the shelves behind him, then pulled down a book. As he thumbed through the volume, looking for a reference, he said: 'I want to show you how, early in our history, Muslims did what their Prophet commanded them.' Finding what he was searching for, Kamal said, 'The clear evidence of this is this Covenant that was signed by the second caliph, Umar Ibn al-Khattab, Commander of the Faithful – may God be pleased with him – with the Christian Patriarch Sophronious. This Covenant is an example of tolerance and an honest contract among people. The inhabitants of the holy land, Muslims and Christians alike, take pride in it because it firmly established the form of the relationship between the sons of the one Palestinian people. It is not predicated on a sectarian or confessional basis, but rather on a sublime basis built on the respect for the religion and beliefs of one party by the other party, and the complete freedom of this party to practise his religion and creeds without criticism or vilification.'

'I am familiar with the Covenant of Umar,' said Andrew. 'History remembers this caliph for his refusal to pray in the Church of the Holy Sepulchre so it would not be claimed as a mosque. But are we not also talking about the same Caliph Umar who ruled that Christians could not build new churches or repair existing churches in towns inhabited by Muslims? The ringing of church bells to call Christians to prayer was forbidden. Christians were required to distinguish themselves from Muslims by their dress, and could only travel by donkeys while Muslims used horses. Muslims look back on this code with pride, but for Christians, this covenant demonstrates the limits of Muslim tolerance.'

Kamal returned his book to the shelf as he said, 'Man is not a Muslim unless he truly loves his fellow man, for there is no need for envy and hate. Ali bin Abi Talib, the Fourth Rightly Guided Caliph, says, "If you conquer your enemy, forgive him as a sign of your gratitude for having conquered him. Punish your brother with kindness and repel his wrongdoing with grace." The Prophet, peace be upon him, teaches Muslims the following: "My God commanded me to pardon the one who did wrong to me, to maintain ties with the one who forsook blood kindred and to give to the one who did not give to me."'

Andrew shook his head. 'Those are nice words, but I don't see much justice or forgiveness or kindness or pardon going on in the Middle East.'

'No, you are right.' Kamal sat down and said sadly, 'But it would be different if Islam were again in its rightful position in Jerusalem.'

The professor's voice was soft and he looked with kindness at Andrew. But it was evident that they had reached an impasse. Clearly Kamal believed that Islam belonged in the pre-eminent position of power and that Muslim leaders would naturally treat all unbelievers or *dhimmis* with justice and compassion.

Andrew decided to challenge that position carefully. 'Professor, Islam is the authority here in your country. But I've talked to many Christians who do not feel the spirit you just described. They do not feel safe and protected. This past week as I have travelled in your country, I have been told of attacks against churches. Christian businesses have been destroyed. Are you telling me that this is not real Islam?'

'Islam stresses the freedom of worship for non-Muslims,' Kamal replied. 'They cannot be forced to do otherwise. It is forbidden to force them to leave their religion and desecrate their places of worship. The behaviour of the Prophet and his successors serves as a testimony. Islam recognises other religions and earlier prophets. The Quran enjoins Muslims to respect them and whenever the name of a prophet is invoked, whether it is Adam, Abraham, Moses, Jesus or Muhammad, a Muslim automatically says, "Peace be upon him." All are carriers of the Message of Heaven, this one eternal message with the basic objective: the worship of God and the kind treatment of human beings.'

'My friend, you must admit that many of your fellow Muslims seem not to have heard this message of Islam. Many in the West see Islam as an aggressive religion, waging war . . .'

'War in Islam is an exception,' the professor interrupted. 'It is only used for self-defence against aggression.'

'Would you consider the attacks by groups like Hezbollah and Hamas and Islamic Jihad a legitimate Islamic use of war?'

'That is their only means of self-defence against aggression. Yes, that is legitimate.'

'Professor, this perspective is hard for us Christians to accept. I know you have another class to teach. You have given me much to think about. I thank you very much for your time. I wonder if I may pray for you?'

'Yes.'

Brother Andrew lifted his hands, palms up, as he prayed: 'Lord God, I thank You so much that You brought me to meet my dear friend Kamal. We search for truth. We search for solutions. We search for peace. We search for justice and righteousness. Lord, I ask that You will operate in our lives – how can we bring peace if there is no peace in our own hearts? I thank You for Jesus who brought us peace, who brought us forgiveness, who made known His grace and access to the throne of God. Thank You for my friend, for his input, for his willingness to talk about solutions. Bless him, Lord, protect him, his family, his work. Bring us together again in Your good and perfect time. In Jesus's name. *Amin*.'

─◦◊◦─

The next day Andrew and Butros waited for their appointment with Kareem in an ornate reception area on the top floor of a large government building. A man dressed in a starched *jallabiya* served coffee from a silver pot as they relaxed on a lush leather sofa. A Persian rug covered the floor of the large room. Opposite them sat a male secretary who prepared documents for the minister's signature, each in a thick leather binder. After Butros and Brother Andrew had waited for a few minutes, the secretary took a stack of the binders into the minister's office and returned to escort them to their meeting.

Kareem rose and came around from behind a huge carved wood desk to welcome them. The stack of leather binders sat in the middle of the desk, along with a row of fountain pens. On the right side of the desk were several phones. There was also a vial of perfume, and Andrew detected the strong aroma of frankincense. The office was in the shape of an L. In front of Kareem's desk was a seating area with lush couches and another large Oriental rug. To the left of Kareem's desk was a dining area and against the wall a table with several warming dishes. There a waiter prepared a tray of coffee and pastries.

As the sheikh showed them around his office, he pulled a leather-bound edition of the Quran off a shelf and offered it as a gift to Brother Andrew.

'I have several nice copies of the Quran,' Andrew said with a chuckle. 'However, this is the nicest one I've ever received.'

In turn, Andrew offered the minister a leather-bound Arabic Bible and four of his books that had been translated into Arabic.

Kareem indicated that Andrew and Butros should sit in the chairs near his desk, and after the waiter had served refreshments and departed, closing the doors behind him, he said, 'It is a pleasure to meet you, Brother Andrew. Please tell me, what can I do for you?'

Butros had warned Andrew that Kareem was seeing them in an official capacity, so he would undoubtedly be cautious in what he said.

'I want to thank you for seeing us today,' Andrew began. Kareem smiled and nodded. 'We are here to speak on behalf of those who cannot speak for themselves. Christians in this country are being threatened more and more. Churches have been burned down. Christian businesses have been attacked. Teenage girls have been abducted and forced to convert to Islam. This should be very disturbing to your government and I have come to you to ask what can be done about this.'

The minister shifted uneasily in his chair and finally said, 'You are right. This is very disturbing. I too am saddened by these reports. As you know, there is freedom of religion in this country.'

'Freedom on paper, perhaps,' Andrew protested, 'but apparently not in practice.'

'My friends, I understand your concern and frustration. Everyone should have the right to practise his religion without interference. I wish I could order the police to protect your friends and to put an end to the attacks.

However, I do not have the authority to so order them. And even if I did, that doesn't mean such orders would be obeyed.'

'So there is nothing you can do?' asked Andrew.

'What I can do is bring it up with the king. I will look for an appropriate time to discuss this with him.'

'I'm sure you know that articles have been written about the situation. There are people in the West watching to see how the government handles this.'

'Yes, I am aware of that.'

'Also, there are many Christians leaving the country or trying to leave. Is there anything the government can do to encourage them to stay?'

'I will definitely bring that up with my fellow ministers. It is not good for our image if people want to flee our country.'

Butros gestured, and Kareem said, 'My friend, do you want to say something?'

'Excellency, I want to emphasise that Christians are loyal citizens and a blessing to this country and every country where they live. For example, every Sunday in our churches, we pray for the rulers of this country. We pray also for the economic prosperity of our nation – we pray for rain and for good crops. It is true that we suffer, but we never stop praying for our people. Further, we serve the greater Muslim community in many ways by operating schools, orphanages, and hospitals.'

'Yes, as you know, I was educated in one of your schools,' said Kareem.

Andrew observed the clear discomfort of his host. 'I am sure you will do all that you can to help the body of Christ. I want you to know that Butros told me about you. I will keep that information in complete confidence. And I want you to know that I am praying for you.'

'Thank you very much,' Kareem answered. 'I wish I could say more, but you understand . . .'

'I do understand.'

As they left their meeting, the secretary in the reception area met them with a silver tray. On it were two beautiful ceramic plates decorated in gold calligraphy, one for Butros and the other for Andrew to take home to Holland.

Later, while riding back to the hotel, Andrew observed to Butros how hard it was for one man, even one so significantly placed in a government, to make much of a difference. 'Kareem was obviously uncomfortable with our conversation,' Andrew said.

'Yes, but at least he didn't lie to us,' Butros said. 'In this culture it is common to pay lip service to visitors like you. They will say whatever you want to hear, but with no intention of doing anything.'

'Our friend didn't do that. He seems to want to try to help.'

'I think he will try, but he must operate within a system. He cannot change the culture. Even the king is limited in what he can do. He walks a fine line, trying to maintain good relations with western democracies while appeasing the growing influence of fundamentalists in this country. He will say this country officially recognises the UN Declaration of Human Rights, but in reality Islamic law is supreme, and he will never do anything that contradicts that.'

'So realistically, is there anything Kareem can do for Christians?'

'He will be a voice of moderation and perhaps use his influence quietly in certain specific cases. But he must be very careful. He cannot stick his neck out. Remember, no one knows that he is really a follower of Christ.'

Andrew thought about that as Butros pulled up to the hotel. 'You're right,' Andrew said as he put his hand on the door handle. He hesitated, then said, 'We must not put too much trust in one government official. However, we must pray for him. God has him in that position for a reason, and some day he will have a chance to be used in a unique way. We must pray that he will be ready when that time comes.'

22

One year later

The staff of Al Kalima in Suq al Khamis met on Monday mornings in Ahmed's ground floor office below the apartment where he and Salima lived. Ahmed, who led the team, managed the budget that Butros provided – paying the salaries and obtaining books and other resources as needed. Mustafa and Hassan had successfully established literacy centres among the Christian community in the villages where they lived. Each man taught an adult men's class on weeknights after the work was finished in the fields. A woman, a pastor's wife trained in the first training programme for literacy trainers at Logos Training Centre, taught classes for women that included health and hygiene, basic maths and writing skills, as well as reading.

For the most part the teachers had been welcomed. The Christian community in the villages recognised the need for these classes, had provided church facilities for them, and encouraged their congregations to participate. During the first few months, there had been no protests. Recently, however, Mustafa and Ahmed had received threatening notes and phone calls. The team had talked about the threats and took precautions, but they saw no reason to stop their work.

Salima also attended the meeting. Salima had become a critical part of the mission. Five afternoons a week she taught a literacy class for women. In the evenings she had started a programme for teenage girls who had not finished primary school. This morning, as was her practice, she joined the men for the meeting when they evaluated the various programmes and talked about any problems they were facing.

Nadir was the final member of the team. He had benefited from the coaching for his business, which had expanded from candy to include drinks and a very popular ice cream stand. He had made a strong effort to eliminate credit, with some success. Now he was teaching two young MBB men basic business principles.

These meetings were also a time for spiritual renewal. The five spent some of their time in prayer for the people to whom they ministered. Mustafa and Hassan were leading small congregations of MBBs in their villages, and the group in Suq al Khamis had grown and divided into three groups of about a dozen each. For safety and security it had been decided to keep the congregations small. One group consisted mostly of members of Ahmed's extended family. Ahmed's father had heard of the meetings and had made it clear to Ahmed that he didn't want this to become known to any of his friends. The health of Ahmed's father was clearly failing. Ahmed prayed constantly for his father and longed for a softening and complete reconciliation.

Besides leading the team in Suq al Khamis and the surrounding area, Ahmed was also helping Butros in other parts of the country, specifically meeting with other MBBs and coaching them in their discipleship. In fact, as soon as this team meeting ended, Ahmed was to spend the rest of the week travelling to several towns and encouraging newly forming congregations of MBBs.

The meeting ended with a light lunch that Salima had prepared. Hassan shut down his laptop and packed it into his shoulder bag. Nadir helped Mustafa load two boxes of booklets and Arabic New Testaments into Hassan's tiny Japanese-made saloon. Ahmed hugged his two friends before they climbed into the car and drove away.

Within a few minutes they were outside Suq al Khamis, and Hassan turned on to a hard-packed dirt road that split two large fields. A narrow canal ran down one side, providing irrigation from a deep well.

Suddenly from among a grove of trees, several motorcycles burst on to the path. Two cut in front of him, and Hassan jerked the wheel of his car to avoid a collision and swerved towards the canal, stopping in mud just before it plunged into the water. Hassan quickly shifted the car into reverse, but the rear tyres of his car were off the ground and he wasn't going anywhere.

Two men jerked open the driver-side door and pulled him out. Mustafa jumped from the passenger seat and started to run, but one of the motorcyclists fired a shot and ordered him to stop. The two men were grabbed. Two more cars drove up. Mustafa was shoved into the back seat of one; Hassan was shoved into the other. Meanwhile two of the attackers started to rummage through Hassan's car and pulled out his shoulder bag.

—◠◠◠—

After a two-hour drive Ahmed had just arrived at his destination and was searching for the address where he was to meet with two MBB leaders when his mobile phone vibrated. He pulled the phone out of his pocket and opened it. Before he could speak, Salima screamed into his ear: 'They've got Mustafa and Hassan. You've got to get away. Now . . .'

Ahmed had never heard his wife in such a state. 'Salima, calm down. Tell me what is going on.'

Ahmed waited for Salima to gain some control of her emotions. Finally, she said, 'I just received a phone call. A voice said, "We have your husband's friends. And you are next".'

'They threatened you?'

'No, I mean they wanted me to give you a message.'

'I'm on my way . . .'

'No, they want money.'

'I can be home in two hours.'

'No, don't come. I think this is a trap.'

'Salima, you'd better slow down and tell me exactly what they told you.'

'The voice told me not to call the police, or Mustafa and Hassan will be killed.'

'Honey, please. Start at the beginning.'

'I'm sorry. I'm scared.'

'Of course you are. But I need to understand exactly what is going on.'

Salima took a deep breath. 'He didn't say much.'

'Did he give you his name?'

'No name. No group. He just said, "Tell your husband we are holding his friends." Then he said, "Do not call the police or you will never see your friends alive again." '

'Okay, we won't call the police. For now.'

'He said they want money.'

'How much?'

Salima told him.

Ahmed sighed. 'I don't know if I can get that much . . .'

'He seemed to think we have a lot of money.'

'I just paid salaries. You saw me do that this morning.'

'Maybe Butros can help.'

'How long do we have?'

'He said he would call me back tomorrow morning with instructions.'

'Okay. Please, I need you to be calm. Listen: I want you to call my sister and stay with her tonight.'

Salima sniffed and said, 'Okay, I'll call her.'

'And I will call Butros. Together we'll work out what to do next.'

'Ahmed, I'm really afraid.'

'Of course you are, my darling. But you must remain calm . . .'

'You can't come home. The man said if you don't do exactly what he said, he will kill you.'

'Salima?'

'Yes?'

'I love you.'

'I love you too. You will be careful?'

'This will work out for good. We must not panic but pray and trust God. I will keep my mobile on. Call me if anything happens.'

—◈—

Mustafa didn't know where he was. He had been forced to lie on the floor in the back of the car, as it bumped along a dirt road. Hassan had been taken in another car. The group, he guessed eight men were involved, had pulled into a remote farm and driven into a barn where farm animals and equipment were stored. Hassan had been led to the opposite side from him. Both of them had been stripped of their clothes. As two men held Mustafa's arms, another man stood six inches from his face and shouted, 'Apostate! Why are you fighting against Islam?'

Mustafa started to protest, but the accuser continued: 'What are you doing with my sister?'

'I'm sorry, but who is your sister?'

A punch in his stomach took his breath away. 'Fatima. Do you recognise that name?'

Another punch caused him to retch, and Mustafa would have fallen over if the two men hadn't held on to his arms.

'You apostate!' the man screamed. 'Why are you putting infidel thoughts into my sister's mind?'

Mustafa had no idea who this man's sister was. He assumed she attended one of the literacy centres being taught by the pastor's wife. His policy was to allow only Christians to participate in classes, but there were also Muslims who wanted the instruction. He had been told that several Muslim women had started attending, and the pastor's wife didn't have the heart to turn them away.

Another blow to Mustafa's head nearly knocked him out, but he still heard his accuser say, 'All my sister needs is Quran. She doesn't need any of those thoughts from the Christian West.'

A shout from the other side of the shed distracted everyone's attention. 'I've found something on the infidel's computer!'

The leader ordered the two men holding Mustafa: 'Tie him up.' Then he strode to the other side of the barn.

Mustafa didn't try to resist as the men tied his hands behind his back, tied his feet together, and shoved him on to a rickety wooden chair. He heard the man with the computer say, 'See – their NGO, Al Kalima. Here are the names of this infidel's students.'

'Good,' said the leader. 'Copy them down and we'll deal with them later. I'm more interested in finding out who runs this organisation. Does he have addresses and phone numbers in there, perhaps a list of key contacts?'

'I'm looking.'

Mustafa heard the clicking of computer keys as the man rifled through the files on the laptop. 'There are a lot of documents,' the voice said. 'Here's something: "How to become a Christian". It's a translation from English. This is proof they're proselytising.'

'Okay. But I want names of the leaders, their network. Who supports them?'

'I don't see that on here.' After a few more moments, the voice said, 'I think that's all. What should we do with the infidel?'

'Shoot him,' said the leader.

Mustafa winced and shouted, 'No!'

One of the guards who'd bound him hit him on the side of the head. Mustafa heard the click of a pistol, and then the roar of a single shot reverberated throughout the barn.

—◦◦◦—

Ahmed prayed more fervently than he'd ever prayed before. He was astounded as he felt a supernatural calm descend over him, as if he were being wrapped in a warm blanket on a bitter cold night. *My Lord Jesus, protect my friends Mustafa and Hassan. Protect my wife, Salima. And give me a clear mind and direct my steps.* Immediately he determined he needed to attend the scheduled meetings that afternoon and evening. Before entering the home where he was to meet the MBB leaders, he dialled Butros on his mobile and quickly briefed him on the situation. When he had finished, he asked, 'What should we do?'

'I can get you the money.' Butros sighed. 'But I don't think it's money they want.'

'Why not?'

'I think this keeps the police away until they finish their terrible work.'

'What *do* they want?'

'You. Me. Anyone with connections to our work. Ahmed, I'm afraid you're in serious danger. Can you drive to the city?'

'I think so, yes. But what about my meetings?'

'Good point. Don't change your plans. Meet with the leaders. Go to the gathering tonight, but after it's over, drive here immediately. Call me when you enter the city, and I'll tell you where to meet me.'

'What about Salima?'

'You must not tell her where you are going. The less she knows, the safer you both are. Can she stay with anyone in your family?'

'I told her to stay with my sister.'

'Good. Have Salima move in with your sister for the time being.'

—◆◆◆—

There was no time for Mustafa to grieve Hassan's murder. He felt strong arms pull him up and when he opened his eyes the leader was again six inches from his face.

'You don't remember me, do you?'

Mustafa racked his brain. The face, with a heavy beard, did look familiar.

'No, you wouldn't remember me. You were the bright, future leader of our movement. I was just a new recruit. The imam couldn't say enough about the great Mustafa. You were the faithful Muslim who set the example for the rest of us.' The man spat in Mustafa's face and pushed him back into the chair, which crumbled under the sudden weight and shattered into several pieces. Mustafa landed on his side.

'You were such a good writer,' the man said. 'I read every one of your booklets. You were so persuasive. You are the reason why I'm now part of Muslim Brotherhood. You were supposed to write the great argument against Christianity.'

Mustafa didn't see the kick coming and took a full blow to the stomach. The two thugs picked him up, but Mustafa bent over and wanted to throw up. The room spun around him. He tried to think clearly, realising he probably had only a few minutes of life remaining. Now he understood why he was here. He had betrayed the Muslim Brotherhood, and this young fanatic was exacting revenge.

'So what went wrong?' the interrogator sneered.

The two thugs pulled Mustafa up, forcing him to stand straight and look at his accuser, who now held a scimitar.

'You read that corrupted book, didn't you? How could someone so smart be so deceived?'

Quick as a cat the accuser struck with his knife, plunging it into Mustafa's stomach. As he removed it, he said, 'This is what happens to apostates. Allah will reward us for wiping you off the face of this earth.'

The knife struck again. As it was removed, Mustafa summoned all of his strength to look at his attacker and say, 'I've found the truth. Isa . . . He loved the world. He died for you.'

The attacker didn't seem to hear his words. How he wished he could tell this man the Good News! He was surprised and grateful that he didn't feel more pain. The words poured into his soul: *He humbled Himself and became obedient to death – even death on a cross.*

The accuser, judge, and executioner continued his merciless attack. 'You can be sure that we do the same to your friends . . .'

Mustafa could barely breathe and his mind was fuzzy as the world around him faded. *Therefore God exalted him to the highest place and gave him the name that is above every name.* He thought he could see the Lord he loved, lifted high. He wanted to go, longed to go to Him. The God who was shamed was now honoured above all others. *That at the name of Jesus every knee should bow, in heaven and on earth and under the earth.*

Some day his attackers would bow and confess that Jesus Christ is Lord. But now Mustafa revelled in the joy of seeing Him face-to-face.

23

Something felt wrong. Salima started to unlock the door to the Al Kalima office, with Farah hovering at her elbow, when she realised that the latch was broken; the door swung open as she attempted to turn the handle.

Salima had hurried away from the two-storey building the previous afternoon, frantic to escape to a safe place, anxious for Ahmed, praying desperately for Mustafa and Hassan. She hadn't taken time to pack carefully – she needed to go upstairs to the flat and gather some clothes and toiletries. She didn't want to come back, but she had to wait here for the phone call.

As the door opened, it banged into a fallen chair. She stared at the scene. The room was a total mess. The phone was on the floor. Books were strewn everywhere. The desk drawers were open and papers were scattered. The computer printer was smashed on the floor beside the desk, and the spot where Ahmed's computer should have been was empty.

Cautiously Salima stepped into the room. Then she screamed and collapsed. Sprawled under the desk was the body of Hassan.

———※———

Abuna Alexander discovered Mustafa's body at the top of the steps leading into St Mark's Church. The body was wrapped in a brown blanket and blood from the wounds had left it soaked with huge rust-coloured spots. Pinned to the blanket, flapping in the breeze, was a note. The priest shuddered as he bent down to read the message:

> In the name of Allah the Merciful. Thanks to God the Lord of the worlds and prayer and peace be on the one He sent as mercy to the whole world, our Prophet Muhammad. God said, 'Say that God is one. He is the strongest. He did not give birth or was born and no one equals Him.' All God's creatures, mountains, skies and earth are against the lies of Christians who said that God has a son. We must make a revolution against those evangelistic centres that change people's religion to Christianity and spread atheism through distributing books that arouse God's anger. *Allahu Akbar!* God is Great!
>
> Listen and be aware. To the priest who associates with apostates, you now see what happens. You will cease all contact with the apostates. You will not proselytise. Obey or we will blow up this church and send the priest to hell.
>
> To the apostate Ahmed, don't you fear the eternal fire? We will hunt you and kill you. If you will return to Islam, perhaps Allah may be merciful.
>
> To the infidel Butros, your crusaders' centre fights Islam and teaches against the religion of God. You are spreading heretical thoughts and teachings through books and activities that are supported by the crusaders' countries who are atheists and full of hatred. That is why we warn you from what they do and from their being here. We want you to know that we are capable of destroying your buildings but first we warn you.

Father Alexander nearly fainted. He stood up and felt the world spinning. He had to call Butros immediately. The note clearly threatened the Logos Centre. He had to warn his wife not to leave the flat. Where was Ahmed? He had to warn him. Where was Salima? What should he do? That decision was made for him, as at that moment a police car rounded the corner and parked at the base of the church steps.

—⟨∞⟩—

A slow fan tried to move air through the police station of Suq al Khamis. Butros wiped the sweat from his face and looked at the police officer across the desk. He was feeling the effects of a sleepless night. He'd quickly gathered the money – if there was a call to come and pay a ransom, he was ready. Ahmed had arrived in the capital city after midnight, and Butros had arranged a safe place for him, at least for a couple of days. Abuna Alexander had called from the police station in Suq al Khamis to inform him that the police wanted him to come in for questioning. That's when he'd learned that his friend Mustafa was dead. But there wasn't time to even think about him.

'They want to know why your name is on that note that was on Mustafa's body,' said the priest. A few minutes later Salima had called to tell him about Hassan. She was also at the police station, where she had learned that Nadir had been arrested.

Butros could barely remember the drive to Suq al Khamis. His mind was a jumble of thoughts and questions. He tried to pray but all that he could manage was to repeat the phrase *Lord, have mercy on us*. He'd arrived at the police station and seen Salima briefly before an officer escorted him to this office. The priest had been asked to make a statement and was released. In the hall, before entering this office, Butros had heard a scream coming from the basement. He imagined it could be Nadir and prayed that God would not allow this brother to suffer more than he could endure.

He expected a harsh interrogation from the police officer, but this man seemed calm and talked in a rational tone. 'We need to locate the man Ahmed. His wife says you may know where he is.'

Butros was instantly alert and felt he had to buy some time before he revealed much information, until he knew what would happen to Ahmed if he turned himself in. 'Ahmed works for me. He is on assignment. He had meetings yesterday in' – he named the town – 'one in the afternoon and another in the evening. He was expected to spend the night there and to drive to some more appointments today.'

'You can vouch for this?'

'Yes, of course. Why?'

'Because he is our primary suspect.'

For a moment Butros's mouth hung open. He stammered, 'That's not possible. I don't understand.'

The policeman set his elbows on the desk and leaned forward. 'Look, two men are dead. The last man to see them alive was your NGO employee, Ahmed. So we need to talk with him.'

'I understand, but that doesn't make him a suspect.'

The policeman said nothing. He leaned back in his chair and studied Butros. Finally, he said, 'We have no other suspects.'

'But I was told you found the victims' car and motorcycle tracks and car tracks. Surely the evidence shows the two men were abducted.'

'And who were these abductors?'

'I don't know. You must have some idea.'

The policeman turned up his palms. 'That's my problem. Who saw these men last. The young man Nadir – we're talking with him right now. The woman Salima and her husband, Ahmed. And Ahmed's missing. You see my problem? Until I see evidence otherwise, your NGO must be held responsible.'

'But . . . but that makes no sense.'

—◦◦◦—

Butros and Salima met Abuna Alexander in his living room to debrief after their all-day ordeal at the Suq al Khamis police station. Nadir, they were told, was being detained overnight. The priest's wife, Nour, worked in the kitchen, preparing a meal. The three in the living room appeared to be in shock.

It was Butros who broke the silence. 'May I see the message?'

Father Alexander rose and walked over to a small desk and picked up a piece of paper. 'This is a copy,' he said as he handed it to Butros. 'The police have the original.'

Butros read through it slowly, twice. 'There is no name on this message. No group or individual. Do you have any idea who wrote this?'

'No, I don't know who did this,' the priest said.

'Salima?'

She shook her head and said nothing.

'So we don't know who to talk to.'

None of them knew what to say.

'I think they will not act right away on their threats. They've issued their warning. Now they will wait and see what we do.'

'They want Ahmed,' Salima blurted, tears flowing down her face. 'When they called, the voice, he said it was Ahmed he wanted.'

'Do you think they expected Ahmed to be in the car?'

No one could answer that question.

'Where is he?' the priest asked.

'Ahmed is in a safe place,' Butros answered, 'for now. What do you think? Should we let the police talk to him?'

Alexander's wife brought in a tray containing a plate of pitta bread sandwiches, some biscuits, and three glasses of iced tea. Butros and the priest each accepted a sandwich, but Salima shook her head. The older woman set the tray down on the coffee table and sat next to Salima, who buried her head on Nour's shoulder and wept.

No one knew what to say. Butros took a bite of sandwich. Alexander sat, holding his sandwich, staring at it as though it ought to provide an answer.

Butros took another bite, put his sandwich down and drank some cold tea. Staring out of the living room window, he spoke again. 'What about St Mark's Church?' he said. 'The threats against you. What does it mean? What can we do to protect you?'

'Historically we've had good relations with Muslims,' Alexander said. 'But this . . . Butros, remember when we first met?'

'Yes, I remember the day well.'

'I complained about the building and how we couldn't get permission even to repair the toilet.'

'The building *is* falling apart.'

'But you also asked about the spiritual condition of the congregation. I haven't forgotten that.' The priest paused, before saying emphatically, 'The building isn't important. If they destroy it, they haven't destroyed the real church.'

Alexander's wife looked up in surprise. 'But our congregation. Where would we worship?'

'It is time for us to stand up for Christ.' Alexander turned to Butros. 'Our Lord talked about separating the sheep and the goats. I want to be on the right side. I want my Lord to say, "You fed My sheep." Maybe this is what we need to awaken the congregation.'

'What are you going to do?' Nour asked with a tremble in her voice.

'I'm going to call them to pray. I'm going to tell them about the threats. And I'm going to say we have a choice. We can cower in fear at the threats of the enemy or we can stand up and confront this evil.'

'It's hard to confront a threat when you don't know who is issuing it,' Butros said.

'The challenge is not from the outside enemy but within our hearts,' he replied. 'Many who have the means run away. Others have simply tried to hide and not cause any problems, hoping that protects them. One family, their daughter is being held by Muslims and they seethe in anger but are powerless to do anything. And none of us is willing to stand up and state the truth.'

The priest paused before adding, 'And I'm the biggest coward of all.'

—◦◦◦—

That night Butros received a brief call on his mobile.

'Mr. Butros, you had better be careful,' said the voice.

'Who is this?' Butros asked.

'What is important is that we know who you are. We have the computer from your office in Suq al Khamis. We found your name and others.' The voice said eleven names.

'What do you want from us?' Butros tried to remain calm.

'What we want is for you to leave. I'm warning you. If you don't leave this country, we will search for you, we will find you, and we will kill you.' There was a click and the line went dead.

Butros knew he needed time to think, to sort things out. He called Nadira and made arrangements for his family. Then he called the national airlines and made plane reservations for himself and his wife and children.

—◦◦◦—

Butros met Nadir the next morning when he was released from jail and drove the terribly shaken man to Alexander's flat so they could talk privately. Meanwhile, the priest was calling on members of his congregation.

Before they sat down, Nadir asked Butros to touch his face. 'Do you feel how hot it is?' Butros nodded. 'They slapped me so many times. It hurts if I press it even slightly.'

Then he turned around and lifted his shirt. 'Look what they did to me. I think they've beaten me over every part of my body.' His back was a mass of red welts. But there didn't appear to be any cuts or infection.

'I'll get you some ointment,' Butros said.

Nadir didn't seem to hear. He pulled down his shirt and sat down on the sofa. 'I didn't tell them anything,' he declared.

'I'm so sorry you had to go through this.'

'They are barbarians.' The young man had a defiant look. 'They've told me not to leave Suq al Khamis. I'm to stay home so they can call me if they have more questions. But as you can see, they have a brutal way of asking questions.'

Butros felt helpless. 'What do they want?'

'Ahmed is what they want. They clearly intend to pin the murders on him.'

'Are you sure?'

'They told me, "He's a blasphemer. Tell us where he is and you go free." '

'What did you tell them?'

'That I don't know where Ahmed is. And I don't. I saw him yesterday morning. After lunch he was leaving, and I don't know where he was going.'

'You did well.'

'I asked the questioner what will happen to Ahmed. I hoped I'd misunderstood. Maybe they only had a few questions to ask him. But that's not at all what they want.'

'What do you mean? What did they tell you?'

'They said, "What happens to blasphemers? They get what they deserve."'

Butros was still trying to process this when Nadir added, 'One of the men said they should have finished Ahmed off when he was in prison. He said, "Here we're not afraid to apply Sharia law."'

At that moment Butros knew he'd done the right thing by hiding Ahmed. The police had no intention of finding the real murderers of Mustafa and Hassan. They were going to use this as the pretext to find and kill Ahmed.

Clearly Ahmed had to be taken out of the country or he was a dead man.

—⁓—

Two days later

The familiar Dutch voice answered, '*Goeien avond met* Andrew.'

'Brother Andrew?'

'Butros.' It was late night and Brother Andrew was in his office preparing to watch the news. 'How good to hear from you. Where are you?'

'In Cyprus.'

'Is everything all right?'

Butros hesitated. 'No, it is not.'

'What's wrong?'

'I wanted to call you earlier, but I think the phones are probably tapped back home. That's why I flew to Cyprus. I needed to get away to a safe place and figure out what to do. I'm afraid we're in big trouble.'

'What happened?'

Butros reported the news about the murders, the written threat, and how Ahmed was in hiding. 'I've had to shut down the NGO, at least temporarily. I've closed the Logos Centre. Nadira and the children have gone home to be with her parents. I've warned the MBB communities to be extra careful. I received a personal message in which I was one of twelve people named who are targeted for execution.'

'From whom?'

'They haven't identified themselves. But I believe it is the Muslim Brotherhood. Mustafa and Ahmed used to be part of them, and the way they tortured Mustafa . . .' Butros broke down and couldn't speak for a moment. 'It was a revenge killing. Brutal. They cut open his stomach . . . I can't tell you any more. It was gruesome.'

'What about Ahmed? Is he safe?'

'For now. He's moving around but in hiding. I need to get him out of the country.'

'Is that possible?'

'I've called our friend Kareem. I'm waiting for him to call me back. He thinks there may be a way.'

'Do we need to publicise this?'

'No, I don't think that's a good idea. It wouldn't be good to embarrass the government right now. I want to see if we can quietly get Ahmed and Salima out of the country.'

'I'm sure there are plenty of countries that would have him. Maybe I can help.'

'Thank you, Brother Andrew. But right now, what we need most is prayer.'

'You know you have that,' Andrew replied. 'What happens after Ahmed and Salima are safe?'

'I don't know.' Butros struggled to control his emotions. 'I really don't know what to do. I feel the work has been destroyed. I don't know if Nadira and I can ever go back.'

'Butros, my dear brother.' The way Andrew spoke caused a surprising surge of hope in Butros. 'You have lost a battle, but you have not lost the war. The enemy is fierce and he would like you to think that he has won. Don't believe his lie. However, there is something very important you need to do.'

'What is that?'

'I want you to stay where you are and rest. You're exhausted. You've lost two precious soldiers. You're wounded spiritually. I will fly down tomorrow. Let me pray with you and minister to you. Take some time to let God heal you and speak to you. That is the next step.'

Butros was surprised by the feeling of relief that washed over him. He almost felt guilty for starting to experience hope in the midst of this tragedy. 'Brother Andrew, I accept.'

'I will be on the next flight from Amsterdam.'

24

Larnaca, Cyprus

The balcony of the hotel room felt like a refuge. The gentle roll of waves off the Mediterranean Sea had a soothing effect. Brother Andrew and Butros gazed off into the clear blue water. In the distance a freighter steamed its way towards Egypt or some other Middle Eastern destination.

Andrew had arrived late the previous evening, and now, as the temperature was rising, the two men sipped coffee and enjoyed the peaceful scene.

Butros felt the stress of recent days begin to lift a little. Here there would be no threatening phone calls. No mob of Muslim extremists would attack. He was thankful his wife and children were safe at her parents' home. Finally, he could relax.

Until, that is, he thought of the ruins of his life work. 'Everything I've worked for is gone,' Butros said. 'Well, maybe not everything. The Logos Centre on our farm still stands, but we dare not use it right now.' He felt compelled to list his losses. 'The work in Suq al Khamis is shut down. Several of our Al Kalima centres have been attacked or threatened. And two brothers are dead.'

His tears started to flow again. Butros couldn't pretend to hide his pain. The words poured out, 'They bound Hassan hand and foot and executed him with a shot to his head. And Mustafa . . .' He couldn't speak as the tears spilled down his face.

'It's okay,' Brother Andrew said. 'You need to talk about it. Whatever you want to say, you are safe here.'

'Brother Andrew, they carved Mustafa up! It was brutal. Over and over they cut him. They sliced open his stomach . . . It must have been horrible.' He looked up and stared at his mentor. 'Is this how it ends? Is that what we get for serving the Lord? I don't want to die like that – tied up, naked, tortured. Is that how our lives have to end?'

Brother Andrew didn't speak. He too felt an ache in his soul. He'd baptised Mustafa and Hassan and heard their testimonies and dreams. Part of him wanted to go and be alone, to weep and pray. But as much as he hurt, he knew his friend was in far greater pain. He had lost his co-workers and friends, and his dream was dying. Butros needed to vent his emotions and he needed to do it with a friend, with someone safe. He wasn't asking for answers, not just yet.

'What about Nadira?' Andrew asked. 'How is she handling this?'

'My wife has been so wonderful, strong, supportive. But this has taken a toll on her. She has terrible headaches. She's broken out in a rash. She doesn't want to answer the phone. I wonder if she can ever come back after this . . . At least she and our children are safe with her parents right now. Maybe we all need to move there permanently – just shut the work down. I'd dissolve the NGO right now if I could – but because of the murder investigation, I can't do that. Andrew, is this what ministry means? If so, I don't think it's worth it.'

Andrew just listened, deeply moved.

'I shouldn't have said that.'

'On the contrary, you need to express how you're feeling. After all, God already knows. The Psalms are full of statements that, taken out of context, many Christians would probably find offensive, even lacking in faith.'

'Well, I think my faith is gone, finished. There's nothing left.'

On the sand below their balcony, a group of children squealed with glee as they ran toward the surf. As they started splashing each other, Andrew spoke: 'Do you mind if I ask you a few questions?'

Butros nodded.

'Do you remember when God called you to this work? What did He call you to do?'

'I was called to return to my home country, to strengthen the church there. I remember it like it was yesterday when you wrote to me – I've kept that letter all these years. You said, "One man with God is the majority." But Brother Andrew, this one man has failed!'

Andrew let that exclamation hang in the air for a moment before gently asking his next question: 'Butros, how has God used you?'

'You assume that He has?'

'Oh, there is no question about it. God has definitely used you. But right now, understandably, it's hard for you to see how. You said you went home to strengthen the church. Is the church stronger today than ten years ago?'

Butros thought about the question for a moment. 'Well, I suppose we've done some things, some good activities. You've helped, Brother Andrew – I know that.'

'What are some of the good things you've done?'

'We've encouraged pastors. I think almost every priest and pastor in the country has attended at least one refreshment conference.'

'Well, that's something. What else?'

'The NGO, Al Kalima, has helped a few adults learn how to read.'

'And each graduate gets a Bible. So more Christians are now able to read the Scriptures and as a result are stronger in their faith.'

'We've also trained lay leaders.'

'Good. Keep going.'

'We had so many dreams. I wanted to establish a programme at the Logos Centre to train Christians for better jobs. I hoped we could have a computer centre – we need good computer operators in our country. And Nadira wanted to start a women's centre – that's a huge need, to help battered women. But now I don't think any of those things will happen.'

Andrew ignored the despair in his friend's voice and instead asked, 'Butros, has the church grown since you started the work?'

'No. I don't think so. There are many Christians, those who have the means, who have left the country. The church has probably shrunk.'

'You mean that no Muslims have come to faith in Jesus?'

Butros was taken aback, realising he'd neglected a big part of God's work. 'Yes, there have been many converts. I know of at least one thousand myself, and there are probably many more I don't know about.'

'That's fantastic! They are part of the body of Christ.'

'But most churches still don't welcome them.'

'So the Muslim-background believers have started their own fellowships. Whether the established denominations know it or not, these are their new brothers and sisters. This is a growing church!'

'But the extremists are trying to destroy them. When a fellowship is discovered, they attack the leaders. Mustafa and Hassan – they're dead. Ahmed is running for his life. How can the church survive without its leaders?'

'Can God raise up more leaders?'

'Yes, but I don't know if I can start again.' Butros let out a big sigh. His eyes were no longer wet with tears, and he was trying to think rationally. 'It's too dangerous for my family. I don't know what to do.'

'Butros, listen to me.' Andrew leaned forward in his plastic patio chair to make his point. 'If you stay at your post, what is the worst thing that can happen to you?'

'I don't know. I may not be able to do anything.'

'Is that the worst thing that can happen?'

Butros was angry: 'No, they could kill me. Then it's really over.'

Andrew paused for a beat before saying, 'Really? It's over? The worst thing that could happen is you are killed serving God in your home country?'

'Actually, it would be worse if they killed my wife or children.'

'If that happens, then what?'

'Then what? What do you mean?'

'If you are killed or your wife or your children, what happens then?'

'The work dies.'

'Does it? Are there no others that God can raise up and use? And what about you and your family? Why have you served God so faithfully? If they do kill you, what have you lost?'

The light went on. 'If they kill me, I'll be with the Lord!' For the first time in days, Butros smiled. 'Nadira and I have talked about how we long some day to hear the words of our Lord: "Well done, good and faithful servants."'

Brother Andrew sat back in his chair. There was no need for him to say more. Butros's mind was focused in the right direction. There was a long way to go, but the healing had begun.

—◦✧◦—

That evening as the sun began to set, Butros sat for a long time on a park bench and stared at the sea. The children were gone, probably exhausted from a day of play in sun and sand, but some older men had swum into the surf and were bobbing up and down in the water as they talked. Mesmerised by the scene, it was easy to let his mind linger in neutral.

Finally, he rose and headed east along the palm tree-lined promenade. He passed by a marina and a bust of the Greek General Kimon, who had driven out the Persians from this area 450 years before the birth of Christ. He continued along the beach towards the old Larnaca Fort, built by the Turks in 1625. Across the street from the fort, he could make out the sixteenth-century mosque, which reminded him he needed to process the many thoughts running through his mind.

Brother Andrew had reminded him of another time, riding on a train through the lush farmland of England, with God speaking to his heart and mind. That ride, the encounter with a Muslim evangelist, and the letter from Brother Andrew had shoved him into an adventure, a work he hadn't planned for but had found rewarding and, he had to admit, productive.

But what now? Was this work finished? Was it time to move on to another country and a new assignment? Maybe he should fly to London and renew the contacts he'd made during university days. Surely he could find work in one of the mission agencies there. Or he could pursue a doctorate degree, something he'd thought about doing for some time. *Lord, what would You have me to do?*

His mind went to the Great Commission. *Go and make disciples of all nations.* Brother Andrew had reminded him, 'God said to go. He didn't promise that you would come back.' Okay, he was coming to grips with the possibility that this assignment might cost him his life. So he would not leave his post until or unless God released him from that assignment.

Still, how would he know when the work was over? If ever circumstances demonstrated that a work was finished, wasn't this it? What was he going back to? *In this world you will have trouble. But take heart! I have overcome the world.* Again the Holy Spirit was speaking to him, this time reminding him of the words of Jesus on the night before He was crucified.

And here was the problem. He was concentrating on the first half of the promise – *you will have trouble*. There was no question about that. However, the second half of the promise needed more of his focus. Did he really believe that Jesus has *overcome the world*? Did he believe that Jesus was greater than the spirit of Islam and Muslim extremism? Did he believe that Jesus could resurrect His work that the devil had tried to destroy? Did he really believe that the church was worth fighting for, worth strengthening, that a strong church was the hope for his nation? Did he really believe that those Muslims who had risked their lives to declare their love for Jesus were part of the body of Christ and that Jesus loved them and would protect them?

Jesus had said not to be afraid of those who kill the body but cannot kill the soul. *Are not two sparrows sold for a penny? Yet not one of them will fall to the ground apart from the will of your Father.* Yes, God surely cared for Mustafa and Hassan. He knew what had happened to them. God knew who had murdered these dear brothers, and eventually they would be held to account for their deeds. God also knew Ahmed and, whether he was also martyred or lived many years, this precious brother belonged to God. Likewise, God knew Butros and the number of his days. He remained God's servant, waiting for the next assignment.

The remembrance of Scripture and the application of God's promises were like ointment to his aching soul. He knew now that he *had* to go back. But what was his mission? Had it changed in any way?

Feed My sheep. That was his call – to feed the pastors who laboured faithfully in a country hostile to Christianity, to feed the many who were coming to believe in King Jesus, forming kingdom outposts in villages and towns where Islam had once known no competition, and perhaps most important, to identify and feed the leaders of those little flocks.

'But, Lord, what about Nadira? What about my two children?' Butros was surprised to hear the sound of his own voice. Expressing his prayer this way jarred him back to the biggest struggle he faced. It was one thing for him to go into hostile territory and possibly give his life in service for his Lord Jesus, but did that mean he should endanger the lives of his family as well? A good question. He waited for the Spirit to speak, but this time he heard no reply.

—◦◦◦—

The next day the two friends walked through the streets past the ancient bazaar to the Church of St Lazarus, where supposedly the remains of the man Jesus raised from the dead were housed until 901 AD, when they were moved to Constantinople. According to local legend, Lazarus had come here after the death and resurrection of Jesus and had become bishop of the church in Cyprus until his second death. As they gazed at the building, more than eleven hundred years old, with the Latinate belfry added during a seventeenth-century renovation, Butros told his mentor that he'd just received word that Ahmed would leave the country within forty-eight hours. He would fly to Larnaca and meet Butros. 'Would you meet us, Brother Andrew?'

'Of course, I'd love to. But how is he able to leave the country, and what about coming through immigration here?'

'Kareem is providing him with a special document. I don't know the exact details, but it is guaranteed to let him into Cyprus. However, he can't stay here for long – maybe sixty days at the most. So we need a long-term solution.'

'What about Salima?" '

'The government won't let her leave the country until the investigation is completed.'

'How long will that take?'

'The police believe Salima will lead them to Ahmed. But she really doesn't know where he is. After a few weeks, they will relax their control over Salima, and Kareem thinks he can find a way for her to leave the country as well.'

'When they're out, then what?'

'I wanted to ask you that question. Is there any place you know that would take him? Holland or some other European country? Or even in North America?'

'It's possible.' Andrew hesitated. 'There are a number of groups that handle such situations. I can check with some friends. Would they be asking for refugee status?'

'I don't know if that's best.'

'Probably not. They'd have to seek asylum.'

'And if it becomes known that Ahmed is being investigated for murder . . .'

'Exactly – they'd expel him.'

The two men went into the ancient church and silently observed the eclectic mix of Byzantine, Romanesque and Gothic styles. Three small domes were supported by four pillars. From one pillar a three-hundred-year-old pulpit hung. On another was a famous icon of Lazarus emerging from his tomb.

As they left the building, Andrew said, 'I wonder if moving to the West is best for Ahmed.'

'Why do you say that?'

'He's Arab. He doesn't speak English.'

'He's smart. He learns fast.'

As the two strolled along through the old streets of the Turkish quarter, Andrew said to Butros, 'Actually, my concern is deeper. I want to ask you to think about something that's very challenging. Jesus said, "Unless a kernel of wheat falls to the ground and dies, it remains only a single seed."'

Butros completed the verse: 'But if it dies, it produces many seeds.'

'Duty before self-preservation – that is a very important principle in Scripture. Do you remember when David confronted Goliath? He said that when a lion or bear attacked his father's sheep, he went after it and killed it and rescued the sheep. Now to our thinking, we can't imagine a father allowing his son to be put in such danger, but that wasn't Jesse's attitude nor David's. Duty before self-preservation. Both father and son expected that David would do his duty to save the sheep. The heavenly Father had the same attitude toward Jesus.'

Butros thought about Andrew's words. He mentioned how he had taught Ahmed, Mustafa and Hassan from Philippians 2 to have the same attitude as that of Christ. 'He humbled Himself and became obedient to death.'

'It is natural that we want to rescue those who are suffering for Christ,' Andrew continued. 'But I wonder, is that what God calls us to do?'

'I couldn't rescue Mustafa and Hassan, but I can help Ahmed. We can't force Ahmed to stay and face certain death.'

Andrew walked several strides before answering. 'You are right. That is not for us to decide. We need to ask Ahmed what he feels called to do.'

Butros changed the subject. 'Last night I was thinking about the Muslim believers. We don't have many strong leaders, and we have lost three of them. I think we need to identify a dozen or more men from the MBBs around the country – maybe as many as twenty – and call them to be shepherds and train them in the Bible. I'd like to teach them one week out of each month. Perhaps at the Logos Training Centre, if it's safe, or else at various locations around the country. I wondered what you thought of this.'

'Butros, that is a good vision.' Andrew stopped and grabbed his friend by the shoulders. 'I see God is healing you. You are going back!'

'Yes, Brother Andrew. I have no choice. I must go back.'

The room in the hotel had a spectacular view of the beach and the Mediterranean Sea. But Ahmed had no interest in the view. He paced the room, wanting to know what had happened to his life, and when he could see Salima.

Butros tried to calm the agitated man. 'Ahmed, we need to be patient. We're working on a solution.'

'It's easy for you to be patient. It's not your life that's being uprooted.'

Butros couldn't help but smile, thinking about the struggle he'd had the past few weeks, and especially the lonely battle with God about his own future. But this was one of the Lord's sheep and he was scared. 'Have you talked to your wife?' he asked.

'Not since you deserted me and left the country. I don't dare call her on my mobile phone.'

'You can call her on my phone. But don't . . .'

'Don't tell her where I am. I know. She's frantic with worry, intimidated by the police, unable to stay in her own home. And she can't see me, doesn't even know where I am.'

'I'm sorry, Ahmed. I really am. But my contact said it had to be this way.'

'Who is this contact?'

'A friend of yours very high in the government.'

'I don't have any friends in government.'

'None that you know personally. But you have a brother in Christ who is helping you. And I can never tell you who he is.'

Ahmed wasn't happy with that but, as he continued to pace, he asked, 'So what's next? I mean this hotel room is nice, but it's not home. Is it really not possible for me to go home?'

'I'm afraid not. At least not for a long time. We're now convinced that the Muslim Brotherhood wanted to kill all three of you. And some of the local police are supportive – they'll kill you or allow you to be killed.'

Brother Andrew outlined one option for Ahmed while Butros translated. 'There is a group in Canada that has identified a businessman who will sponsor you. He will provide you with a flat and a job. He said, if you're interested, once you learn English, you can continue your college education and maybe go to Bible school or seminary.'

Ahmed listened carefully, then announced. 'I'm not moving to Canada. I'm not going to Europe or North America or anywhere else in the world.' He stopped pacing and looked at the two men. 'Brother Andrew, I really do appreciate all that you have done for me. You have encouraged me. I remember how Mustafa was so excited when you talked with us after we got out of prison. Do you remember how he said he wanted to go on the *hajj* and witness for Jesus?'

Andrew smiled and said, 'He was enthusiastic. Do you think he would really have done it?'

'He talked about it all the time. He was making plans. That was his dream. And Brother Andrew, that dream of his *will* be fulfilled.' He stared into Andrew's eyes. 'I don't know how many years it will take to make it happen, but I'm going in his place.'

Butros and Andrew were stunned. 'Is that really practical?' said Butros.

Ahmed stared at his mentor. 'No, it's not practical, but Brother Andrew said to us, "Tell me where you cannot go as a Christian, and I will tell you how you can get in." You remember saying that?'

Andrew laughed. 'Of course. I've challenged many people with that statement. But you remember the other half of what I say?'

'Yes. "I may not be able to tell you how to get out." God told us to go. He didn't promise that we would come back.'

Butros could barely control his emotions as he said, 'My brother, you challenge me. For those are the very ideas God gave me, convincing me I must not give up and that I must continue my work.'

'So you understand what I feel. Look, I know you want to help me and it makes sense for me to go somewhere that's safe. And I'm sure God can use me in Canada or Europe or wherever.'

He stopped, walked to the big picture window, stared out for a few moments, and continued. 'But I'm Arab. I speak Arabic. I'm a Muslim who loves Jesus.' He turned around and faced his two friends. 'These are my people. I want to reach Muslims for Jesus. I *need* to stay in the Middle East.'

Andrew and Butros looked at each other to be sure they were in agreement. Then Butros spoke: 'Clearly this is where you belong. I don't know how we'll do this, but we will find a way for you to live and work in the Middle East.'

25

Six months later

A noise woke Abuna Alexander. It took him a moment to realise that someone was knocking on his front door. He threw on a robe and hurried downstairs. He peered out of the window and saw a woman holding what looked like a small package. And he heard her speaking, softly, for fear of drawing attention from neighbours.

'Abuna Alexander, please, can you let me in?'

Quickly he unlocked the door, and Layla stumbled into the room. From the bundle she carried came a sound – the cry of a baby.

The story emerged slowly. Nour helped Layla settle the baby in the room where Salima had lived while in hiding. Then they talked until daybreak. Layla started from the day of her abduction. Initially she didn't know who the kidnappers were, but gradually it had emerged that there was a distant cousin who was attracted to her, and after the conversion of her uncle to Islam, he had become increasingly interested in having Layla for himself.

'At first they tried to be nice, to have me say the *shahada* willingly, but of course, I refused.' Layla's words spilled out, as though the pressure had built up and suddenly the cap was off and her emotions overflowed. 'They locked me in a shed. They beat me. They made me work as a slave – I was forced to get up as soon as the rooster crowed and often I didn't get to sleep until midnight.'

Tears spilled frequently and the priest's wife provided comfort for the frightened girl who had grown into a young woman during her years of abduction.

'One day they were very impatient; they dragged me to a mosque and told me to say the *shahada*. They promised to kill me if I resisted. Abuna, will God ever forgive me? He knows that I didn't mean those words. I didn't really become a Muslim.'

'Of course, our Lord forgives you,' the priest assured her.

'Father, they told me that once I said the words, I was always a Muslim and could never go back.'

'You didn't mean it in your heart,' said the priest.

'They told me I could be killed for blasphemy if I ever went back.'

The priest raised the intensity of his voice as he said, 'Layla, they are intimidating you. Our Lord Jesus is stronger than their threats. Do not listen to their lies. You belong to Jesus!'

Layla thought about these words and seemed to take comfort. She continued her story: 'My father and mother came to see me and I so much wanted to tell them the truth. But the boy was right behind me and he had a knife and he promised he would kill me if I didn't say exactly what he told me to say, that I was a Muslim and I was happy. Oh, Father, it was horrible!'

The priest asked about the baby.

'After my family left, those people decided to move me to another farm. The boy who had kidnapped me was tired of me now, and he "gave" me to a friend. He told me that Abdul-Qawi was now my husband and he would beat me if I didn't obey him.' She wept as she told about the brutal way he came upon her every night. She dreaded the evenings. At least during the days, even though she had to work hard, she could lose herself in her work. But at night she thought of her family and endured the horrors of her attacker. Even after she realised that she was pregnant, her nightmare didn't end. She was never allowed to let up in her work, and she often had to do her chores while sick. And when the contractions began, she had the baby on a couch in the family farmhouse. Of course, her 'husband' was very proud to have a son and considered him a Muslim.

'Abuna Alexander, I will never let my baby be a Muslim. Never! I don't care what anyone says. Every day I pray for him. I've tried to remember all that you had us read in the Bible and I told the child the stories of Jesus, whatever I could remember. Of course, I know he's too young to understand, but I won't let him be forced to believe that awful religion. I won't!'

'How did you escape?' the priest asked.

'They locked me in my room every night. I always checked the door, and three nights ago Abdul-Qawi was away and his sister didn't lock the door. I took the baby and ran into the field. I've been hiding during the day and moving around after dark. It's a miracle I wasn't caught.'

'We are so glad you have come home,' said Alexander. 'We have prayed every day for you.'

'What is the child's name?' Nour asked.

'His father calls him Abdul-Azim, but I call him Alexander.'

Abuna Alexander trembled as he stood in front of the packed sanctuary. This was the third parish meeting since he had discovered Mustafa's body, with the threatening note, in front of the building. There were even more people here than at the first two meetings – in a quick visual survey of the assembly, he thought every family in the parish was represented. He noted with satisfaction that more than twenty of the teenagers were sitting in a group in one corner of the room. Layla was in their midst, and her friend Fanziah was hugging her while another girl held baby Alexander. He also noted Layla's family on the other side of the aisle, her mother wiping her eyes with a handkerchief, her oldest brother sitting with arms folded and a furious scowl.

Layla had hesitated to go home to her family – she was afraid of their reaction, especially her brother when he learned about the baby. So the priest had called and asked Layla's parents to come to his home and he had exhorted them to embrace their daughter.

'Please don't focus on the honour and shame of your family, but rather on the fact that your daughter was captured by agents of the devil. She is now free. She needs healing and she desperately needs your love.'

The father had wondered about the reactions of his extended family if he allowed her back into their home, so the priest and his wife had offered to care for Layla and her child for a period of time until something better could be worked out.

The anger in the church sanctuary was palpable. Clearly the congregation had reached breaking point, and many of the men almost seemed to want an excuse to attack the Muslims. The priest prayed that God would give him words to somehow defuse the anger.

'They have threatened to destroy our church.' One of the parish council members was speaking. 'They steal our daughters. They burn our shops. It's time for us to take a stand. We must not let them push us around any more. The government will not support us. The police will not defend us. We must stand up for ourselves.'

'Is this how Christ has taught us to respond to persecution?' Alexander asked.

But it was as though no one had heard him.

Another businessman stood. 'I have talked with other Christians in town. They agree that we must stand together. We need to make a statement. I propose that we all gather here on Friday at noon and demonstrate outside the main mosque.'

One voice protested: 'That's during Friday prayers. We'll be in the streets when they come out of the mosque.'

'Exactly. Everyone will know we mean business.'

'But what if they attack us?' said a voice from the back of the church.

'Then we fight back,' said the parish council member.

'We have guns too,' shouted one of the men.

'No!' shouted the priest. Everyone grew quiet. 'That is *not* how we will respond. We ought not to lower ourselves to their standards. We are Christians. We should be different.'

'We can't let them intimidate us,' said the council member.

'And we won't,' Alexander answered, 'but neither will we send a message of hate. I know we're all scared. We're angry, and that's understandable. But if we react with guns and violence, we are no better than the fanatics of the Muslim Brotherhood. There is another way, a better way.'

The parish council member sat down and everyone waited intently for the priest's alternative.

'As you know, for two years now we have had a prayer meeting every week involving people from every church in town. I have talked with my fellow ministers about this situation. We propose to call a special assembly. We will erect a tent and invite all Christians to come. And we will also invite Muslims to attend. And we will tell them that we forgive them . . .'

There was an eruption of voices in protest. Finally, one man gained the floor and said, 'How can we forgive? People have died. Our shops have been destroyed. They rape our daughters and threaten to destroy this building. How can you speak of forgiveness?'

Alexander felt a surge of energy as he answered, 'Because of Christ in us, the hope of glory.'

The protestor reluctantly sat down.

'Why do we gather here on Sundays? Why do we celebrate Eucharist? Because we are forgiven. Most Muslims know nothing about forgiveness. We are not going to seek revenge, because our neighbours need to be shown the love of Christ.'

One woman raised her hand meekly, and Alexander nodded for her to speak. 'Father, we're afraid,' she said.

'Of course you are, sister,' the priest said gently. 'We are all afraid. But what is the promise God gives us? Perfect love casts out all fear. Brothers and sisters of St Mark's Church, we must demonstrate to the Muslims in Suq al Khamis the love of Christ. That is our only answer.'

26

Six months later

Ahmed checked his watch. It was after 1 a.m. – still a lot of time left. This was prime time for talking about spiritual things with seekers from all over the Muslim world. Ahmed redoubled his attention on the screen of his laptop computer and pounded away at the keyboard. He was in a chat room enjoying a lively discussion with four Arabs. This was an ongoing conversation. Over the last three months, they had discussed the Bible versus Quran, the claims of Muhammad versus the claims of Jesus, the issues of Christian lifestyle, and much more.

Butros had worked hard to find a job for Ahmed and succeeded by making an arrangement with the Bible Forum. As their employee, he was able to obtain a residency permit in this Middle Eastern country, and the Forum had helped him and Salima locate a flat in a high-rise building near the centre of this large city. They had joined a Protestant church – since they were unknown here, there was no problem caused by their Muslim background in this congregation. In fact few in the Christian community knew their story.

But Ahmed hadn't lost his heart for Muslims and he hoped soon to start an MBB gathering. After work at the society he usually stopped at a café to seek conversation with young Muslim men, and he often didn't get home until 9 p.m. for dinner. His outreach had yielded some fruit, as several men were interested in talking about Isa. After dinner it was on to the computer for more evangelism online.

Ahmed hadn't given up hope of returning home to encourage the growing MBB church in his country. He missed Suq al Khamis, but he realised he might never see his home town again. His sister, Farah, stayed in touch via email – they used a special account with disguised names just in case the *Mukhabarat* was snooping. They agreed it was too dangerous to talk by phone. Shortly after the murder of Mustafa and Hassan, their father had passed away. That had been hard. How Ahmed had longed for one more talk with his father, one more opportunity to help him see the truth about Jesus. But his father had rejected all such discussions, and Ahmed tried to comfort himself with the hope that somehow his life and words and those of his sister and others in the extended family had caused his father to have a change of heart even on his deathbed.

It was on the computer that Ahmed found his greatest joy. On an Arab website that provided Christian resources for Muslims, Ahmed talked with people all over the Arab world. He kept a running list of countries where he had contacts and it now numbered more than twenty, including Saudi Arabia. Yes, even in the heartland of Islam, a country where the practice of Christianity was absolutely forbidden, there were numerous seekers and many secret followers of Jesus. Clearly the Holy Spirit was not restricted by borders and the restraining policies of the Wahhabi *matawain*, the religious police who vigorously enforced Sharia law. There were even Christians in Medina and Mecca, Islam's two holiest cities where supposedly no infidel was allowed to set foot. It renewed his intention to someday go on the hajj, to fulfil the dream of Mustafa, who wanted to witness for Jesus to the pilgrims. He would do that and he would seek for his brothers in those two cities.

There was only one problem for Ahmed, who was living out his dream of witnessing for Jesus. While he was thriving in Christian ministry, his wife was lonely and struggling to adjust to a new country and a new home. Many nights after dinner he had tried to comfort her, but she seemed to be drifting further away, into a dark region that he couldn't reach. It troubled him when he thought about it, but then he was distracted by yet another person entering the chat room, eager to talk about the claims of the Prophet Isa.

———≈———

Salima was curled up in bed. She longed for her husband to join her but she heard him tapping away on the computer and knew it would be at least a couple of more hours – he rarely came to bed before 3 a.m. Quietly she wept; she didn't try to hold back the tears. In the last month she'd cried herself to sleep most nights, and Ahmed didn't seem to notice. She knew she should be happy. Her husband was alive and he did a wonderful work for God. Many people were interested in Isa, and Ahmed never lacked for people to talk with in the coffee shops or on the Internet. But that left him little time for her. And he was all she had.

Often she thought of home, her parents and brothers and sisters. They'd had a wonderful family. There had been servants to meet her every need and Daddy brought home books from his travels for her to read. She had girlfriends who enjoyed shopping with her. Why had she given that up? Now there was very little money and no friends, and they were living in a foreign country where people spoke Arabic with a different accent. For what? For Jesus? She hadn't meant to give up so much. If she'd known . . . Of course, she had fallen in love with Jesus, but why did she have to give up everything she loved for Him?

She'd begged Ahmed for permission to call home; if only she could hear her mother's voice and see if there was any chance of reconciliation. But her husband had said it was not safe. 'We'll be discovered and forced to come home,' he protested. Salima had suggested she call from a public phone, but Ahmed said that would still betray where they lived.

A couple of times Ahmed had preached to her about trusting God and quoted Bible verses, but that only made her angry. He didn't know what she was feeling nor was he trying to understand. He had suggested that she take a computer course and then she could help him or get a job of her own. They'd had an argument about that. Salima felt her husband wanted to put a sticking plaster on her problems, so he could get on with life.

How she longed for someone to talk to, someone who understood her story and the pain of her losses! But there was no one. She had made no friends at church and she was afraid to tell anyone about her background.

After all, look what had happened to Mustafa and Hassan in Suq al Khamis. No, at all costs she felt she had to keep her story a secret.

The one person she could talk to was Jesus, and she did that often. But He didn't have flesh and blood. She couldn't hug Him and cry on His shoulder. What good was giving up everything for someone she couldn't see or hear? This was agony, and she felt her spirit slipping deeper into a darkness she'd never known. She was frightened of the depths to which she'd descended, and yet she saw no way of escape. Was there any hope?

All she could do was breathe a prayer: *Jesus, are You there? Is there any hope for me?*

—◦∾◦—

Abuna Alexander was talking in the market with one of his parishioners when a prominent businessman approached him. He stopped and they exchanged greetings.

'I wanted to tell you that the meeting you organised was very much appreciated by the community,' said the sheikh.

'Shukran. Thank you for coming and supporting us.'

The sheikh leaned forward, almost touching the priest. 'You know, not all of us Muslims agree with the fanaticism of the Muslim Brotherhood.'

'I understand.'

'In fact I was hoping to run into you sometime. I have a question for you.'

Alexander had to listen carefully as the businessman was speaking softly so as not to be overheard.

'You gave a speech at the meeting,' he said. 'You spoke about forgiveness. I have never heard such a message, and I was wondering . . . he looked both ways and said in a whisper, 'Could you give me something in printed form about the Prophet Isa? I would like to know more about this Prophet who forgives.'

After their brief conversation, the sheikh went on his way.

The parishioner looked at Alexander with a stunned expression. 'I never expected . . .'

'That a Muslim would be interested in our Good News?' The priest chuckled at the situation. 'It's the love of Christ. That's the hope for Suq al Khamis.'

—⁓—

Nadir and Samir looked around the Logos Training Centre grounds as Butros came out of the building to welcome them. At that moment a *muezzin* began his call to prayer from the mosque built right against the wall opposite the building. 'They put it up last year,' Butros explained, noticing the questioning looks.

'There are no homes around here, just fields,' Nadir observed.

'Exactly. But when I asked, they told me that a mosque was needed for the workers in the field. They explained that according to Islamic doctrine, every Muslim had to be within listening distance of a mosque.'

'But right against your property?'

'They apologised – but they said this way they weren't losing much in the way of crops. The placement was most efficient.' Butros shook his head in amazement. 'Of course, they've managed without a mosque in these fields for hundreds of years.'

'Look at the loudspeakers,' Samir said. 'They all point at you, at this property.'

'That's right. And sometimes they crank up the volume extra loud when we have a meeting. It's all for the purpose of intimidation.'

'To drive you away?'

Butros laughed. 'They're trying. But this is where God has planted us.'

The three men walked along the wall for a few moments before Butros said, 'Thank you for coming today. I have a very important question to ask both of you. I have identified several men who I believe can lead the MBB communities. I would like each of you to be trained for this ministry.'

Nadir nodded, almost as though he'd expected this invitation. In fact he sensed that God was prompting him to greater service for the kingdom. 'I deeply miss Ahmed and Mustafa and Hassan,' he said. Butros smiled his sad agreement. 'But the work they began must not die. We have continued to meet, but frankly we're lost without them.'

'Like sheep without a shepherd?'

'Yes, exactly.'

'Nadir, I want to train you to be a shepherd. It is an honourable calling and I believe God has His hand on you to do it.'

'What would be required?' Samir asked.

'I will meet with you and a dozen others like you. We will meet for five consecutive days each month to study Bible, theology and ministry. I will also bring instructors for special classes on such things as discipleship, Christian family life and other subjects you need to know.'

'I would very much like to learn these subjects,' Samir said. He walked on for a moment, then asked, 'What about the NGO?'

'We had to stop it for a while. You understand.'

Nadir and Samir nodded.

'Would you like to continue that work?'

'Yes, very much,' said Samir.

'We need it,' Nadir said. He hesitated, before adding, 'I want to finish the work that my friend Ahmed started.'

'Good. I will train you both.'

—∾∾∾—

Butros and Nadira took a stroll around the grounds later that evening. It had become their habit after their children were asleep. It was a time for them to talk about the day, to pray together and to dream about the future. Recently they had decided to make the Logos Centre their home. Butros enjoyed the peaceful country compared to the constant noise of the city – except of course when the mosque by the wall decided to crank up the volume of its loudspeakers. Still, he worried about his family's safety. Twice his family had fled to the home of Nadira's parents, and he still wondered if she was comfortable living here, with the constant threats. 'So, how is my wife feeling, here at this centre?' he asked as the sun set, causing a colourful show of red and orange produced by the dust from the desert beyond the farm fields.

'I am fine, my dear husband. It is good to have our family together. Wherever you are is my home.'

Butros loved the way Nadira expressed her affection for him. It made him want to be all the more protective. 'You no longer seem afraid. Are you just hiding it better?' he asked.

'I prayed a lot while we were apart. God has made it clear that we belong to Him.' She waved her hand over the property where they were walking. 'And this land belongs to Him. This work we're in is His work. Butros, did you really envision this fruit, what we've seen happen, when we were married?'

'No, I can't say I really knew what God was going to do. I just knew He had called me.'

'And He called me to be your helper. He called both of us to ministry. Do you remember when we prayed over this land with Brother Andrew?'

'Oh yes.'

'I've been thinking about the next phase of this campus.'

'And what do you think that should be?'

'I would like us to build a women's centre.'

'You may be right. I've been thinking about what we should do next here. Why do you think a women's centre should be the priority?'

'Remember when Abuna Alexander told us about the girl in his church?' Nadira's eyes watered, and she hesitated before saying, 'There are too many girls, Christian girls, Christian women, who are suffering in this country. Some have been kidnapped and terribly abused. But even Christian families, many of them don't know how to have a Christian marriage or family.' Nadira grabbed her husband's hand. 'Like we do. Too many Christian men think just like Muslims when it comes to their women.'

'Of course, there are good as well as bad marriages among Muslims.'

'Yes, that is true. But there should be something special, something different for committed Christian couples. So one of the things I want to do is help Christian women be godly wives.'

'Like Paul instructed Titus, that older women should teach younger women to love their husbands and children.'

'Actually, women tend to do that naturally, at least initially. But when they live under constant verbal and physical abuse, they come to believe that they have no worth. It's hard for them to believe that God really and truly loves them. And so they begin to live in fear of their husbands rather than believing they are given to their family out of love.'

'I believe men need to learn how to love their wives sacrificially, as Christ loves us. That is one of the areas I plan to teach the men who will become shepherds of the MBB gatherings.'

'There is more to my dream,' Nadira added. 'For those who have suffered abuse, they need a place to come, for healing, to be cared for and to be taught the real way of Christ.'

'I like this vision of yours. However, they can't stay here forever. What happens to them after they leave the centre?'

'I have thought of that too. I want this centre to provide vocational training for the women – teaching them skills that will enable them to survive on their own, or in a family, to provide additional income.'

'Of what skills are you thinking?'

'More and more businesses need computer operators. I would like to train women to use computers so they could work in offices or at home, typing documents or spreadsheets.'

'Secretaries.'

'Office workers. The women who are literate could earn a decent living in the city with such skills.'

'This is a good vision. Let's pray and if God continues to lead us, we will draw up a plan for the building and programme and see if we can find funding.'

—⁓—

The ring of the telephone jarred Ahmed out of his intense concentration on the chat room conversation on his computer screen. Quickly he picked up the receiver so that his wife would not awaken. 'What are you doing up so late?' said the cheerful voice on the other end.

'Zaki? It's past midnight in London.'

'And 3 a.m. where you are. I saw you were online.'

'So why didn't you instant message me?'

'Because I need to hear your voice. Why are you up so late?'

'I'm saving the world,' Ahmed responded. 'It's amazing how many Muslims are interested in Isa. And what are you doing calling me at this ridiculous hour?'

'I was thinking of you.'

'Thanks. Say a prayer and go back to bed.'

'How is Salima?'

'Okay. She's asleep.'

'Are you sure?'

'Actually she's been very quiet lately.'

'Take her to the doctor.'

'Why?'

'Listen to your friend Zaki. I'm a trained physician. Your wife is depressed. She needs medical attention.'

'How can you tell?'

'You've been emailing me about your concerns. Trust me, she's depressed and she needs help. She's suffered terrible trauma and too many changes. Think of all she has lost. You must help her.'

'Okay, I will.'

'Most important, she needs your love.'

'So you've become a marriage counsellor?'

'Timothy, you work too hard.'

Ahmed winced. He knew his friend was right. 'So, what do I cut out?'

'You can't save the world by yourself. Today skip the café. Go home after work. Take a walk with Salima. Take her out for dinner. Spend an evening with friends. And you don't have to stay up all night every night.'

'But there are so many people who need to talk. They have so many questions.'

'You aren't the only one who can answer those questions.'

Ahmed sighed. 'I get the point.'

'Do you? You are passionate and that is good. But the most important person in your life is your wife. Please, take care of her.'

Ahmed's mind flashed back to the glorious starlit night on the roof of the flat in Suq al Khamis. 'I will be your rock,' he'd said to his wife. He'd promised to love her. And two days later, he'd made the same promise before God, to lay down his own life for his wife. It was time for him to live out that promise.

'I will slow down and look after her,' Ahmed said. 'In fact, I will start by taking tomorrow off. I'll make her breakfast and spend the day with her.'

'That's a good start.'

'I realise it will take time. I've neglected her and I need to let her know that I'm here for her, that I'll listen to her.' He knew that of all the people God called him to love, Salima had to be first.

Zaki affirmed his friend's resolve to focus on his wife's needs and put her first. He was glad that it hadn't taken much for Ahmed to recognise his failure in this area.

'Now, what about you?' Ahmed asked. 'Have you thought about what I said?'

'I have a great medical practice here in London,' said Zaki.

'Your country needs you.'

'I can do a lot for my country where I am.'

'You can do more if you go home.'

'And suffer like you did? Look what they did to our friends, to you.'

'Go home and take our place.'

'To Suq al Khamis?'

'Yes. You are a doctor. You can witness in ways we never could. There is a community of frightened MBBs who need your leadership.'

'Is this the Holy Spirit talking?'

'If you believe that, then yes, maybe God is speaking through me.'

'Actually, I think He is.'

'Then go home.'

'But I hardly know where to start.'

'There are two men who will help you.'

'Who?'

'One is Brother Andrew. He lives in Holland. Fly to Amsterdam and talk to him. The other is his protégé Butros. Believe me, he can use your help.'

'Now I know why I couldn't sleep.'

'Because I needed a kick in the pants – to take care of my wife.'

'And I needed confirmation that God wants me to go home.'

'Zaki?'

'Yes, Timothy.'

'I never thanked you.'

'For what?'

Ahmed suddenly felt a surge of emotion and found himself momentarily unable to speak. He thought back to his youth, to the terrifying dreams of judgement, to the questions that had tormented him, and to the fact that his friend took a huge risk to point him toward the Bible and Jesus. That had started him on a journey, one that had landed him in jail and almost killed him, but that had also brought him more joy than he ever thought possible. 'Zaki, hold on just a moment.'

Ahmed stepped across the room and grabbed his notebook, the one in which he recorded his poetry and thoughts from Scripture. 'Listen to this,' he said back on the phone. 'There is no escape from a better life, an abundant life and full freedom. There is no escape from the revolution – the revolution of love. And there is no escape from God – God in the fullest sense of the word. A God who loves His creatures, all of them. A God who has mercy. A God who heals. A God who liberates. A God who is just. There is no escape from a God with flesh and bones. We need a real person, a real Father, someone who is really holy, someone who really loves. There is no escape from a real God. There is no escape from Jesus Christ. There is no God like Him. He created us, loves us with a passion, and longs for the same from us in return.

'That is what I want to thank you for; for introducing me to the God from whom I cannot escape, from whom I never ever *want* to escape.'

Part 2

HOW SHALL WE RESPOND?

The Binding

They had buckled his bomb-
belt. Thought it was their duty,
headed for the place.
Halfway he said, 'I don't want to die.'
Stuck to it. They turned
to the road on which they had come.
Ishmael who spared himself,
and Isaac.
With shocked relief his parents saw
him back safe from the height of Moriah's
mount. Held him, and kept him closely watched.
They wait for the God of Abraham
to provide a sacrifice.

Pem Sluijter

Prologue

How do you feel after reading about your brothers and sisters in the Islamic world? Excited about what God is doing? Worried about the ongoing situation and how Butros and Nadira, and Ahmed and Salima, and Layla and Abuna Alexander will do in the coming years? Both responses are appropriate. I hope also that you want to get personally involved. At the minimum I hope you are willing to pray for these people, realising that this story represents thousands of others in similar or worse situations around the world. Maybe you will have the opportunity to encourage some of them with your letters. Surely we can't continue on blithely with life as usual when we learn about a part of the church suffering so severely.

Maybe you're also thinking about the condition of the world these days, and wondering what the role of the church in the West should be. This is a growing concern as more and more Muslims make their home in Europe and North America. I'm concerned that currently the most common reaction to Islam is fear. I see it in public comments by various Christian leaders who malign Islam and the Prophet Muhammad. I see it in the war rhetoric spoken by politicians and military generals. It's expressed in the use of labels like 'Islamofacism' and comparisons of Islamic fundamentalism to the rise of Nazi Germany in the 1930s.

One respected Christian commentator, Gary Bauer, wrote the following on the fifth anniversary of the 9/11 attacks:

Critics . . . are complaining that the Iraq war and the misnamed 'war on terror' have now taken as long as World War II and we haven't won yet.

Perhaps that is because we still haven't started fighting the way we did then – to win. We are still more afraid of ACLU lawsuits and *New York Times* editorials than we are of the enemy who is dedicated to destroying Western civilization.

This war has a long way to go – perhaps a generation. The day five years ago that we are commemorating may not be the worst day we will experience before it is over. Surely more horror lies ahead and more testing before we will know whether we, the heirs of a great civilization, have inherited the courage and resolve to defend it.[1]

Gary raises important questions for us. He is right that we are in a war, but are we fighting the right enemy? Should we *fear* the worldview of Islam? Is the only option to view it as a 'life and death' struggle, as several writers have put it? Didn't the psalmist promise that the one whose heart is trusting in God, 'he will have no fear of bad news' (Ps. 112:7)? Again and again the Scriptures exhort us not to fear, as Paul wrote to Timothy: 'God has not given us a spirit of fear, but of power and of love and of a sound mind' (2 Tim. 1:7 NKJV). 'Do not give way to fear,' said Peter (1 Pet. 3:6). 'Perfect love drives out fear,' stated the apostle John (1 John 4:18).

After reading the story in the first part of this book, I believe you understand better the challenges to the worldwide church that Islam presents. But it would be tragic if all we do is respond with fear and retreat. In these next few pages, I want to suggest what the persecuted church in the Islamic world is saying to Christians in the West. I (Andrew) believe the story you have just read presents us with four challenges: to love all Muslims by giving them the Good News, to forgive when we're attacked, to live lives totally committed to Jesus Christ, and to engage in the real war – the spiritual war.

To set up the first challenge, Al and I need to take you to a secret location on the border between Afghanistan and Pakistan.

1

It was early in 2002, shortly after coalition forces drove the Taliban from power in Afghanistan. Fighting still raged in the region, and a couple of times we heard American bombers fly overhead to targets in the nearby Tora Bora mountains where Al-Qaeda leaders were hiding. We travelled to this meeting in an SUV through a narrow, winding mountain pass. Often we had to grab on to the handles above the passenger windows to keep from being thrown about as we bounced over the rocky, uneven ground or swerved to avoid oncoming traffic on a road that was rarely more than a lane-and-a-half wide.

But our travels were easy compared to those of the men and women we met. Several of them had walked all night or endured hours crammed with twenty others in a van that might comfortably seat twelve. They came from Jalalabad and Kunar and Kandahar – rugged areas where the Taliban had arisen, and to which these extreme practitioners of Islam had retreated, thinking they might elude capture for years in the caves of the rugged mountains of Hindu Kush.

On our arrival the men approached us one by one and welcomed us with huge smiles and handshakes, often followed by big hugs. We could smell the sweat on them and knew many hadn't bathed in days. All but two of them had a beard and all wore the traditional *shalwar kameez* – baggy, one-size-fits-all pants and knee-length shirts, usually brown or tan. Some wore jackets or sweaters over the shirts to ward off the cold mountain air. One old man was wrapped in a rough, brown woollen cloak. Several also wore distinctive tribal hats, a rough, brown woollen *chitrali* or a white, knitted *nimazi*. Staying back in a dark corner were two women, both completely covered in their *burkas*. Our host didn't introduce them but said they were wives of two of the men.

There was no electricity in the house where we assembled, and blankets covered the windows to prevent unwanted observation. Apart from a little sunlight leaking at the edges of the window coverings, candles provided the light. As I looked at the men around me, I couldn't help but wonder what would happen if the CIA suddenly barged into this house. Judging by appearances, all of these men would probably have been carted off to cells in Guantánamo Bay, Cuba, but only because soldiers look at outward appearances. God looks at hearts, and He allowed us to get a glimpse of what He saw. For the next few hours, we were transported into a world few have experienced, and in the process we became convinced that there is a genuine Christian solution to the scourge of terrorism.

We started our meeting with singing. This was Pashtun territory where tribes from the dominant people group of Afghanistan lived. These men were memorising and singing Psalms in Pashto, and the song leader was a former mullah with a hauntingly beautiful chanting voice. His face radiated joy, and once he spoke to us in broken English – 'I want to be a mullah for Jesus!'

Naturally we needed an interpreter to translate into English, so it took a while to learn their stories. The first man to speak was Alef.[2] He had a receding hairline and, instead of the traditional Afghan beard, he sported a droopy mustache. He explained that under the Taliban, all men were required to wear beards, and that enforcers would accost them in the street and measure their beard. Alef held up his fist to indicate that a passing grade was a fist full of chin hair. Often those who failed the test were beaten. He had shaved his beard after the fall of the Taliban.

Until he became a refugee, Alef was a farmer and his cash crop was opium. He also raised barley and vegetables, but he admitted sheepishly that the only way to support his family was to grow poppies from which opium is produced – it's a tragic fact that today 90 per cent of the world's opium supply comes from Afghanistan.[3] He survived during the war with the Soviet Union in the 1980s, but the subsequent civil war drove him and others south to the refugee camps surrounding Peshawar. At the time of the invasion of coalition forces in 2001, some three million Afghans lived in northern Pakistan, on the edge of the tribal territories. Alef lived there for nine years. Many like him learned about Jesus in those camps.

Alef was a student of literature and loved to listen to news on the radio. One day he found a new channel and heard an announcer speak about Jesus Christ being like a shepherd. He contacted the people who produced the programme and acquired some Christian literature in Pashto. 'I read about the miracles of our Lord Jesus Christ,' he told us proudly. 'He raised the dead. He gave sight to the blind. He walked on water. When I looked at the miracles, I said, "There is no *man* who can do these things." These are divine characteristics.'

He described the changes in his life as entering into another world – perhaps not unlike the feeling I as a Dutchman felt entering into the Afghan culture.

'I lost the fear of death,' Alef said.

Naturally he wanted to tell those closest to him about the transformation, but he was shrewd. He told his wife he had found a new book but didn't tell her what it was. He started reading stories to her from the Gospels. Gradually his wife responded and wanted to know what book he was reading. In time she joined him in his new journey, following Jesus.

Like all the Pashtun men in the room, Alef had been a devout Muslim, but he insists he had no choice. 'Unless you have a choice, you can't choose. Then I was given the other option, and I chose the right one.' And now Alef was spreading the Word. Proudly he took out a piece of paper. On it were sixty names. 'These are the people I am discipling,' he said.

As soon as Alef finished his story, others wanted to tell us about their spiritual journeys. Geem told about a dream he had. There was a large pond and Geem was trapped in the middle of it, unable to swim to shore. A man dressed in white and riding a white horse galloped up, reached out, grabbed Geem's hand, and pulled him to safety.

'Why did you rescue me?' Geem asked the man.

The rider in white replied, 'I wanted to save you and I've saved you.'

But who was the rider? Geem pressed the man to reveal his identity. Finally, the rider announced that He was Jesus Christ.

Bea was a burly man with a thick black and grey beard. He was a secondary-school teacher, and told about living through the civil war and his growing disgust at the atrocities committed by Muslims against fellow Muslims. 'Thievery, adultery, stealing, corruption – this was taking place all around me,' Bea said. He determined to make a comparative study of other religions and in the process learned about Jesus. But he didn't understand the significance of the Prophet Isa until Alef visited his village and gave him some books that opened up the truths of the gospel.

When Qaf met his first Christian, he was a boy living in a refugee camp. Apparently his English teacher was a missionary, and Qaf was so impressed by him that he invited the teacher to become a Muslim. The teacher smiled at the student and said, 'You are too young and I can't talk with you now. But I will pray for you that you will read more and make a good choice.' In Peshawar, Qaf discovered a church with a small library that allowed him to read about Christianity. But the more he came to understand the Christian faith, the more curious he became about his own faith. So for several months he studied and faithfully practised Islam. Gradually he grew restless and returned to the church reading room where he met a teacher who could answer his questions and help him understand the Christian faith. 'I now disciple others,' he announced proudly, 'and eighteen people have come to know the Lord.'

But there was also a sad element to his report. His father-in-law had conspired with Qaf's father to take away his wife and three children. His family was being forced to live with his wife's father until Qaf returned to Islam.

'I haven't seen them now for the last two months,' he said.

Then there was Sheen, a short, sinewy man who wore a black *shalwar kameez*. His testimony was simple yet elegant: 'There is a way of peace and that's the way of Jesus.' Sheen knew the mountain passes like we know the streets in our neighbourhood, and for years he transported guns on mule trains via treacherous trails from Pakistan to the *mujahideen* in the Jalalabad area. With loads of opium he retraced his route back into Pakistan. Today he smuggled a very different sort of contraband – Christian books and Bibles. Avoiding border stations and checkpoints, he spent up to two weeks transporting each load of precious cargo. When Al asked if he carried a gun,

Sheen gave him a curious look. Of course he carried guns – a Kalashnikov and a pistol. I could imagine him wearing a bandoleer across his black shirt, with his machine gun slung over a shoulder, as he led his mules and kept alert for a possible ambush that might endanger his mission.

Though he couldn't read what he smuggled – like more than half of all Afghans, he was illiterate – he had spent seven months in prison after he was caught with a load of New Testaments. He didn't understand why the authorities would be upset with him. What did they prefer – for him to transport good books, or guns and drugs?

'There is a dignity and respect of human life in the Christian faith,' he said. 'That has brought great consolation and peace to me. In this faith I am not ignored or neglected, but God is interested in me.'

A voice spoke from behind one of the *burkas*, and we were told that one of the wives was requesting prayer. Kaf, her husband, explained they had been married for nine years and had no children. I asked the woman if she would like to tell her testimony. She spoke very softly, saying, 'My husband saw a dream and talked to his brother who told him about this new system. I knew they wouldn't tell me to believe in something wrong.'

I prompted her to talk a little more. She explained that Jesus 'changed my husband's life and his behaviour toward me, his barren wife. I try constantly to please God and not make him angry. But I am barren and of no use.' My heart went out to this woman. I knew it was a very sensitive situation. In this culture a woman's worth and honour were directly tied to the number of her children. I prayed for this couple, asking that God would hear their cry just as He heard the prayer of Hannah, the mother of the Old Testament prophet Samuel. Silently I also prayed that this woman would know the love and comfort of Jesus whether or not God blessed this couple with children.

The primary reason for this meeting was to baptise a dozen men and two of their wives who were the leaders of the developing church in Afghanistan. Before we started the ceremony, I delivered a short message that seemed so appropriate in this setting. My text was 2 Corinthians 5:17: 'If anyone is in Christ, he is a new creation; the old has gone, the new has come!' How I wished everyone could witness the amazing transformation of these people. Each of them lived in a radical Muslim society. They had all endured war and the terrifying rule of perhaps the most fundamentalist, legalistic Islamic sect.

Many had lost everything because of tribal warfare and had lived for years as refugees. But they were all transformed by the gospel.

Alef was a poet and had written a hymn that expressed the transformation of these people. As I listened to Alef and then the rest of the men sing, I experienced so thoroughly the emotion of the chant that I felt I had been transported out of this world into heaven. When they had finished, our translator tried to convey the words of the poem. After hearing the rhythmic beauty of the song in Pashto, the English words seemed somewhat pedantic.

It was a long poem that recalled many of the miracles of Christ. Then it switched direction, praising God for the miracles in their own lives: 'You are the only One, the holy One without sin. Only through You can we experience cleanliness. You became our substitute. You saved us from our sins. Your grace is on us and we experience it. The way You used to love Your disciples on earth, You love us also. The way they loved you, we want to love You too.' The refrain, repeated many times throughout the song, went something like this: 'There is power in You, in Your hands.'

After the baptism service, the man opposite me, who wore a white beard and a white *nimazi*, started talking and waving his right hand.

'What is he saying?' I asked our translator.

The man looked seventy years old, but I knew that he was probably much younger. The average life expectancy of men in Afghanistan was only forty-five years. My interpreter explained, 'He says that he had a stroke a few months ago and his right arm was paralysed. He prayed that when he was baptised God would heal him. He is waving his arm to say that God has healed him.'

This was Nazim, a man who loved learning and shortly after this service returned home to his village and started teaching children to read and write, primarily using stories from the Injil. One morning about two years later, the local mullah, a member of the Taliban, entered Master Nazim's home with others from the local mosque and beat him severely, yelling, 'Why do you teach our children from the Injil and not from the Quran? All they need is Quran.' The mullah threatened to return and kill Nazim if he didn't stop.

When the mullah and his thugs had left, Nazim asked his wife and two children to quickly run and call together family and friends, along with his students. Within a few minutes there were approximately twenty-five people crowded into his home. Despite the pain from his injuries, he gathered the strength to say to the assembly: 'I want to tell you something very important.' He then recounted his journey to faith in the Lord Jesus Christ. He concluded by reading from the Gospels and saying, 'Jesus, by giving His life for us, releases us from the burden of sin and links us with God.' He challenged his listeners to follow Jesus, then he fell over and died.

When that disturbing news reached me, at once the thought flashed through my mind – *unless a grain of wheat falls into the ground and dies, it remains alone. But if it dies, it produces much grain* (John 12:24 NKJV).

Nazim's wife was expelled from the village, but she has relocated to another area where she teaches young women to read and write.

To my knowledge there was no church in the Pashtun area of southern Afghanistan before 2000. As I write today, there are several thousand believers in Jesus in that region. They are the church in Afghanistan. They meet in secret, but they are exuberant in their joy.

Does this story change the way you view Muslims? When you see pictures of large Muslim crowds protesting cartoons of Muhammad in London or Lahore, do you see them as a threat? Or do you see them as a mission field?

The first challenge I want to propose is this:

Challenge 1

Do we view Muslims as enemies? Or are we seeking to win them to Christ?

Is it possible that we are concentrating too much on the threat of Osama bin Laden and Al-Qaeda and other Muslim fundamentalist groups? Perhaps it is time for us to ask if God is working in the hearts of these men.

In the Sermon on the Mount, Jesus challenged the common thinking about how to relate to the soldiers of the Roman occupation (see Matt. 5:38–48). 'You have heard that it was said, "Love your neighbour and hate your enemy." But I tell you: Love your enemies and pray for those who persecute you' (vv. 43–44). Jesus illustrated this with three practical situations. The first was if someone struck you on the cheek, loving your enemy meant turning to him the other cheek. Second, if someone sued for your tunic, you were to give him your cloak as well. And third, if a Roman soldier forced you to carry his pack one mile, you were to go with him two miles.

Now why would Jesus suggest carrying the soldier's heavy burden a second mile in the hot Middle Eastern sun? Because the first mile was compelled by law. But when the victim offered to carry it a second mile, naturally the Roman soldier would want to know why he was willing to carry the pack beyond the legal requirement. That provided the man an opportunity to tell the soldier about Jesus.

Today we walk the first mile by following Jesus. I propose that we walk the second mile by sharing the love of Jesus with Muslims. Jesus said we are to *love* our enemies. To our minds that just doesn't make sense. How can we love someone we hate? But that's the brilliance of this command, for if I decide to love someone, that person cannot remain my enemy. Often I have said that the best way to disarm a terrorist with a gun is to go up and hug him – then you are too close for him to shoot you. If I love someone, surely I will attempt to give him or her the greatest gift imaginable. That means sharing the Good News of the gospel.

The call of the church is to 'go and make disciples' from all peoples and nations (see Matt. 28:18–20). In *Light Force* I told about my outreach to Hezbollah, Hamas and Islamic Jihad. Surely this demonstrates that Muslim fundamentalists are reachable, and anyone who is reachable is winnable.[4] Maybe you have had no opportunity to meet such extremists, but surely there are Muslims in your city. Do you know any? Have you made friends with them? Consider this: you may be the only Jesus they will ever meet.

Some people may object to my statement that I seek to *win* Muslims to Christ. But I point you to the words of the apostle Paul who said, 'Though I am free and belong to no man, I make myself a slave to everyone, to win as many as possible' (1 Cor. 9:19). He goes on to say that to Jews he became like a Jew to *win* Jews. To those under the law he became like one under the law so as to win those under the law. And to those not having the law he became like one not having the law so as to win those not having the law. Finally, to the weak Paul became weak to *win* the weak (vv. 20–22). Paul's passion was to win as many people as possible to Jesus Christ. Shouldn't that be our passion for Muslims?

Please understand that this does *not* mean we force anyone to follow Christ. That is not our responsibility, and we cannot do so anyway, for it is God Himself who draws people to Christ, as we've seen from the testimonies of our Afghan brethren. In centuries past some Christians have attempted to convert people at the point of a sword. That goes against every command of our Lord. It is love that wins people to Christ, never force!

In March 2006 the world seemed to awaken for a moment to the possibility that a Muslim could change his faith when we learned about the case of Abdul Rahman, who was arrested and accused of attacking Islam for the simple reason that he had converted to Christianity sixteen years earlier. If convicted, he would be executed under Afghan/Islamic law. An outcry rose from western countries that had spent billions of dollars and sacrificed hundreds of lives to set Afghanistan free from the draconian rule of the Taliban. This was not the behaviour expected from a freely elected government. The administration of Hamid Karzai needed to find a face-saving solution. It was determined that Rahman was 'insane', and he was released and allowed to slip out of the country and take refuge in Italy.

The world breathed a sigh of relief and moved on to other news, but all was not well. Away from the spotlight, two more Christian converts from Islam were immediately arrested. Another was severely beaten and hospitalised. Several more were subjected to police raids on their homes or intimidated by threatening telephone calls. I wondered how many of these persecuted brothers were ones Al and I had met in that mountain town in the vicinity of Tora Bora.

We really should not have been surprised by what happened to Abdul Rahman. In December 2003 I received a copy of a letter from my Christian brothers in Afghanistan addressed to President George W. Bush, pleading with him to intervene to prevent the confirmation of an Afghan constitution that would impose Islamic law on the nation. I learned later they had fasted and prayed for many days before sending this letter. Please hear their heart as I quote just one section of the letter:

> There was no concept of freedom during the time of Taliban, and after
> the fall of Taliban we thought that with the coming of US there will be

a new constitution that would give freedom to choose religion to every person, which is a basic right of every human being, and Muslims are converting hundreds of Christians and other religion people in to their religion, but when a Muslim is converted to Christianity or other religion, they are threatened, persecuted and killed. Now we have that draft of the new constitution, which is almost the same as the Taliban time.[5]

The letter was sent to a person who had connections with a senior official in the White House who promised that he would get it on the President's desk. Unfortunately that's the last I heard. I could never confirm that the President ever saw or read the letter.

I quote this letter to demonstrate that we in the West need to recognise there are many Muslims who may want to come to Christ if they are given the chance. Are we doing everything in our power to make sure they have that opportunity? Certainly we owe them that much!

2

There is a second challenge that emerges from the church in the Islamic world. It concerns a power Christians are uniquely privileged to use, but one that Muslims don't understand and rarely see. I observed this power several years ago in a village in Pakistan.

As evening prayers were concluding on 5 February 1997, someone tossed a hand-scribbled anti-Islamic slur into a small mosque that bordered a canal near the Christian village of Shantinagar in Pakistan's Punjab province. No one actually saw the culprit, but immediately the mosque's loudspeakers were used to gather a group of young men. Someone claimed the pages of the Quran had been burned. The assumption was that this had to be the work of Christians, since obviously no Muslim would desecrate a Quran. The news spread quickly, and soon all mosques in the region were broadcasting calls for local Muslims to teach the Christians a lesson. The town of Khanewal, fifty miles east of the city of Multan, became the focal point for the growing mob. Rumours and accusations flew. A police officer reported that Christians were making alcohol and selling it to Muslims. Others said the Prophet Muhammad had been blasphemed. And now the Christians had desecrated a copy of the Quran. With each accusation the mob's anger grew.

The crowd began to march towards the Christian villages. One of the local police leaders, using a megaphone, pleaded for them to turn back. The plea was ignored. St Joseph's Catholic Church and the Church of Pakistan in

Khanewal were set ablaze. Stacks of Bibles and hymnbooks were tossed in a pile by the altar and burned. The mob gathered again, this time equipped with rocks, knives and guns. They began marching towards Shantinagar. Some had more sophisticated weapons: hand grenades, petrol bombs and incendiary chemicals. Word spread quickly: 'Destroy buildings and property only. We will not kill the infidels this time. We will teach them a lesson.' By the time the rampage ended the next morning, fifteen thousand Christians had lost their homes and property – cattle, fruit trees, wheelbarrows, tractors and bicycles were all destroyed.

A team from Lahore quickly packed a van and made the four-hour drive to Khanewal. They first stopped at the Catholic church, which was still smouldering. The walls and ceiling were black. Pews were smashed. The parish priest, Father Darshan Theodore, told the team that the village of Shantinagar had been completely destroyed. 'Every house is burned out,' he reported.

Quickly the van headed towards the village, driving down the narrow one-lane street that was just a dirt path with an oil coating. They passed a few bicyclers and a cart pulled by a water buffalo. The fields were empty, green with shoots from recently planted spring wheat. They passed through the village of Tibe and could see in the distance, half a mile ahead, numerous columns of smoke rising from the village of Shantinagar. The Pakistan army, its lorries parked around the village, was keeping watch over the proceedings.

The devastation was total. One store had foodstuffs scattered on the floor. Ashes and bits of rupee notes floated in the air. A metal rolltop door was bent from the heat of the fire. The Shantinagar Clinic, founded in 1973 according to a plaque on the outside wall, was only a shell. Next to it stood a scorched ambulance, its tyres melted by the heat. Every church had been destroyed. One was simply a pile of charred bricks. Another had scorched walls but no roof. In a third, smashed sound equipment was littered among the charred and twisted seats. A Bible, with singed pages, lay open at Psalm 82. Birds perched on the blackened iron beams of another church building. Next to the Full Gospel Assembly was a van sitting on charred wheel rims. Clearly, these fires burned extremely hot. One church building was still burning, flames pouring out of the roof.

The scene at the homes was even worse. Not one had been spared. 'How many homes were destroyed?' the team leader asked.

'All of them,' answered the pastor. 'A thousand, fifteen hundred homes. All destroyed.'

In front of the homes, children stood dazed. A woman sifted through a pile of burned books. Nothing was salvageable. The contents of pantry shelves were scattered. Pottery was broken. Furniture was burned. Clothing had been piled up and burned. An old man stood gazing at the devastation, a stunned look on his face. Beside his house stood a tractor, black and useless.

But soon these villagers learned they were not alone. A van drove in with the markings of a church from another village. It was filled with blankets. Other cars and carts arrived throughout the day. The surrounding Christian community was responding with food and water and warm clothing. It was going to be a cold night, and everyone would have to sleep outdoors, but no one would go to sleep cold or hungry.

—◦◦◦—

Two months later, at the request of national Christian leaders, I visited Shantinagar where a tent had been set up for a meeting with community elders. The commissioner of the Salvation Army, which had founded the village eighty years ago, was joined by local pastors. Other delegates included the district commissioner, the Bishop of Sialkot, and the retired chief justice of the Pakistan Supreme Court. Justice Nasim Hassan Shah, representing many in the government, greeted me warmly, saying, 'I want you to know we are very upset over what has happened here. The Christian community has been disgraced. We must do something to restore their confidence.'

I asked one of the bishops of the Church of Pakistan, 'Do you have any idea who instigated this riot? Surely it wasn't spontaneous.'

'No, it was well organised,' the bishop agreed. 'I've asked many of the local pastors. They seem to think it started with three Muslim police officers who ripped a villager's Bible during an arrest. That caused a major protest from the Christian community, and the officers were suspended for two weeks. Many believe they started the accusation about a Christian desecrating the Quran. But there may be more to it than that.'

The bishop reflected for a moment before he spoke his heart: 'There has been a growing movement of Muslim fundamentalism in this area. There are four Christian villages here, and I believe they intended to create a reason to destroy them all and drive the Christian community away for good.'

All of us gathered in the tent where some three hundred people were seated, and several hundred more stood at the back. Soldiers carrying machine guns were conspicuous along the sides. I was one of many speakers, and I had been asked to give a message from the Bible. This was, of course, a traumatic experience for these families. We can all imagine the feelings we would have if everything we owned was destroyed in a single, senseless rampage. So how should these people respond? How should I respond? What could I possibly say that might bring healing and peace to this community? I needed to speak to the Christians yet remember that many Muslims were also listening.

I began by reading the Beatitudes, also called 'the beautiful attitudes' from Matthew 5. The challenge for this Christian community was to reflect Jesus' attitude in the face of disaster. I lingered over these verses:

> Blessed are those who are persecuted because of righteousness, for theirs is the kingdom of heaven. Blessed are you when people insult you, persecute you and falsely say all kinds of evil against you because of me. Rejoice and be glad, because great is your reward in heaven, for in the same way they persecuted the prophets who were before you.
>
> Matthew 5:10–12

'Rejoice and be exceedingly glad,' Jesus said (v. 12 NKJV). Now *that's* a change of attitude. If we who are persecuted are blessed, then why do we complain? But how do we arrive at that attitude? The answer is in Matthew 6, where Jesus gives us the pattern for perfect prayer. It includes a plea for forgiveness, not on the basis of the atonement but on the basis of reciprocity. 'Forgive us our sins,' Jesus said, 'just as we have forgiven those who have sinned against us' (Matt. 6:12 NLT). As I spoke these words, I saw people sit up straight. 'For if you forgive men when they sin against you, your heavenly Father will also forgive you. But if you do not forgive men their sins, your Father will not forgive your sins' (vv. 14–15).

I could imagine what Christians in the audience were thinking. *You ask too much of us. We've lost everything!* And besides, while a number of Muslim leaders had expressed shame for the behaviour of those who rioted, no one had actually requested forgiveness. How can we forgive if no one asks to be forgiven?

The answer is found on the cross. While Jesus was hanging on the cross – I stretched out my arms to make the point – He prayed, 'Father, forgive them' (Luke 23:34). There was no one in that angry mob, watching Jesus die, who even thought about asking forgiveness. Nevertheless Jesus offered it. That is the way of Jesus. By offering forgiveness, He removes the barrier between a sinful people and a loving, forgiving and giving God. Forgiveness breaks down the barrier. That's not normally our approach. We demand that the person who harmed us first crawl in the dust and beg for forgiveness.

I concluded by saying, 'Today, here in Shantinagar, we offer those Muslims who have committed this crime forgiveness.'

Justice Shah and other Muslim leaders were astonished and deeply moved by my words. The chief justice later asked a bishop at the meeting if he could have a copy of my sermon, 'because I've never heard this. I want to read it again.'

However, the process of forgiveness requires more than words. Before the meeting I had asked the church leaders what might be done to bring healing to the community. I knew there were many Christians around the world who had means and wanted to help materially. Community leaders in Shantinagar had reported that one of the greatest losses was to school-children – their books and school uniforms had been destroyed. Most families could not hope to replace those losses, so the children would be deprived of their education for at least a couple of years, if not permanently. So in my speech I offered schoolbags, books and uniforms to every child in the village – Christian and Muslim. Also I announced that we would build a Christian community centre that would house a school and library.

Challenge 2

Are we going to seek revenge when we're attacked? Should we not offer forgiveness instead?

What was the lesson from Shantinagar? Forgiveness is the power that can truly change the world. We saw it happen in this village. A few months later the entire village turned out for ceremonies where more than thirteen hundred children were individually handed a bag and schoolbooks.

A second ceremony occurred just two hundred yards from the mosque where the riots had begun a year before. The son of the late Zia ul-Haq, Pakistan's former president, joined Chief Justice Shah and other dignitaries for the ribbon cutting and dedication of a new building that would become a library and community centre for all of the area. A message from the Archbishop of Canterbury was read. A local choir sang. Balloons and white pigeons were released, and then I was asked to pray a prayer of dedication for the new Prince of Peace Library.

That beautiful building stands today next to a rebuilt village as a testimony to the power of forgiveness. Many adults in the area have learned to read and write within the walls of this library. And, note incidentally, none of the other nearby Christian villages was attacked.

A few years ago I met with a political leader in a strong Islamic country. This man also happened to be the editor of a national newspaper and he had published some 'Open Doors' articles, about the threat of Communism, in his paper. As our meeting ended, the man asked if we could correspond and I agreed. A few weeks later I wrote my first letter to him. I struggled with how to address a man in such a high position and finally decided on a neutral approach, beginning my letter with 'Dear Sir'. A couple of days later, a letter arrived from this man – our letters had crossed in the mail. His letter to me began: 'Dear Brother Andrew. In the name of Allah, the compassionate and the merciful . . .' Suddenly I felt terribly convicted. This man had used his letter as an opportunity to proclaim one of the tenets of his faith, while I had missed my first chance of witnessing to him.

So what would I proclaim to this Muslim leader? After a great deal of prayer, I determined I would open my next letter to him with a declaration from the most important verse in the Bible. But before I reveal what I said, I need to put this in context.

We need to understand that the challenge posed by Islam is very different from the challenge presented by Communism during the twentieth century. Communism made the absurd claim that there is no God, and the result was a horrific system that collapsed after only seventy years. Islam has already been around for fourteen hundred years, and presents a far greater challenge for Christians. It presents us with this question: Who is God? The way we answer this question has a profound implication on how we live our lives.

The situation in Shantinagar had everything to do with the question, Who is God? Muslims reacted to a supposed provocation with anger and rage, and proceeded to destroy churches and homes. Christians then had a decision to make. Would they exact revenge? Would they attack the Muslims? If they had, a war almost certainly would have started between the two groups. There would have been attack and counterattack. People would have died. Most likely the small Christian community would have had to flee in the face of overwhelming numbers, surrendering valuable fields and property to the Muslims.

But God offered them another way. You see this approach all through Scripture, beginning with a remarkable encounter between God and Moses. As we all know, Moses first met God at the burning bush and from that learned God's name: 'Yahweh' or 'I Am.' Some time later God brought the Israelites out of Egypt to Mount Sinai, and there in Exodus 32–34 we read about an amazing situation when Moses interceded for his nation. God was on the brink of destroying His people because of their idolatry. Boldly Moses offered himself as a substitute, and God 'changed his mind' and said He would not destroy the people.[6] Because of that experience, Moses made an incredible request. From the very depths of his heart, Moses asked to know God. 'Show me your glory,' Moses requested (33:18).

God granted this request, and in the process we have what I believe may be the most important verse in the Bible. God passed in front of Moses, *proclaiming*: 'The Lord, the Lord, the compassionate and gracious God, slow to anger, abounding in love and faithfulness, maintaining love to thousands, and forgiving wickedness, rebellion and sin' (34:6–7). Here for the first time a human learned who God is. He is a God who is slow to anger and abounding in love. And perhaps most important, He is a God who forgives.

Some may protest this emphasis on forgiveness. As we saw in Part 1 of this book, Christians struggle with this. Layla's family and the congregation of St Mark's Church had to decide whether to pursue revenge, march in the streets or offer forgiveness. Butros, Ahmed, Salima and Nadir had to confront the need to forgive as they dealt with the horror of a double murder. So let me state that forgiveness does not mean a cover-up. The psalmist noted: 'You were to Israel a forgiving God, though you punished their misdeeds' (Ps. 99:8). We know from experience that sin has consequences. God disciplines, but He also forgives. When it comes to the sins of Muslims – particularly fundamentalists and their terrorist attacks – I wonder if we are far more interested in discipline (we don't call it revenge) than forgiveness.

I realise that none of us has mastered this. For so many, the concept of forgiveness is very shallow. We say we forgive, but the person remains an outcast. Don't we want the forgiven to become good citizens? Forgiveness is the first step to restoration and acceptance (of the person) and rehabilitation. Peter thought he was being generous by asking Jesus if he should forgive a person seven times. Jesus said the standard was seventy times seven. I read somewhere that Dietrich Bonhoeffer explained it this way: 'As long as you are counting, you haven't forgiven once.'

In *Light Force* I recounted a conversation with Dr Abdulaziz Rantisi, one of the founders of Hamas, in January 1993 after 415 Hamas leaders had been deported by Israel to the freezing mountains of southern Lebanon. I asked him, 'Do you think you could possibly forgive Israel for what they have done to you?' He admitted that the Quran says it is better to forgive than take revenge. Of course these leaders did not practise forgiveness when they returned home. During their year of deportation, Hamas were taught new methods of resistance by Hezbollah, including suicide bombings.[7]

Why does Islam appear stronger than Christianity today? It has everything to do with the crucial question posed by Islam: Who is God? At the beginning of each *sura* of the Quran, at the start of important documents, as the first statement in their *fatwas* and speeches, Muslims declare their allegiance to Allah, the God who is One, who is merciful and compassionate.

But in their actions, we find out that this is a God who is merciful only to some Muslims. He is also a God who exacts revenge and who demands that Muslims fight jihad, compelling all to come to Islam or die.

Who is the God that Christians worship? He is the God who loves and forgives. Surely Jesus demonstrated that truth on the cross. But how do we demonstrate this fact in our behaviour? Our lives should be a living demonstration that we know a God who forgives. We can begin by *proclaiming* this truth. In my next letter to the high government official, I began this way: 'Dear _____, In the Name of the Lord, a God merciful and gracious, slow to anger, and abounding in steadfast love and faithfulness, keeping steadfast love for thousands, forgiving iniquity and transgression and sin . . .' Since then I have used that proclamation in every letter I have written to a Muslim.

Many times people ask me, 'Andrew, how long will this conflict with Islam and terrorism last?' My usual reply is, 'It will last until we Christians have found the answer to the question, Who is God? and are able to verbalise it and prove by our actions that God is not the God of revenge but a God who forgives.'

This leads to what I consider the greatest challenge for Christians in the West. It deals with the fact that Muslims around the world despise us. In the next chapter we must address the reasons for this, and confront our third and perhaps most difficult set of questions.

3

I do not know how Sayyid ended up at a church in Greeley, Colorado. Perhaps someone from Colorado State Teachers College,[8] where he was studying, invited him. What I do know is that this event had a major impact on his life.

Sayyid was forty-two years of age, old for a university student. He had already lived an exemplary life in Egypt, where he was a teacher, then an author and critic, and for ten years worked in the Ministry of Education. The government provided him a scholarship to spend two years studying educational curricula in the United States. That's how he found himself at the foot of the Rocky Mountains, lonely and lost in a foreign culture.

Part of his struggle was the dramatic contrast between 'Christian' America and his Muslim background. Born in 1906, Sayyid had memorised the Quran as a boy, but he had grown up with a restlessness that caused him to ponder the meaning of life and death. He was curious, with a mystical bent that motivated him to write several volumes of poetry as a young man. He was also a moralist and, as such, tended to shy away from western influences. He published a comparative study of the Quran and the New Testament in which he argued that European society was little affected by Christian thinking while Egyptian thought and law were greatly affected by the Quran and Islamic law. He was quick to accept the influence of western sciences while rejecting the cultural influences of Europe and the Americas.

Now Sayyid was in America, able to see for himself whether or not his preconceptions were right. He spent time in New York, Washington, DC, Denver, San Francisco and San Diego. But the event that perhaps had the greatest impact on him occurred at the church in Greeley. He attended an evening service followed by a social event for the young people next to the 'prayer hall'. The pastor chose the music and the dancing began.

'They danced to the tunes of the gramophone, and the dance floor was replete with tapping feet, enticing legs, arms wrapped around waists, lips pressed to lips, and chests pressed to chests. The atmosphere was full of desire . . .'[9]

What a shame that Sayyid didn't have a Christian friend, someone to go with him to church, to talk with him about what he was observing in the United States, to exchange thoughts about Christianity and Islam and their impact on morals, daily life and culture. Most tragic, apparently no one ever showed him what real Christianity looks like. Sayyid returned to Egypt with powerful impressions of America filled with violent games like football, primitive music, severe racial discrimination and obsessions with sex. And this was before the social revolution of the 1960s – just imagine what he'd observe today! He concluded that America was soulless and materialistic.

Back home Sayyid became an activist, increasingly dedicated to the study of the Quran. Egypt was emerging from the shackles of British rule and trying to recover from its army's humiliating loss to the newly formed country of Israel in 1948. A group called the Muslim Brotherhood was calling for economic reforms and redistribution of land to counter the increasing western influences in the country. Sayyid used his considerable writing skills to express the ideology of the Muslim Brotherhood during the period when Egypt was going through political convulsions with the dethronement of their king and the rise to power of President Gamal Abd al-Nasser. Along with other radical thinkers, he was imprisoned in 1954, and during the next ten years, he poured his literary skills into writing several books. Most notable was a tract, completed in 1964, in which he declared that humanity was on the brink of annihilation unless there was surrender to Islam. He issued a call to jihad – not a defensive struggle, but a vast offensive that would bring first the Arab people and eventually all the world under the rule of Islam. His thoughts were considered so dangerous that he was executed in August 1966.

That little book called *Milestones* has become the manifesto of radical Islam, as powerful as Adolf Hitler's *Mein Kampf* was to the rise of Nazism, or the writings of Karl Marx to Communism. Virtually every extremist group, from Hezbollah to Hamas to Al-Qaeda, points to this book and its author, Sayyid Qutb, as the man who developed the philosophy of modern jihad.

I have often said that we are the Bible to unbelievers. Would things have been different if Sayyid Qutb had become friends with just one man who demonstrated the reality of a Christian life submitted to Jesus Christ? It could have happened in Egypt. It could have happened in America. The tragedy is that apparently he never experienced the real love of Jesus.

When Qutb visited the United States, few Muslims came to the West. Today there are millions of Muslims living in Europe and North America, and they present us with a challenge.

Challenge 3

What would happen if we accepted the challenge of Islam by striving as Christians to imitate Christ?

As I travel through the Muslim world, I see and hear vociferous anger against Europe and North America. The problem is that Muslims look at the West and think they are viewing Christianity, and they want nothing to do with it. In their minds, religion is not separated from culture and politics. So when the United States invades Iraq, most Muslims view it as Christianity attacking Islam. When they turn their satellite dishes to our media, they see and hear popular entertainers, often wearing big gold crosses while dressed in the most suggestive clothing and singing lyrics that promote violence and sex, and they think they are viewing Christian behaviour. It doesn't matter if you or I protest that this isn't real Christianity.

'*Allahu Akbar*,' which really means 'Allah is greater than any deity', is preached five times a day from millions of minarets around the world. Have you not heard it? By their declarations they proclaim that Islam is the only solution to all societal problems – moral, political and cultural.

Of course we protest and declare that in democratic societies there is freedom of thought and expression, but Muslims are not impressed. Our decadence speaks far louder than any words. I'm sure some of you think we are living authentic Christian lives because we are not behaving like the culture at large. But the challenge to imitate Christ takes us to a much deeper level. Listen to the apostle Paul: 'But among you there must not be even a *hint* of sexual immorality, or of any kind of impurity, or of greed, because these are improper for God's holy people' (Eph. 5:3). 'For you were once in darkness, but now you are light in the Lord. Live as children of light (for the fruit of the light consists in all goodness, righteousness and truth) and find out what pleases the Lord. Have nothing to do with the fruitless deeds of darkness, but rather expose them' (vv. 8–11). That's the challenge. I've already asked the question: Are we seeking to win Muslims to Christ? It won't help to preach the gospel to them if they can't hear us because of what they see and hear from our culture. We need to repent of the activities and behaviours that dishonour our Lord Jesus. I know there are individual Christians who are taking a bold stand against western culture, but the reality is that too many Christians watch the movies and television shows and listen to the songs that celebrate our self-centred decadence. The divorce rate among Christians is no better than that of the society as a whole. If our morals are the same or only marginally better than the society at large, what message do we have for 1.2 billion Muslims who, at least outwardly, uphold a higher moral standard?

Many Christians will conclude we need a revival. I'm afraid that is *not* the answer. Revival only fills the pews. Something far more powerful is needed – a cultural reformation. True surrender of our lives to Jesus means we change our way of living. When enough Christians do this, societal structures will change dramatically, based on the Word of God. We will address poverty and crime and take care of the sick and infirm and address loose living and decadence. The church in the West has shed too many of its responsibilities; it is no longer the guardian of morals.

How do we do this? Paul instructs us: 'Be imitators of God . . . and live a life of love, just as Christ loved us and gave himself up for us' (Eph. 5:1–2). Here's the bottom line: the only chance we have against the relentless growth of Islam is millions of people revealing through their behaviour the love of Christ. We must be imitators of Christ! That was the challenge faced by Ahmed and Butros and the other friends we met in the first part of this book. These people were faithful to proclaim Jesus to Muslims, but it was their lives that gave their message authority. They weren't perfect. They made mistakes. But remember one passage that guided them: 'Your attitude should be the same as that of Christ Jesus' (Phil. 2:5). He was their lodestar. His example showed them how to live in an environment hostile to their faith. And His Spirit gave them the power to persevere even when it could cost them their lives.

Some have suggested that the scourge of Islam may in fact be God's means of judgement on us. If that is true, it doesn't really help to fight Islam. We must repent and *then* God will protect us. Here is the challenge that convicts me: Is there anything in our lifestyle that God wants to protect? If not, then why worry about Islam taking over the West? Why should God protect a society in which He sees nothing worth protecting in our morals, righteousness, ethics or spirituality? Maybe it's time for us to take a serious look at our churches and admit that while they appear prosperous and successful on the outside, in reality they are weak and provide little if any real witness to Muslims.

Several years ago Hamas leaders invited me to dedicate a new lecture hall at the Islamic University in Gaza. They asked me to speak to students and faculty on the topic of 'What Is Real Christianity?' With leaders of Hamas sitting in the front row, I made this statement: 'You Muslims will never fully understand the message of the cross until we put into practice the challenge of Jesus to deny ourselves, take up our cross daily, and follow Him.'[10] If we do not do this, we will not make any impact on the Muslim world; we will have no testimony, and nothing will change except for the worse, because we will keep retreating from their onslaught.

Isn't the problem that we love ourselves more than we love the people in the world whom God loves? Don't we love ourselves more than we love Muslims? Jesus said if we love our lives, we will lose them. But whoever loses his life for the sake of Jesus will find it (see John 12:25–26). If this makes you uncomfortable, know that it also makes me uncomfortable. But really, is there any other way?

This is the challenge of Islam. We must answer the question, Who is God? Muslims have made their declaration and are ready to spread Islam around the globe. How will we respond? The only legitimate response is for Christians to demonstrate who God is by imitating Christ.

It's not too late. If we will repent, we can be renewed. Then we will be ready to participate in the fourth challenge.

4

There is a war raging. I'm not talking about the wars we read about in the papers or watch on the news, but a spiritual war that is reflected in the global conflicts. If we focus only on fighting in the Middle East or responding to terrorist acts around the world, we miss the big picture. The apostle Paul understood that we are in a war, but he said: '. . . we do not wage war as the world does. The weapons we fight with are not the weapons of the world. On the contrary, they have divine power to demolish strongholds. We demolish arguments and every pretension that sets itself up against the knowledge of God. And we take captive every thought to make it obedient to Christ' (2 Cor. 10:3–5).

But how do we gain the understanding we need about the nature of this fight? One excellent way is to listen to our brothers and sisters living under persecution. They are on the frontlines of this war, and they and their loved ones suffer the most casualties. That is why Al met two MBBs in a Cairo safehouse. I had known these men years before, but because I am now blacklisted in Egypt, Al went in my place to meet them. Neither of us knows their real names, so we will identify them simply as Peter and James. Please carefully hear their words.

Peter is a natural leader with an energy that is infectious. He has multiple identities, including business owner, writer and family man. But he was talking to Al in his identity as a Muslim who had become a follower of Jesus

Christ more than twenty years ago. He has suffered terribly for his faith. He told of being beaten in an attorney general's office, and of months spent inside a dark cell where all he could feel were spider webs covering his face. 'It felt like they put me in a grave.' In a sense, Peter did die in that cell, for today he is fearless and confident in his witness for Christ.

Next to him sat James, a small, quiet man who had been following Jesus for sixteen years. When asked about the challenges they face as Muslim-background believers, James said, 'I will tell you about my son. He is seven years old. He is a Muslim. But in his heart he is a Christian. In school he is taught Islam, and everyone relates to him as a Muslim. But at home he is a Christian, and he is raised as a Christian. As he grows older, something terrible is happening. My boy is being torn apart. He doesn't know his identity. All of the boys in the neighbourhood treat him as a Christian – in other words, they reject him. They tell him they will play with him only if he goes to the mosque and becomes a Muslim.'

Both of these men have moved away from their extended families to the anonymity of a huge city. 'I had to relocate because everyone knew I became a Christian,' said James. 'I lost my job. I have to be productive. So what kind of job should I look for? As soon as I apply, they ask me my religion. As soon as they know I'm a convert, they send me away. So I work with missionaries. But last year, they were expelled. And then there are the problems with security officials. Once the police took my father and put him in prison. My father has nothing to do with my work, but they did it to put pressure on me. They made him sign a statement saying that his son was mentally deranged.'

Peter leaned forward and stared intently at Al as he explained, 'We face a legal status that is problematic. The second article of the constitution of Egypt says that Islam is the religion of the state and Islamic law is the only source of Egyptian law. But in Article 46 there is a guarantee of the freedom of belief and the freedom of practice of religion. This is a serious contradiction. Further, Egypt has signed the United Nations Declaration on Human Rights.'

He was referring to the document adopted by the General Assembly in 1948. Article 18 states: 'Everyone has the right to freedom of thought, conscience *and religion; this right includes freedom to change his religion or belief,* and freedom, either alone or in community with others and in public or private, to manifest his religion or belief in teaching, practice, worship and observance' (italics added).

'When Egypt signed this declaration,' Peter continued, 'they put themselves under its application. But as long as we have Sharia law, all other laws are annulled. The only group suffering from this are MBBs.' The implications are clear. Anyone – Presbyterian, Coptic, Catholic – is free to become a Muslim. But a Muslim is *never* free to become a Christian.

Referring to a recently enacted law, Peter showed how bad the situation is: 'Article 98 of the Egyptian criminal code is a new way of putting pressure on MBBs. It speaks of slandering the Muslim faith. By that they mean whatever *they* consider disrespectful. So they tell everyone we have freedom of religion, but we are incriminated because we are Christians and every word we say can be held against us. The paradox is that every day in the media they print things against Christianity, and that is never considered disrespectful.'

A critical problem with the issue of religious freedom concerns the identity card that every Egyptian is required to carry. One line on the card identifies the religion of the bearer. A Christian can go to the government office and officially receive a new card that identifies him as a Muslim. But if a Muslim becomes a Christian, he is stuck with his old identity card, for no government official will change it. And that presents still another problem: a woman MBB cannot marry a Christian because her identity card states that she is a Muslim and no Muslim is permitted to marry a Christian. Thus her only hope for marriage is with another MBB.

'Have any of you thought about leaving Egypt?' Al asked. 'After all, if it is so difficult for a former Muslim to practice his faith here, why not go to the West where there is religious freedom both in law and in practice?' But these two men would have none of that. 'The first ten years of our faith,' Peter explained, 'we looked at Egyptians who fled as traitors to the cause. Now I think we were too strong. We realise that some have to leave because of threats on their lives. But as for us, we look at this as an exception. We are Egyptians and we want to live here.'

James explained that the group has experimented with migration within the country. When they learn about a Muslim who has converted, they help him move to a new community, where people don't know him, and where he can get a fresh start. At safe houses, MBBs participate in nine to twelve months of intense discipleship, and then are introduced into a church fellowship that is prepared to welcome them.'

Peter explained the thinking: 'We encourage all new believers not to share about their faith for a while. They need time to be built in the faith and establish a new life. So in one or two years a person's life will demonstrate change and the family will notice. We have experienced that when new believers are excited and share their faith too soon, they encounter problems they aren't ready for.'

So what is God doing in Egypt? Or to put it another way: Are Christians making any headway in this spiritual war? Are they demolishing any arguments or pretensions that set themselves against the knowledge of God? James said God was moving on two levels. One was with intellectuals. 'Many thinkers have lost faith in Islam. So we're seeing more intellectuals who are ready for a change.' The second level was for the average person – people are being drawn to Christ in a mysterious way. 'In many of my contacts, people are already prepared to listen. They've received a tract or had a dream or heard a Christian radio programme or seen a Christian TV show. But they've told no one. So there is a spiritual shift, and if the trend continues, it will produce a storm from the other side. This will be the start of the spiritual awakening we've been praying for.'

Al asked what these brothers wanted to say to the church in the West. Peter was emphatic: 'Tell the church in the West to wake up to the realities of Islam. We tried to tell them, but they did not believe us. Second, keep pressuring for democracy and freedom and human rights. By that I mean we need more than just elections. We need real freedom – freedom to write, freedom to practise our faith. We need the values of democracy.'

Do you hear their cry? They aren't asking for a western political system; they are asking for the opportunity to proclaim the gospel and for Muslims to have the freedom to hear it. See if that doesn't mesh with these words of Paul: 'I urge, then, first of all, that requests, prayers, intercession and thanksgiving be made for everyone – for kings and all those in authority, that we may live peaceful and quiet lives in all godliness and holiness. This is good, and pleases God our Saviour, who wants all men to be saved and to come to a knowledge of the truth' (1 Tim. 2:1–4).

'So how should we pray for you?' Al asked.

'We need prayer that we remain strong and do not fall back,' Peter answered. 'Also, pray for the second generation of Christians. Our children are really suffering. And pray that the church will be more sensitive to MBBs.'

'And visitors from the West should come,' added James.

'Yes, we need to keep the mission heart here,' Peter agreed. 'But we need understanding of *real* partnership. We need people with maturity. This is not a field for beginners or people who want spectacular results. We need people who will come and serve the church. Their agenda must be the kingdom of God.

'Don't bring Hollywood; bring Christ. Don't bring power. Don't bring just your money. Bring love. Bring the kingdom.'

Do you hear the heart of these brothers? If so, consider this last challenge.

Challenge 4, Part A

Are we really convinced that we are engaged in a spiritual war? If so, shouldn't we commit to a life of prayer?

The apostle Paul writes: 'Be very careful, then, how you live – not as unwise but as wise, making the most of every opportunity, because the days are evil. Therefore do not be foolish, but understand what the Lord's will is' (Eph. 5:15–17). Paul goes on to exhort us to be filled with the Holy Spirit, and in the final chapter of Ephesians instructs us to put on the armour of God and get engaged in spiritual war: 'For our struggle is not against flesh and blood, but against the rulers, against the authorities, against the powers of this dark world and against the spiritual forces of evil in the heavenly realms' (6:12). This war is fought with prayer first of all. Again the persecuted church in the Islamic world can show us the way.

There is a pastor in Cairo who is attempting to prepare the church in Egypt for engagement in spiritual battle. Because of a recent attempt on his life, we will not name him here. Referring to Isaiah 19, a prophecy that says God will reveal Himself to Egypt, this pastor says: 'We're praying for a real awakening. We believe God wants to pour out His Holy Spirit over this nation.' And he is seeing evidence of that. 'We need to love Muslims and to see them loved by Christ. Five years ago I didn't observe that. But in the last five years I've started to see Christians praying for Muslims. We pray especially for visions and dreams and we see answers every day. Christ is revealing Himself in visions and dreams. We see Muslims coming to us, asking us questions because of the visions.'

Of course, that provides new challenges for a church that isn't used to actively engaging Muslims with the gospel. This pastor and other leaders are equipping their congregations for these encounters, but the biggest challenge is one of the heart. 'They have to love Christ more than themselves. They have to be ready to die. A great revival in a Muslim country means a good number of martyrs. You have to expect it.' I expect many Christians in the West will recoil from such a statement. Shouldn't this pastor be more cautious? Shouldn't he protect his flock? But our friend sees it differently. He believes the only way to reach his country is if believers are willing to give everything, even their lives, for that cause.

The question that emerges from this discussion is: What roles can the rest of the body of Christ play, specifically the church in the West? This pastor is blunt. 'First, love Muslims. This is the command, to love our neighbours as ourselves. They are our neighbours. They are not our enemies. If they are our enemies, we have to love them more. We cannot win them to Christ without the spirit of love. If they hate us, we have to love them more than their hate. Otherwise we will be defeated. They need to know we are willing to die for them, not to kill them. This will convict them and they will revise their faith and open their hearts to the love of Christ.'

Then the pastor gives us the punch line. 'Please pray *with* us. Many times I've told the church outside, "Don't pray for us. Pray with us." Can you see the difference? If you pray for me, you will pray for my safety and my prosperity. No, just pray *with* me for the Muslims to know Christ.'

Do you think you can pray *with* them?

Because of the words of this pastor, I must propose a second part to this challenge.

Challenge 4, Part B

In this war are we willing to do anything, even lay down our lives, if necessary, to advance the kingdom of God?

Listen to Jesus: 'Anyone who does not carry his cross and follow me cannot be my disciple' (Luke 14:27). 'Any one of you who does not give up everything he has cannot be my disciple' (v. 33). 'Unless a kernel of wheat falls to the ground and dies, it remains only a single seed. But if it dies, it produces many seeds. The man who loves his life will lose it, while the man who hates his life in this world will keep it for eternal life' (John 12:23–25).

Until we are willing to give up all we consider important in this life – our comfort, our cars, our homes, our families, our careers, our entertainment, our savings, and our retirement accounts, whatever Christ requires of us to be His disciples and accomplish His work – the world will not take the church seriously. That is the challenge posed to me by our brothers and sisters who live under Islam, especially people like Mustafa and Hassan and Master Nazim, who were willing to follow the example of Christ, even though it cost them their lives. They were imitators of Christ. Jesus emptied Himself and became a servant and was obedient even to the most humiliating death (see Phil. 2:6–8). Are we willing to go that far? Muslims are willing to sacrifice their lives in jihad because they believe in a greater life in paradise. Shouldn't we be *more* willing to die than they are – not by committing acts of terror but because by imitating Christ we have so much more to live for? We have the promise of eternity with Jesus; all He asks is that we live in obedience to Him now. I believe that only such radical submission to Jesus can win the hearts of Muslims.

This is what we need throughout the Islamic world. This is the solution to the challenge presented by Islam. And it's not just in Egypt. I could give you similar examples from pastors and MBBs in Indonesia, Central Asia, Pakistan, Iraq, Iran and dozens of other Islamic countries.

I believe we all want to see the victory, but are we willing to pay the price? Al and I have been challenged by these men to ask the question: 'Are we willing to die for Christ?' They are. They are living out the words of Christ: 'If anyone would come after me, he must deny himself and take up his cross daily and follow me. For whoever wants to save his life will lose it, but whoever loses his life for me will save it. What good is it for a man to gain the whole world, and yet lose or forfeit his very self?' (Luke 9:23–25).

Think about this: unless Christ returns first, we can be certain that we will die physically. If each of us will die, is it too much to ask God that He be glorified in our death? What is holding us back? If we are convinced that Jesus paid the price for our sins and that when we leave this life we enter into His presence, we should not be afraid to die.

I call this the third mile. The first mile is yielding to Christ. The second mile means sharing the love of Jesus with Muslims. The third mile means I love Muslims so much that I'm willing even to die for them. Remember Muslims want to die for their own salvation. How can we convince them that Jesus already died for them? By showing them that we are more committed to living for Jesus than they are to dying in jihad.

In this spiritual war there will be casualties. I have no intention of throwing my life away – that is not my decision; my life belongs to Christ. But if following Christ means risking my life so that others may know Him, I don't think that is too great a price. If I am living for Christ, He can take my life any time it serves His purpose.

So are you ready to engage in battle? If so, I want to ask you some very personal and practical questions.

First, have you ever prayed for terrorists in Al-Qaeda or Hamas or Islamic Jihad or Hezbollah? Let me be more specific. Have you ever prayed for Osama bin Laden? I ask because prayer is the primary way we wage this war. If you say you did not pray, I ask you, 'Is that the reason Osama is what he is – because we didn't pray?' Can we pray him into the kingdom? Or can we neutralise his hatred and effectiveness by prayer? Let's go on a prayer offensive! Let's contest with the devil for the soul of the man, not with military might but with the gospel. After all, God is in the business of transforming lives. If our only response is to go out and destroy Muslim fundamentalists, we won't win a single soul. We cannot win the war on terror with guns and bombs because everyone we kill is replaced by dozens more who seek revenge. The only answer is total, radical commitment to Jesus Christ.

Here are a few more questions:

Will you pray for the angry men living in refugee camps in Lebanon and Jordan and Gaza who believe their only hope is fundamentalist Islam and who are being recruited to wage jihad against Israel and the West?

Will you pray for the young men who are preparing to strap on explosives, walk into a crowd in Iraq or Israel or London, and blow themselves up? Will you pray that someone will reach them before it's too late and tell them about Jesus?

Will you pray for the preachers in thousands of mosques, including those in Europe and North America, who incite hatred against Christians?

Will you pray for a harvest of souls among Muslims? Not one or two but *millions*? Will you choose a Muslim country and pray specifically for it – for as long as it takes for God to move in the hearts of men and women there?

Will you pray for the churches in the Islamic world? Specifically will you pray for the churches in the Islamic country you choose to focus on? Do you know their needs? Are they equipped and ready to reap the harvest in their country? We will try to get first-hand reports from church leaders so that you can pray *with* them, not just for them.

And one final question: Are you willing to become the answer to your prayers? If God chooses you to deliver His message, will you go?

Epilogue

Normally a book ends with a conclusion. Al and I want to end with a beginning, with the launch of a major offensive campaign. We want to invite you to strap on your spiritual armour and join in the good jihad. We are calling all Christians to a prayer campaign for Muslims throughout the world. You can choose the part of the Muslim world for which you wish to pray. Perhaps you know of a missionary in the Muslim world and you want to focus there. Or perhaps God has burdened you with a specific country.

We have started a website called www.secretbelievers.org where there is a lot more information than we can present in this book. There we will provide you with the information you need for the country you choose. Also we will have a lot of other helpful material, such as how to reach out to Muslims in your neighbourhood or city.

Let's close with an acrostic that I hope you will remember every day. It brings us back to the core of the message of this book. The word is *Islam*. Here's what we need to remember:

I
Sincerely
Love
All
Muslims

May we conquer the world with the love of Christ!

Appendix

A Letter from the Afghan Persecuted Church in Christ

Near the end of 2003, I received a message from the Christians in southern Afghanistan asking for my help. A new constitution had been drafted and the believers were concerned that provision was not made for non-Muslims. They wondered if this was what the coalition forces intended when they freed the country from the ruthless rule of the Taliban. They were very disappointed and wondered if Christians in the West realised what was happening. In response, they wrote a letter to President Bush. The following is that letter in its entirety. Please listen to their hearts as you read:

> To, The President George W. Bush
> Greetings in the Mighty Name of Jesus.
> We are very thankful to God that He has raised you up and kept you.
> We are also happy that God has given you courage to fight with the
> evil of the world, that has broken the power of evil in our country
> and we have seen a glimpse of hope. We are praying for your success
> and that God will give you the eye to see and ear to hear the plea of
> the ones who are always ignored in our country. They are
> persecuted and killed only because they are seeking to have
> fellowship with the living God through Christ. All the people are
> looking at them as downcast because they are in minority. When
> these people want to testify for the living God, they are hung and

killed, and life is made so difficult for them that their children will die with hunger and diseases and there is no one in our country Afghanistan to fight against the darkness. Our only and only help is God, there is no one else where we can go.

We are the people of Afghanistan, who have seen the bad consequences of our old religion, and after 20 years of war we had started to think that what kind of religion are we following which gives death instead of life. The religion that has pushed many of our friends and relatives in death. At last some people came to us as the messengers of God and told us that in fact God gives life instead of taking. They have introduced us with the living God, and we have restored our relation with the living god. We have find eternal life through them and secretly they have brought God's voice into our areas. Now by the grace of God we are more than three thousand people and we believe that the Lord Jesus Christ is our redeemer and he has released us from the power of sin. We believe that His Cross has reconciled us to God after living so long in the darkness.

We were praying for so long that we would be able to bring our voice to you, and now God has open this way today. We have fasted today and we are praying that God will lead us to write a few words to you.

We want to bring your kind attention to the problems which are faced by the persecuted church in Afghanistan:

There was no concept of freedom during the time of Taliban, and after the fall of Taliban we thought that with the coming of US there will be a new constitution that would give freedom to choose religion to every person, which is a basic right of every human being, and Muslims are converting hundreds of Christians and other religion people in to their religion, but when a Muslim is converted to Christianity or other religion, they are threatened, persecuted and killed. Now we have that draft of the new constitution, which is almost the same as the Taliban time.

Taliban belonged to the Sunni sect of Muslim, all the constitution made by them was based on the Hanfi Sect. It was expected that the monopoly of the Sunni Muslim will be broken. This not happening, instead the same flag is introduced which has the Sunni creed written on it. This proves that not only the Christians but, the big minorities like Shiates, Sikhs etc. will be exploited.

In the Muslim world all the commentaries made by the Hanfi Sect say that who ever leaves Islam is Murtid and should be killed. The blasphemer against Mohammad is killed. The Creed on the flag proves that Afghanistan is coming under the Saudi Islam and this type of Islam has no concept of human right of freedom.

In Afghanistan Shiats, Sikhs and Christians are persecuted and troubled since the time of Taliban. Specially Afghan Christians have no protection at all. Taliban were exploiting all the minorities with the tool of Islam and now the same thing is expected to be repeated again. The sword of Islam should be removed from Afghanistan and Afghanistan should be a democratic country instead of Islamic, where all the sects would have freedom.

The new constitution which is being formed by 35 people, after seeing the draft it is felt that the government is fearful of Taliban and trying to appease them by giving them all that they wanted and the minorities are ignored. With this all the minorities will fall into the darkness and there will be no future for them.

All of the people who are martyred or persecuted in the past were because of Taliban, but now in the future all the such incidents will be because of the new constitution which is being processed and the minorities are totally ignored.

You have courageously fought against Taliban and now it is time that with the wisdom that God has given you, very wisely you should try to avoid the rule of the same group over Afghanistan and put a new foundation of hope for every person for the freedom of choice. We are whole-heartedly with you, and if there is anything we can do for you we are more than willing to do for you. We can even sacrifice our lives for the freedom of the coming generations and for the spreading of the good news through Jesus Christ.

There are people among Muslims who are kind of liberals and they don't want to practise and follow the same type of Islam, which is introduced by Taliban. Now after bringing such a constitution *would not allow these people to prosper and there will be no hope for the future of Islam. In a way these people can help to fight against the fundamentalist type of Islam.*

Today there are Sikhs temples in Afghanistan but no churches. Zahir Shal had made a church for the missionaries in Kabul, long ago but that was destroyed by other people later on. Even today there are guards on that place and the Afghan Army has built some of the barracks. Our question is that if it is possible to make mosques in US and Rome, why there could be a church in Afghanistan???

Our last point is this, that the God who has made you the president of US, the God who has kept you for so long instead of all the threats and attacks of the enemy. Now it is a good chance for you to help spread His kingdom in Afghanistan, we are constantly praying for you and we believe that God has given you wisdom and power to spread His kingdom and serve Him. You are a chosen man of God, and we believe that God has a special purpose for your life, and that is to help spread His kingdom. We pray that the Holy Spirit our best helper and guide will help you to serve the King of Kings and Lord of Lords, Jesus Christ the Son of God in these last days.

This is the word of God for you, Mr George W. Bush:

The Lord will extend your mighty sceptre from Zion; you will rule in the midst of your enemies. Your troops will be willing on your day of battle (Ps. 110:2–3).

May God bless you and keep you. If you want to get in touch with us for any assistance, please use the same channel through which you have received our plea.

May the grace of the Almighty Living God and His son Jesus Christ be with you by the presence of His Holy Spirit. Amen.

The Afghan persecuted Church in Christ

Notes

1. Gary L. Bauer, 'End of Day', received from garybauer@cwfpac.com on 11 September 2006.
2. This is not his real name. 'Alef' is the first letter of the Pashto alphabet. With one exception, each of the Afghan men in this chapter are identified by a letter of the Pashto alphabet.
3. See Sebastian Junger, 'American's Forgotten War' (2006), http://www.vanityfair.com/commentary/content/printables/060327roco02?print=true. Junger writes: 'According to a recent internal report for the American Special Forces, opium production has gone from 74 metric tons a year under the Taliban to an astronomical 3,600 metric tons, an amount which is equal to 90 per cent of the world's supply. The profit from Afghanistan's drug trade – roughly $2 billion a year – competes with the amount of international aid flowing into the country and helps fund the insurgency.'
4. See Brother Andrew and Al Janssen, *Light Force: A Stirring Account of the Church Caught in the Middle East Crossfire* (Hodder & Stoughton, 2004); see especially chapters 2, 11, 17–20, 22, 25–6.
5. See the Appendix for the complete (and unedited) text of the letter to President Bush from 'The Afghan persecuted Church in Christ'.
6. See Brother Andrew with Susan DeVore Williams, *Prayer Works* (1990; reprint, Grand Rapids: Revell, 2006), pp. 30–5.
7. Andrew and Janssen, *Light Force*, pp. 146–52.
8. Today the school is known as the University of Northern Colorado.
9. *All Things Considered*, NPR, May 6, 2003. Also see Adnan A. Musallam, *From Secularism to Jihad* (Westport, CT: Praeger, 2005).

10. For the story of Brother Andrew's lecture at Islamic University in Gaza, see Andrew and Janssen, *Light Force*, pp. 213–17.

Selected Bibliography

We have read many books over the years in our attempt to understand the world of Islam, and more books are coming out every month. There are so many options available that we thought it might be helpful to recommend a few. The following are books that will help you as a Christian as you consider the challenge of Islam.

Accad, Fouad Elias, *Building Bridges: Christianity and Islam* (Colorado Springs: NavPress, 1997). An excellent little book to help you in dialoguing with Muslims.

Bawer, Bruce, *While Europe Slept: How Radical Islam Is Destroying the West from Within* (New York: Doubleday, 2006). There have been several books written on the changes happening in Europe, in large part due to the influx of Islam. Bawer is a journalist and has an easy-to-read style. Also easily readable is Claire Berlinski, *Menace in Europe: Why the Continent's Crisis Is America's, Too* (New York: Crown Forum, 2006). If you want more focus on the situation in England, you might take a look at Melanie Phillips, *Londonistan* (Gibson Square Books, 2006).

Brother Andrew and Al Janssen, *Light Force: A Stirring Account of the Church Caught in the Middle East Crossfire* (Hodder & Stoughton, 2004). This is our book, but we recommend it because the Middle East conflict is the focus of much attention in the Muslim world and the West, and this book attempts to show how that affects the church. Also it tells how I (Brother Andrew) attempted to reach out to groups like Hezbollah and Hamas.

Caner, Ergun Mehmet, and Emir Fethi Caner, *Unveiling Islam: An Insider's Look at Muslim Life and Beliefs* (Grand Rapids: Kregel, 2002). These brothers grew up as Muslims and are now followers of Christ. As such, they provide an insider's perspective on Islam.

Esposito, John L., *Unholy War: Terror in the Name of Islam* (New York: Oxford University Press, 2002). Esposito is a respected historian. His book *What Everyone Needs to Know About Islam* (New York: Oxford University Press, 2002) is considered an excellent introduction to the Muslim world. He is also editor of *The Oxford History of Islam* (New York: Oxford University Press, 1999).

Gabriel, Mark A., *Jesus and Muhammad: Profound Differences and Surprising Similarities* (Lake Mary, Florida: Charisma House, 2004). Gabriel grew up a devout Muslim in Egypt and earned a doctorate in Islamic studies at Al-Azhar University in Cairo. In this book he tells about his conversion to Christianity and then examines the lives and teachings of the founders of Islam and Christianity. He also wrote *Islam and Terrorism: What the Quran Really Teaches about Christianity, Violence and the Goals of the Islamic Jihad* (Lake Mary, FL: Charisma House, 2002).

Geisler, Norman L., and Abdul Saleeb, *Answering Islam: The Crescent in Light of the Cross* (1993, reprint, Grand Rapids: Baker, 2002). An excellent resource for those who want the apologetics for the Christian response to the claims of orthodox Islam.

Hadi, Abdul, *The Cross and the Crescent: Understanding Islam.* This book is written by a dear friend who is pastor of a church in a Muslim country and a renowned Bible scholar. He writes under a pseudonym. There is no copyright date or publisher listed on the book, but it can be ordered online through the Haggai Institute. Go to: http://www.haggai-institute.com/Information/InfoItem.asp?InfoID=48.

Huntington, Samuel P., *The Clash of Civilizations: Remaking of World Order* (New York: Simon and Schuster, 1996). This was the book that caused a sensation by proposing that, after the fall of Communism, 'civilisations' replaced nations and ideologies as the driving force in global politics.

The Koran, translated with notes by N. J. Dawood (New York: Penguin Books, 1995). Reading the Koran is not easy for most Christians, but when talking with Muslims, it helps to have read their holy book. Of course you should also spend a lot of time reading your Bible!

Lewis, Bernard, *What Went Wrong? The Clash Between Islam and Modernity in the Middle East* (New York: HarperCollins, 2002). Lewis is Emeritus Professor of Near Eastern Studies at Princeton University and has written many well-researched books on the Middle East and Islam.

Marshall, Paul (ed.), *Radical Islam's Rules: The Worldwide Spread of Extreme Sharia Law* (Lanham, Maryland: Rowman and Littlefield, 2005). A collection by Freedom House's Center for Religious Freedom in which various contributors look at the growth of Sharia law around the world.

McCurry, Don, *Healing the Broken Family of Abraham: New Life for Muslims* (Colorado Springs: Ministries to Muslims, 2002). Don is a long-time friend who has faithfully served for years in the Muslim world. This is an excellent resource for any Christian with an interest in ministry to Muslims. You can order it online at WorldChristian.com. Go to: http://www.ywam.org/books/default.asp. Also Don has an excellent little booklet called *Now You Can Know What Muslims Believe: A Muslim World Overview*. Available through Ministries to Muslims, 4164 Austin Bluffs Parkway, 357, Colorado Springs, CO 80918.

Sheikh, Bilquis, with Richard H. Schneider, *I Dared to Call Him Father: The Miraculous Story of a Muslim Woman's Encounter with God* (1978, reprint, Grand Rapids: Chosen, 2003). I (Brother Andrew) had the privilege of knowing this remarkable woman from Pakistan. This is her testimony, one of the best you can find of a conversion from Islam to a follower of Christ.

Open Doors

This book is a challenge. It is a challenge to understanding and a challenge to commitment and action. It is a challenge to individuals and churches to live as authentic disciples of Jesus Christ.

Open Doors has been part of that challenge and part of the response for more than fifty years. It started in 1955 with a Dutch missionary discovering that Christians in Communist countries were desperately longing for supplies of the Bible – and so he took a suitcase full of Christian literature behind the Iron Curtain. He became known as Brother Andrew – 'God's Smuggler' – and he is one of the authors of this book.

Fifty years later, Open Doors is serving persecuted Christians in around fifty countries. This book has given an insight into its work in Muslim countries; similar work is supported in countries in Africa, Asia and Latin America, whether the oppression comes in the name of communism, Buddhism, Hinduism or Islam. Where the people of God are under pressure, Open Doors stands with them, responding to their cries for help and shaping its response under their guidance.

Right now Open Doors is ready to give you information for your prayers – the authentic voice of the Persecuted Church brought to you in print, by email, on the Web, so that your prayers are timely, informed and effective weapons in the spiritual battle.

Right now Open Doors can channel your gifts to where they will make a significant difference to our sisters and brothers in the Persecuted Church. Providing the Bibles and other Christian literature they have requested. Training pastors and congregations so that they can stand strong through the storm. Strengthening the church in its commitment to mission, so that even under pressure it can reach out with the Gospel of Jesus Christ. Enabling those who have lost so much to receive material help and spiritual encouragement.

Right now Open Doors is enabling many Christians around the world to build personal relationships with the Persecuted Church, as they travel to share encouragement, to pray, to bring Bibles and other literature. And many also volunteer to bring the Persecuted Church into the life of their own church family, sharing news for prayer and exploring the lessons to be learned from our sisters and brothers.

Getting involved with Open Doors is not, in itself, the answer to the challenges posed by this book. But we are committed to encouraging and supporting those who do want to rise to the challenge – by linking you to God's Persecuted Church around the world. So that you can pray with them and not just for them. So that you can learn from them as well as give to them. So that, together, we can all play our part in God's great plan and purpose for His world.

It would be a privilege to be part of your response to *Secret Believers*. For further information, simply contact the national office listed below.

And may you know God's blessing as you follow Him in faithful obedience and radical commitment.

'Our very mission is called "Open Doors" because we believe that any door is open, any time and anywhere . . . to proclaim Christ.'
    Brother Andrew

International Website: www.od.org

Australia: www.opendoors.org.au

Brazil: www.portasabertas.org.br

Canada: www.opendoorsca.org

Denmark: www.forfulgt.dk

France: www.portesouvertes.fr

Germany: www.opendoors-de.org

Italy: www.porteaperteitalia.org

Korea: www.opendoors.or.kr

The Netherlands: www.opendoors.nl

New Zealand: www.opendoors.org.nz

Norway: www.opendoors.no

Philippines: http://ph.od.org/index.php

Singapore: www.opendoors.org/ODS/

South Africa: www.opendoors.org.za

Spain: www.puertasabiertas.org/

Switzerland: www.portesouvertes.ch

UK: www.opendoorsuk.org

USA: www.opendoorsusa.org

Or, go to www.secretbelievers.org

Addresses

Open Doors
P.O. Box 53
Seaforth
New South Wales 2092
AUSTRALIA

Åbne Døre Danmark
P.O. Box 1062
DK-7500 Holstebro
DENMARK

Missao Portas Abertas
C P 55055
CEP 04709-011
Sao Paulo
BRAZIL

Portes Ouvertes
B P 130
F-67833 TANNERIES
Cedex (Lingolsheim)
FRANCE

Open Doors
30-5155 Spectrum Way
Mississauga, ON
L4W 5A1
CANADA

Open Doors Germany
Postfach 1142
DE-65761 Kelkheim
GERMANY

Porte Aperte
CP45
37063 Isola Della Scala, VR
ITALY

Open Doors
P.O. Box 50
Dongjak-gu
Seoul # 156-600
SOUTH KOREA

Open Doors
P.O. Box 47
3850 AA Ermelo
THE NETHERLANDS

Open Doors
P.O. Box 27630
Mt Roskill
Auckland 1440
NEW ZEALAND

Åbne Døre Danmark
Barstølveien 50 F
4636 Kristiansand
NORWAY

Open Doors
P.O. Box 1573
QCCPO
1155 Quezon City
PHILIPPINES

Open Doors
8 Sin Ming Road
#02-06 Sin Ming Centre
SINGAPORE 575628
Republic of Singapore

Open Doors
P.O. Box 1771
Cresta 2118
SOUTH AFRICA

Puertas Abiertas
Apdo 49
18100 Armilla (Granada)
SPAIN

Portes Ouvertes
Case Postale 147
CH-1032 Romanel
SWITZERLAND

Open Doors
P.O. Box 6
Witney
Oxon OX29 6WG
UNITED KINGDOM

Open Doors
P.O. Box 27001
Santa Ana, CA 92799
USA